The *Star Wars*
Radio Dramas

The *Star Wars* Radio Dramas

Brian Daley and the Serialization That Saved NPR

Maria Jose Tenuto *and* John Tenuto

McFarland & Company, Inc., Publishers
Jefferson, North Carolina

Library of Congress Cataloging-in-Publication Data

Names: Tenuto, Maria Jose, 1975– author. | Tenuto, John, 1969– author.
Title: The Star wars radio dramas : Brian Daley and the serialization that saved NPR / Maria Jose Tenuto and John Tenuto.
Description: Jefferson, North Carolina : McFarland & Company, Inc., Publishers, 2024. | Includes bibliographical references and index.
Identifiers: LCCN 2024010854 | ISBN 9781476695631 (paperback : acid free paper) ♾
ISBN 9781476653372 (ebook)
Subjects: LCSH: Science fiction radio programs—United States. | Star wars (Radio program) | Daley, Brian—Criticism and interpretation. | National Public Radio (U.S.)
Classification: LCC PN1991.8.S34 T48 2024 | DDC 791.44615—dc23/eng/20240320
LC record available at https://lccn.loc.gov/2024010854

British Library cataloguing data are available

ISBN (print) 978-1-4766-9563-1
ISBN (ebook) 978-1-4766-5337-2

Printed in the United States of America

McFarland & Company, Inc., Publishers
Box 611, Jefferson, North Carolina 28640
www.mcfarlandpub.com

For Brian

Table of Contents

Acknowledgments

A heartfelt thank you to these generous individuals who contributed their time and memories to help us celebrate Brian Daley and the *Star Wars* radio dramas:

Kale Browne
Anthony Daniels
Myra Daley DiBlasio
Keith Eyles
Joshua Fardon
Rhonda Herman
LaReine Johnston
Perry King
Lindsey Loeper and the University of Maryland, Baltimore County Albin O. Kuhn Library & Gallery Special Collections
James Luceno
John Madden
Dan Madsen
Layla Milholen
Alex Newborn
Marc Rosenzweig
Ann Sachs
Samuel Sachs Morgan
Lucia St. Clair Robson
Nicholas Tenuto
Nicholas Jose Tenuto
Richard Toscan
Tom Virtue
Tom Voegeli
Will Wright

Thank you, George Lucas, for creating *Star Wars* and for letting Brian Daley expand your universe with his words.

Preface

It's open skies from now on, partner![1]
—Han Solo, Star Wars: *The National Public Radio Dramatization*

Consequential, innovative, audacious, inspirational, and more—the *Star Wars* radio dramas have many descriptors. Consequential because without them, the trajectory of National Public Radio (NPR) would have been very different, and likely, not for the better. Innovative because they employed state of the art technology and a revolutionary audio aesthetic that, despite time and budget constraints, reformulated radio serializations. Audacious because the idea of transforming a special effects extravaganza into an aural medium was thought impossible. Inspirational because a generation of podcasters, vloggers, and authors have shared how their imaginations were infused with new possibilities because of George Lucas' universe and the words added to it by the radio dramas' scriptwriter Brian Daley. These reasons alone brand the making of the *Star Wars* radio dramas a story worth exploring.

But the radio dramas were something more.... They were an act of philanthropy, driven by the desire of those involved to reignite the radio drama format in an era where visual entertainment dominated, and more importantly, to give those without means or ability the chance to experience *Star Wars* for free on radio. Many of the radio dramas' artists, technicians, and actors contributed because of this charity-minded motivation.

The radio dramas were also intertwined, figuratively and literally, with the life of their writer. To tell the story of the making of the *Star Wars* radio dramas is to also tell the story of Brian Daley. Always a science fiction and comic book fan, Daley was forever changed by *Star Wars*, in ways that many other fans who were inspired by that galaxy could likely relate to. *Star Wars* was formative for Daley, who, because of his authorship of a trilogy of Han Solo books, was one of the first writers to expand upon Lucas' universe. His fascination with *Star Wars* would lead him not only to the radio dramas, but, in the roundabout of happy coincidences, to the person who would be the love of his life. When Brian dealt with his terminal illness, finally being able to write the long-delayed *Star Wars: Return of the Jedi* audio drama script gave him hope and something else to focus on beyond the emotional and physical pain.

The radio dramas, then, have as much heart as art, and to chronicle their origins and production has been a privilege.

After more than 40 years, too many of those who contributed behind the scenes and in front of the microphone to one of radio's most important events have been lost. Because getting their remembrances firsthand was not possible, archival research became essential. Most beneficial was the access granted to the Brian C. Daley Papers collection at the Albin O. Kuhn Library & Gallery at the University of Maryland, Baltimore County, which contains Daley's scripts, personal correspondence, photographs, and newspaper clippings. To supplement this library research, invaluable newspaper archival resources were consulted. The NPR *Star Wars* radio dramas were heavily advertised in newspapers and magazines, featuring interviews with creatives.

The many more creatives who worked on the radio dramas were generous with their time, granting new interviews for this book, sharing memories of their own experiences and of interactions with Brian. With gratitude: Anthony Daniels (C-3PO), Ann Sachs (Princess Leia Organa), Perry King (Han Solo), Joshua Fardon (Luke Skywalker), Kale Browne (Biggs Darklighter), Tom Virtue (Bren Derlin), John Madden (Director), Richard Toscan (Executive Producer and Story Editor), Tom Voegeli (Sound Designer and Editor), James Luceno (*Star Wars* Author), Dan Madsen (*The Official Star Wars Fan Club* President and Publisher), Lucia St. Clair Robson (Author and Partner of Brian Daley), Myra Daley DiBlasio (Sister of Brian Daley), LaReine Johnston (Film Editor and Cousin of Brian Daley), and Marc Rosenzweig (Son of Joel Rosenzweig). Their contributions are the foundation upon which this text rests.

It is hoped that after reading this book, the credits heard on each episode of the *Star Wars* radio dramas, spoken by narrator Ken Hiller, will come alive for fans, giving an appreciation for the art, creativity, and dedication that was required to create these radio dramas. Perhaps the book may inspire new fans to seek out the radio dramas and experience them for the first time or remind those who were there at the time what it is like to hear the adventures of Luke Skywalker, visualized in their own imaginations.

When Brian passed, his family, friends, and fans lost not only his charm, compassion, advice, and presence, they lost all the future characters and narratives his imagination would have created. But, like us all,

Brian lives in the memories of others and in that which he left behind. By reading his books, both *Star Wars* and his original novels, and most especially by listening to the *Star Wars* radio dramas, fans can get to know Brian. He lives there now.

The story begins ... a long time ago...

Prelude

In 1977, National Public Radio (NPR) was in real trouble, plagued with too little funding and low ratings.

In 1981, the phenomenal success of the original *Star Wars* radio drama gave NPR the needed ratings, national and international publicity, and boost in donations to keep it afloat at exactly the time it was threatened the most. The radio drama and its sequels would become a staple on local NPR stations and be used for decades as fundraising programs. Most importantly, *Star Wars* brought a new audience to NPR. As it did in theaters, where George Lucas' films redefined movie making, so, too, did NPR's *Star Wars* redefine the artistic world of radio drama. Everything from its revolutionary use of sound to its limited use of narration, relying instead on atmosphere to create context, would become the standard for a new modern age of audio storytelling. It was, simply, the most ambitious radio drama ever produced, and there had never been that kind of reaction to a radio drama since *The War of the Worlds* panicked the East Coast in 1938.

That a radio network, dependent exclusively on audio for its format, would find a lifeline in the most visually dynamic movie ever released is the stuff of irony. This is the story of the making of the three *Star Wars* radio dramas and how they saved NPR. It is the story of how an unlikely alliance of academics, radio executives, Lucasfilm employees, actors, and behind-the-scenes artists banded together, despite the obstacles, to create a unique and consequential work spanning forty years. In turn, it is also the story of how writer Brian Daley was the fulcrum, making it all possible.

1

The Opening Crawl

The origins of the *Star Wars* radio dramas are not found in a galaxy far away. Rather, events transpired within the more prosaic chambers of the U.S. Congress, with the help of a little cellophane tape. Created as part of President Lyndon B. Johnson's Great Society plan, National Public Radio (NPR) was an afterthought to the Congressional Public Broadcasting Act of 1967. The act established the Corporation for Public Broadcasting (CPB), a nonprofit, independent company funded primarily by the U.S. government and whose directors would be nominated by the president and confirmed by the Senate. Unlike private broadcast stations that derived income from commercials, nearly 90 percent of the CPB budget was to come from taxpayer dollars, with the rest through grants and donations. The mission of the CPB was to create programs that would educate and affirm the public good. Speaking on the establishment of the CPB, President Johnson said, "So today we rededicate a part of the airwaves—which belong to all the people—and we dedicate them for the enlightenment of all the people."[1]

Originally, the 1967 act authorized the CPB to create only television programs. That was until the proverbial last-minute revisions common to legislation, Michigan Senator Robert Griffin literally "used Scotch tape" on the paperwork "to add a provision permitting the CPB to expand into radio. Without this addition, NPR could not have been formed."[2] Balancing focus and funding between the radio and television responsibilities of CPB would be a continued tension for the company that endures today.

National Public Radio was incorporated on February 26, 1970, with eighty-eight stations joining the network. Its first broadcast was on April 20, 1971, covering the Senate Foreign Relations Committee Hearings on the Vietnam War. Early on, NPR scored a success with the creation of the afternoon news program *All Things Considered* on May 3, 1971, a program that still airs as one of the highest-rated radio programs in the United States.

From its inception, NPR faced challenges. Starting in the 1950s and

1960s, radio in the United States had become both dominated by and synonymous with music. Gone were the glory days of radio dramas so prevalent during the 1930s to 1940s when radio was king. Americans turned to their radios then—as they do smartphones and streaming services now—for purposes as diverse as news and entertainment. It used to be common to adapt movies for radio plays, bringing the stars and stories of Hollywood to parts of the United States, still heavily rural, without easy access to movie theaters. In 1947, for example, the popular CBS *Lux Radio Program* adapted *It's a Wonderful Life* for radio starring James Stewart and Donna Reed from the film's original cast.

These adaptations were frequently shorter than their source material, conducted in front of live audiences, and without much sophistication. The radio version of *It's a Wonderful Life* runs only 60 minutes instead of the 130 minutes of the original film. The reality, though, was that by the 1970s, unless it was music, news, or sports on the go, Americans had little interest in radio when they could turn to TV. Of all the radio formats, the one that had suffered the most was radio drama, as Americans became especially devoid of any appetite for audio-only narratives.

By contrast, the NPR equivalent in England, the British Broadcasting Corporation (BBC), was producing two thousand hours of radio drama per year for an audience that still thrived on the format. Of course, there were still fans of radio dramas in the United States, even if only as a niche. But even a niche when measured among a population of 203 million Americans could add up to enough people to create a sustainable radio show. During the late 1960s and 1970s, fans who knew where to look found a few modern programs that harkened back to the Golden Age of Radio, from the CBS *Radio Mystery Theater* to the *Saturday Night Live* precursor, *The Credibility Gap*.

Without the ability to depend on rock or popular music for its programming, NPR also turned to radio dramas as a programming strategy. Karl Schmidt, a founding board member of NPR, University of Wisconsin communications professor, radio host, and station manager of WHA-AM 970, was one of those fans of radio dramas. He had the idea to revitalize the format in a program called *Earplay* by bringing together talented playwrights and actors with modern sound technology. Schmidt's mission was two-fold. One was to create "a more personal kind of medium and we try to bring the words, noises, and the music together in a kind of sound poem."[3] The other goal was to cultivate a new generation of radio playwrights and a new market for radio dramas. In 1976, Schmidt told journalist Susan Toller, "We received over 3,000 scripts, but the quality in no way reflected the quantity. Some were plays written in the '30s, taken out of a trunk, dusted off and sent to us. Others were plays written by dramatists who didn't know how to construct a play that would be produced on radio."[4] The CPB funded the endeavor beginning at $150,000, eventually growing to $250,000, with the National Endowment for the Arts providing another $200,000.

When they began, *Earplay* radio dramas were running as vignettes of less than fifteen minutes, partially because of the idea that it could capture a commuter audience with limited time and partially because of problems finding suitable scripts. Eventually, better playwrights were found, and as the program grew in popularity and funding, the running time grew concomitantly, with some reaching two hours.

Tom Voegeli, who would eventually become the sound mixer, engineer, and editor of the *Star Wars* radio dramas, remembers Schmidt:

> I have a graduate degree in marketing from the University of Wisconsin–Madison [UWM] that I've never used. I met Karl Schmidt there. He was really my mentor. We started together on *Earplay*. He was the primary force, but I was the legs behind it. When people think of radio drama it may be *The Shadow* or things like that. Instead, *Earplay* was the kind of radio dramas that would be on Radio 3 of the BBC. Very high end, about existential crises. We had some really great playwrights who wrote for that project. David Mamet wrote *The Water Engine* for that radio project, and then it went on to be a Broadway play. Arthur Kopit wrote *Wings* for that project. I remember it fondly and Karl was the primary instigator behind it.[5]

Voegeli's father, Don, a music professor at UWM, composed the various themes for *All Things Considered* and also had an influence on his son's interest in sound engineering. "I fell in love with audio and even radio because Dad worked at Wisconsin public radio as a music director a long time. I was the board operator by the time I was probably 14."[6]

Tom Voegeli spent time learning about radio drama, too, at the BBC. "I spent some time at the BBC when the BBC was really active in radio dramas, which they did because it was a really inexpensive way to realize a dramatic idea. All the best actors in London would come in and do their part in a radio play. You didn't have to memorize lines. It was a wonderful, wonderful time. And I got to see the very tail end of that. And I learned a lot about the conventions of radio."[7]

It was while working on *Earplay* that Voegeli would meet his best friend and lifelong radio collaborator, director John Madden:

> He was flown in from England as a script editor initially on *Earplay*. He had been script editor at the BBC which used to have these great training jobs that you could only keep for a year. We glommed onto him and brought him to Madison, Wisconsin. We were housed in Madison, but we really did not do any of the productions in Madison. *Earplay* was done in New York or LA, or someplace where we had enough actors. I remember it so well, he getting off the plane with Penny, his wife, and we just bonded. John is still my best friend.[8]

Although eventually becoming better known as a film director, earning best director nominations from both the Academy of Motion Picture Arts and Sciences and British Academy of Film and Television Arts for his 1998 film *Shakespeare in Love*, Madden actually began his career in radio and theater. He would become the director of all three *Star Wars* radio dramas, working closely with Voegeli. Madden recalls his start in radio:

> Everybody in England grows up with radio drama to a degree. Most probably the widest ranging program is *The Archers* which has been going for years and which is an absolutely indefatigable soap. I ran a theater company after leaving Cambridge, which was based at Oxford and Cambridge, related to the University. After about three or four years of doing that. I joined the BBC on a series of short-term contracts. It was in a period of time where they didn't have a traineeship, although they did have before that, and they did after that, but not at that moment. I was just really moving from one position to another and I landed in radio drama for a period of time working as essentially a script reader, and I did some production while I was there.
>
> During that tenure, which was probably no more than about eight, nine months, as I remember, the BBC was approached by National Public Radio about a project called *Earplay*. They turned to the BBC for some help in setting up a public radio drama industry, in terms of commissioning scripts, and so forth. I held my hand up when they were looking for somebody who might be interested in going. The play that put us on the map was *Wings* by Arthur Kopit which was a drama about a woman suffering a stroke and had been in her earlier life an aviatrix, which is where the name of the play came from. Tom and I did *Wings* together. I directed it, and we put it all together. That created a little bit of a stir because it won the international Prix Italia Award, which is the preeminent radio drama prize.[9]

Even with the successes of *All Things Considered* and *Earplay*, NPR was still finding it a challenge by the mid–1970s to find a sustained audience and reliable funding. In a 1977 *Cincinnati Enquirer* newspaper article, journalist Willets Prosser, Jr., summarized the sorry state of affairs, "Nationally, public radio has about 3.3 million listeners, according to a 1976 'Arbitron' survey by the American Research Bureau. Of the 7,000-plus radio stations now broadcasting in the United States, but 201 are NPR outlets. And only 60% of the U.S. population is within reach of an NPR station."[10] To illustrate the problem, Prosser detailed how WGUC-FM 90.9, the public radio station owned by the University of Cincinnati, only attracted 3 percent of the total listeners available in a thirty-mile radius. Despite the small number, WGUC was still the sixteenth highest rated NPR station in the nation, a clear sign of public radio's challenges.[11]

Simply put, people either did not know about NPR or they did not find anything appealing on the network except *All Things Considered* and *Earplay*. Neither program was enough on its own. Plus, there were never-ending financial limitations as NPR had to fight for what it considered its fair portion of CPB's monies. Some years, NPR received 25 percent of CPB's budget, while the rest was earmarked for the favored television networks. These problems resulted in NPR not being able to supply its member stations with enough programming to cover an entire day.

Clearly, a new model was needed, but that model would have to conform to the confines of the fact that the CPB and NPR were, despite being independent, actually quite dependent on laws and lawmakers. Someone was needed at NPR who understood the worlds of both broadcast communications and politics. That someone was Frank Mankiewicz.

The same summer of 1977 that the film *Star Wars* had become a metaphorical meteor strike on the cultural landscape and a literal blockbuster with lines that transcended one city block to the next, Frank Mankiewicz was determining his next career move. Mankiewicz was born May 16, 1924, to Sara Aaronson and Herman J. Mankiewicz, and from the get-go, his was a life steeped in politics and media. Father Herman was a Hollywood screenwriter, eventually winning an Academy Award along with Orson Welles for the screenplay of *Citizen Kane.* It had been Herman who originated the idea that *The Wizard of Oz* use black-and-white imagery for the Kansas sequences to contrast with the colorful Oz in his uncredited contributions to that film. His interest in politics had emerged partly from his time as a journalist before starting his career in Hollywood. Known as "Mank" and the "Central Park West Voltaire," Herman Mankiewicz had a singular wit and creativity that made him a much sought after script doctor. Herman's brother was Joseph, a writer and director responsible for such classics as *All About Eve.* Home was a place, then, for Frank where politics and Hollywood collided, and it was at the dinner table and at parties hosted by his parents that his education began.

After serving in the European theater of war for the U.S. Army during World War II, Frank Mankiewicz earned a bachelor's degree in political science from the University of California at Los Angeles in 1947, a master's degree in journalism at Columbia University in 1948, and a law degree from the University of California in 1955. His careers were varied and impressive. He served as an entertainment lawyer, the Latin America regional director of the Peace Corps, and press secretary to Senator Robert F. Kennedy. It was Mankiewicz who informed an anxious public and press about the status and eventual death of presidential candidate Kennedy, which occurred on June 6, 1968, as a result of Robert Kennedy's being shot after delivering his California primary victory speech. Mankiewicz later served as the presidential campaign manager for Senator George McGovern. The Senator said of Mankiewicz, "I never got any bad advice from Frank. I found him just fascinating to travel with during the campaign."[12]

In April 1977, Ronald C. Bornstein, general manager of the WHA radio station and director of NPR's committee responsible for finding a new company president, met with Mankiewicz. Ironically, Mankiewicz was not familiar with much of NPR's programming, having only learned of *All Things Considered* three weeks earlier while driving.[13] But Mankiewicz liked the challenge and certainly was able to navigate through politics and broadcast realities. When he assumed the presidency of NPR on August 1, 1977, he found the situation even worse than imagined. Not only were ratings a problem and funding deficient, but Mankiewicz was immediately faced with workers claiming low wages and threatening a possible walkout. Recognizing the value of talent both on air and behind the scenes, Mankiewicz negotiated a union contract for better wages and solved his first NPR crisis.

Mankiewicz had a bold plan with two priorities. The first, increasing nonfederal funding, produced immediate controversy and debate among the NPR ranks. Since its founding, NPR had relied most heavily on federal funding. Now, Mankiewicz was altering the rules, bringing in more corporate sponsors to public broadcasting. The fear of critics was that public radio would become influenced by corporate goals or, worse, be transformed into a shill for business interests. The whole reason for public funding was so that NPR could be insulated from corporate sponsorship and influence.

Mankiewicz thought NPR had enough wherewithal to avoid that problem. "What public broadcasting needs," he argued, "is not so much insulation from underwriters as courage on the part of management to say, 'We're going to do it anyway.' I suppose there are some listeners who wish we didn't have underwriters, but the only other option is not to be on the air."[14] Corporate monies began to flow more readily to NPR from companies such as IBM, the Mellon Foundation, the Marshall Foundation, and Xerox, easing a bit the burden of depending on the federal government.

The second part of Mankiewicz's plan was to improve NPR's ratings. This goal required a multipronged approach. Innovative technologies could improve the reach of NPR, and NPR would make history in 1980 by becoming the first radio company, public or private, to have its own satellite distribution network. Another idea in the spirit of the past being prologue was Mankiewicz's notion to duplicate NPR's two ratings successes. If *All Things Considered* was a winner in the afternoon, then perhaps a morning news program would duplicate those numbers. *Morning Edition* would be exactly that, a rating giant, and Mankiewicz hired Cokie Roberts as NPR's congressional correspondent and other journalists to build the NPR news brand.

Could the visibility of *Earplay* also be duplicated? Mankiewicz was really more interested in the news as the venue by which to improve NPR's fortunes, but he realized that NPR needed more than that. Radio dramas could provide NPR with something unique that was not readily available on commercial networks. Mankiewicz turned to John Houseman, an old friend of his father Herman and of the family. Known to audiences for his Academy Award–winning role of Professor Charles W. Kingsfield in *The Paper Chase* (1973), Houseman's roots were in theater and radio.

In 1937, Houseman and Orson Welles formed The Mercury Theatre, adding The Mercury Theatre on the Air the following year, which would produce radio dramas for the CBS radio network in addition to their live performances. One of their collaborations was perhaps the most influential radio drama of all time, the October 30, 1938, adaptation of H.G. Wells' *The War of the Worlds.* The panicked reaction by American audiences to the realistically presented drama about a Martian attack on Earth, some of it real, some of it media hype and fantasy, left an inedible mark on radio and even led to Congressional hearings and new laws about what could and could not be broadcast by radio networks. By 1968, Houseman was the founding director of the Drama Division at the Juilliard School, which would educate actors such as Christopher Reeve and Robin Williams, as well as Perry King, who would play the role of Han Solo in the *Star Wars* radio dramas. Of Houseman, King said, "I love John Houseman, but I can't call him John or even John Houseman. I have to call him Mr. Houseman. He was the leader of Juilliard. He led it with a powerful hand."[15]

In addition to his acting schedule, at the time that Mankiewicz called on his friend for advice in 1977 about new radio drama ideas, Houseman was a university artistic director. He did have a suggestion. Mankiewicz should talk to his colleague at the university, Associate Dean Dr. Richard Toscan. That university just happened to be the University of Southern California, alma mater of *Star Wars* creator George Lucas. And there upon turns the tale.

2

Giants Marking Time

If the University of Southern California were a location in the *Star Wars* universe, it might arguably be most similar to the Massassi Base on Yavin 4. Both were safe havens for innovators, creative thinkers, and, yes, rebels of one sort or another. Both were hubs where challenges to the status quo occurred, and at each location, future leaders were forged and found. One was student George Lucas, who transferred to the University of Southern California (USC) School of Cinematic Arts in 1964 from Modesto Junior College. At USC, he gained a reputation as a promising *cinéma vérité* editor and filmmaker, producing experimental student films such as *1:42:08*, *The Emperor*, and the inspiration for his first professional film, *Electronic Labyrinth: THX 1138 4EB*.

Other graduates of USC who would work on the *Star Wars* films included producer Gary Kurtz; sound designer Ben Burtt, whose audio effects would become an essential ingredient in the *Star Wars* radio dramas; visual effects supervisor and writer John Knoll; and John Moohr, a vice president at Lucasfilm. While not a USC student, director Steven Spielberg once joked about how many USC graduates worked in the film industry: "If all of the alumni didn't show up for work tomorrow morning, Hollywood would grind to a halt."[1] What was true for the *Star Wars* movie, that USC was a network for talent, would also be true for the *Star Wars* radio dramas.

If USC was the Massassi Base, then Richard Toscan was its General Jan Dodonna. Toscan was born during the 1940s, "a Manhattan brat" as he describes himself, until his parents moved to Connecticut for its better schools. In yet another connection between Orson Welles and the *Star Wars* radio dramas, Toscan's uncle was an investor who was friends with the actor. "My uncle owned an apartment building downtown around Washington Square and he ended up getting to know Orson Welles, who rented an apartment there. He was much younger and loved to spend money. Every year Welles would run out of his trust fund before the 12 months rolled around for the new deposit and my uncle would write off his rent for a month or two to help support him because he liked the work that he and John Houseman were doing at the Mercury Theatre."[2] Connecticut would also be, where at the age of 11, a much deeper introduction to the technology of radio and sound editing would begin for Toscan. He recalls:

> It was the height of the Cold War then and a handful of us kids were selected to be backup ham radio operators in the event of a nuclear attack so we all got FCC licenses, and for the first time I understood how radio waves were transmitted and how those radio dramas I listened to in Manhattan got to my ears. And then one day a van drove up our driveway and unloaded this huge box that turned out to be an early hi-fi console with record player, radio, and most importantly for me, a reel-to-reel tape recorder. And I discovered I could put together tracks from different albums on tape. The tape kept breaking on those early decks, so my parents gave me a simple tape splicing thing and I taught myself how to do my first editing of analog audio tape.[3]

In high school, Toscan began working for a rock DJ at a local radio station. "Both the station and DJ were both strangely similar to the character played by Wolfman Jack and his station at the center of Lucas' *American Graffiti*. The DJ taught me how to use professional turntables and cue 45-rpm discs. That's also where I got my first hard lesson in the business of radio: audience size matters. He was fired by station management for not delivering the listener numbers the owners expected, ending my gig as a radio rock-jock assistant."[4]

While Toscan started his college studies at Purdue University as an engineering student, he quickly realized that what he enjoyed, tinkering around with technology, was not quite the same thing as modern engineering. Instead, he changed to English, political science, and journalism for his undergraduate program, where he also translated the work of poet and playwright Bertolt Brecht. After earning a Woodrow Wilson Foundation fellowship, Toscan realized that his passion was theater history and dramatic literature for which he earned a PhD at the University of Illinois (UI) in Urbana. At UI, he spent time at the electronic music studios where computer scored and synthesized music was being developed.

He remembers, "There was very little interest in sound and sound effects in the theatre department, so I became the sound designer, creating sound effects reels for theatrical productions. Then one day a student named Tomlinson Holman stopped by the sound lab and asked me to teach him how to edit tape for sound effects. I was overjoyed to finally have someone interested in sound so we worked together in that tiny lab for several months."[5] Years later, Holman would develop the THX system for Lucasfilm that ensured the quality of sound for the *Star Wars* films in theaters across the country beginning with *Return of the Jedi*.

It was one of many coincidences prefiguring the *Star Wars* series for Toscan. Perhaps that choice to study the arts was in the genes, as Toscan tells it, "I only learned much later, after I was involved in Hollywood, that my grandmother had been a screenwriter back in the late 20s to the 30s during that transition to talking films. My parents had always been actively involved in the arts one way or another. I was taken to what I think was my first theater production of *Porgy and Bess* in New York when I was about six years old. I still remember the mechanics of the revolving stage and the amazing music, kneeling on the seat so I could see."[6]

Toscan applied for a National Endowment fellowship, which led to a job teaching in Fresno, California, which he had been told was scenically located between the mountains and the ocean.

> I said yes and ended up going out to Fresno, discovering it was a long haul from either the mountains or the ocean. I spent three years there doing a mix of directing, running the experimental college, which was about new approaches to instruction, and getting more involved in experimental theater in America during that time. One of the things I did, which prompted me eventually to move to the University of Southern California, is that I hired Luis Valdez, the founder of El Teatro Campesino, which began as the theatre arm of Cesar Chavez's farm workers union. In the middle of a college in Fresno, California, in the middle of the central agricultural valley, this was not viewed as a great move for a young junior professor to make. But I got to know Luis Valdez and it led to my being offered a position in USC's theater program as their American theatre person.[7]

By 1977, Toscan was associate dean of the School of Performing Arts. He was also tasked with a double responsibility: temporarily taking on the role of chair of the theater department, replacing Alex Segal, a renowned director of *Playhouse 90*, who had become seriously ill.

> The issue was who could we have be the next head of the theater program? A friend of mine Ed Kaufman, who was professor in USC's Cinema program, and I went to a show at the Mark Taper Forum one night. At some point, Ed said, knowing what happened with the former head of the theater program, "John Houseman is sitting about five rows back. Why don't we ask him at intermission if he wants to be head of the theater program?" At intermission, John was staying in his seat. So we worked our way five rows back to him and pitched him on this idea. And, as I got to know John much better in later years, one of the many things that John loved was money [laughs], but he also loved training young talent for theater and film. He founded the renowned theater program at the Juilliard School and developed the curriculum there. And obviously, USC had a major theater reputation, so the request wasn't like it was coming out of the blue. He was intrigued right away and said, "Let's have a discussion." John and I met with the Dean and John agreed to be artistic director if I would manage the place. And the deal was done. We got to be very friendly

which is what eventually led to the radio dramas and his putting his two cents in on the productions of those radio dramas.[8]

While at USC, Toscan was able to bring his passion for radio to the college, especially through its radio station, KUSC-FM 91.5, a Los Angeles National Public Radio (NPR) affiliate owned by the university and funded by NPR, the school, and donations.

> When I was a little kid growing up in Manhattan, my parents had one of these small wood-cased radios. And every afternoon or night, I would sit with the volume turned as low as possible, listening to the Golden Age of radio drama, mostly drama rather than comedy. Everything from *Suspense* to *The Green Hornet* to *The Shadow*, all those great productions. And I probably listened to them enough that somehow it altered my brain. I never forgot those radio dramas, no matter how old I got, and can still remember scenes from some of them. While I was at Purdue, I offered my services to the student radio station that was based in the men's dorm. I got this sort of part time gig, running a show involving mostly concept albums, and presenting them as though they were live concerts with narration and music. And people thought they were pretty swell.[9]

Toscan began having conversations with Wallace A. Smith, who had been a graduate student at USC when he became general manager of the KUSC radio station.

> I don't know what prompted it, but Wally and I started talking about radio drama. NPR gave $10,000 or something like that to KUSC and me to do a couple of radio dramas with the understanding that these were not going to sound like *Earplay*. John Houseman suggested I should be the producer of these things. John knew a guy from his New York days of radio drama named Fletcher Markle. He was to be the director and the writer of the series. The idea was suggested to adapt the Raymond Chandler short story "Red Wind." Through John, I went to Chandler's widow and got the rights for some small amount of money, $50 bucks. She was reasonably happy to let us do that. We recorded it as a one-hour adaptation with Richard Widmark as Philip Marlowe and followed that with a sci-fi adaptation of Damon Knight's "Stranger Station" with Richard Thomas playing the astronaut stranded in a malfunctioning space station. I think those two shows are what convinced Houseman I knew what I was doing in radio drama and especially my ability to work with A-list performers.[10]

Richard Widmark was still a grand old name in Hollywood then, and Richard Thomas had just finished his turn as John-Boy on the hugely successful television series *The Waltons*. It was because of his work on "Red Wind" and "Stranger Station" that Toscan refined his ideas about what radio dramas should be like for a contemporary audience. Those lessons would eventually shape the *Star Wars* radio dramas.

I realized then, that one of the distinctions between what NPR had been doing and the way in which it really needed to be done was that radio drama was essentially like film, much more so than it was like theater. It required a production approach that was similar to how actors perform in film. And the great mistake, I think that is made today by a lot of the productions of audio drama that are being done in what I call the New Golden Age—unlike the most successful programs like *Homecoming* and *The Bright Sessions*—is that most of them are falling back on the assumption that because you can't see the performers, they have to push vocally to express to the audience what's really happening. They're performing much more like stage performers who are trying to reach the back row of the theater instead of realizing that they're whispering in somebody's ear.[11]

In the late 1970s, earbuds were still part of a science fiction future. Toscan continued: *Radio* really was the operative word in radio drama then. That's how everyone listened in those days unless you were a sound geek and used those clunky and uncomfortable headphones. So that did require a more active performance style to compensate for the distance listeners were from their radio—the source of the sound. The second lesson from "Red Wind" was a result of the radio drama taking place during a Santa Ana wind, which in those days of LA in the 1940s and 50s, when Chandler was writing, were called Red Winds. Houseman told me they really did drive people crazy. There were many fewer trees to block them or slow down the winds or add moisture to the air. And people really did get psychologically and emotionally affected because of these winds.

We needed a wind. Markle brought in this old Foley artist to do live sound effects for us and who had the wind from that classic Western, *High Noon*, on tape and we used that in "Red Wind." Whenever the wind was embedded underneath the scenes as environmental ambience, whenever that wind was blowing, my ears just perked up. The show seemed to take off in a way that it didn't when they were in some interior location where you couldn't hear the wind. My approach to contemporary radio drama is that environmental ambience is critical to the comfort level and emotional engagement audiences have in listening to it. So radio drama had to match our experience in real life where all the talking we hear actually has some sort of ambience under it. It never takes place in a silent vacuum and when it does in radio drama, it's physically uncomfortable for listeners even if they don't realize it.

And that environmental ambience could also tell you as much about the location where the performers were as the image you see on screen in a film. That means that in the dialogue of a contemporary audio drama, you didn't have to provide as many direct descriptions and clues of where characters are. You didn't have to say, "Let's go to the diner and have lunch." Step, step, step. Plates tinkling around. "Isn't this a nice diner? Let's have a cheese sandwich." You don't have to do that kind of nonsense.[12]

Frank Mankiewicz had contacted Houseman during 1978 about his thoughts on radio dramas and whether NPR's existing radio dramas could attract more listeners. He sent Houseman record albums of *Earplay* episodes, asking him to review them and to let Mankiewicz know if it was worth putting a major public relations (PR) effort into similar radio dramas to help NPR produce on a regular basis the audience it needed for better ratings. Toscan recalls:

> Although John and I had offices across the hall from each other, I didn't know what was going on with this. One day John marched into my office in his usual bow tie and sport coat, carrying this big box of records. He says, "Play these records." The reason he came in is that I was the only member of the faculty who had a 33-rpm record player and speakers and amplifier in my office because of my radio drama work. He plunks down albums representing the entire output of *Earplay* over about seven or eight years. One by one, I would pull out the album, plunk it on the turntable, drop the needle, and the thing began. Within 10 seconds, John says, "Next," which is what he used to say when he would audition actors. They'd open their mouths and say, "Hi, my name is Joe Schmo" and he'd say, "Next." So anyway, we went through about 12 to 15 *Earplay* recordings, and I think the longest he listened to any of them was about 20 to 30 seconds. And he didn't say anything about what this was about or whatever. He just got up, took the box, and was gone.[13]

Whatever Houseman's opinion, he apparently advised Mankiewicz that if he wanted to produce a new radio drama series that could attract audiences, Toscan was the person to do it. On the same day that Toscan signed his contract with NPR, Houseman gave him advice that would eventually lead to the adaptation of *Star Wars* for radio. "I remember John being in my office after I had signed on the dotted line with NPR to be the producer of this thing," Toscan details.

> I said to John, "Now that you got me this gig, how do you think we could create an audience for contemporary radio drama in America?" And he thought for a minute, almost as though he was being Professor Kingsfield from *The Paper Chase* and in his best Kingsfield voice, he said, "Create a scandal." That was the watchword then for whatever we were going to do. I had no idea what we were going to do. But the watchword was *create a scandal*. I was totally unclear how we would do that. But I realized what he meant was the way he and Welles attracted a huge audience for *War of the Worlds* by creating a scandal, though they didn't realize they were doing that when they were making the show.[14]

The ideas flowed, but none of them had the proverbial legs required to sustain the project. Houseman had made some suggestions that for one reason or the other did not manifest themselves. The British Broadcasting Corporation (BBC) had agreed to partner with NPR on the initiative, with the deal being that they would provide the writer and half the funding for the thirteen half-hour episodes, which was the traditional number of radio drama series episodes. Everything else would be produced and supplied by NPR. Toscan's contacts at the BBC were script editor Richard Imison and Aubrey Singer, managing director of BBC Radio and BBC Television. Singer not only was responsible for programming in Great Britain and the Commonwealth but joked that his job was doubly difficult because he had to program in America for PBS television. Toscan recollected:

> I spent a fair amount of time at the BBC palling around with Richard Imison and we talked about various ideas. One of the thoughts I had because we'd done "Red Wind" was maybe we could do a Chandler series, which had not been done in an American production. The BBC had done a UK production with American sounding performers. Initially, Imison was not sold on the idea. But by the time we finished lunch, he said, "It would be interesting to do Chandler with an American feel to it." He was, and this will come back in importance later in terms of *Star Wars*, sensitive to cultural differences between the US and UK.[15]

Despite being responsible for producing radio dramas at the BBC, Imison did not suggest other options for this new producing partnership with NPR. However, he did have something else on a small tape cassette that would be important to what was to come. Toscan shared, "I was leaving the BBC for *Heathrow* and my flight to LA when Richard pulled this cassette out of his pocket and said, 'Play this when you get back to California. You'll be interested.' That's all he said, but he had this sort of mischievous grin that made me want to get home as soon as I could to listen to it."[16] Having returned to Los Angeles, Toscan was astounded by what he heard. "It was a 20-minute radio play without any dialogue, told entirely through sound effects and environmental ambience."[17] The show was *The Revenge*, a controversial production Imison had just completed, one of the first experiments with then new binaural recording techniques for radio drama. "That cassette did away with any lingering doubts I had about sound really being the key to telling audio stories. What it told me was that complex soundscapes combining effects, environmental ambience, and score, were essential for this new sort of radio drama I was imagining. At least for me, it said that the time of this practice being thought of as just a minor add-on in radio drama was over."[18]

But were Chandler's Philip Marlowe mysteries the strategy to realize Toscan's vision? "I once again called Chandler's widow and pitched the idea of a 13-week series based on Chandler's short stories. She was very nice and pleasant about it, but basically said at $50 per show or whatever, and nonprofit public radio, it's too much trouble. She didn't want to do it."[19] Looking back years later, Toscan realized he hadn't fought very hard or really at all for those rights. "Even when I was about to call her, I'd had this tiny warning buzz somewhere in my brain about whether an anthology series could attract the sort of audience we were after. No matter how I looked at it, the Chandler idea would still have come across as a series of

13 self-contained and essentially unrelated stories only held together by a great central character. And along with that worry, there really wasn't any scandal I could see that could be ginned up out of any of this. In hindsight, I was lucky she said 'No.'"[20]

It was tough generating an idea because, as Toscan told journalist Ray Richmond in 1981, "We're hoping to attract a whole generation of listeners who have been raised on visual entertainment and think of radio as something that's used only for background. For about the last 20 years, drama has been done as it was in the 30s and 40s. I'm trying to introduce people to an art form—the radio drama—that's practically vanished and attract them to stay with it."[21] Toscan had the goal. Toscan had the experience. What was needed was an idea, and they just didn't have it. That is until a former USC student named Joel Rosenzweig visited Toscan to say, "Hi."

A native of Los Angeles, Rosenzweig's father Aaron attended the USC's music program, returning to teach there. Aaron learned to play nine different instruments, contributing to many motion picture scores. Because of his father, Joel Rosenzweig had a love for USC, musical theater, storytelling, and film. He was a freshman at USC while George Lucas was a senior, and the two of them met a few times at parties. Rosenzweig's son Marc describes his father Joel as someone who:

> wanted to be an actor, singer, he wanted to perform in musical theater, perform on TV, for film. He had a professor during his sophomore year, say to him, "You know, Joel, be the director. Don't be an actor. You'll get bored being an actor." This professor saw that he had a real interest in integration, and not just the performance aspect, but the storytelling aspect itself, and crafting the story and the way it should be presented and told. He had multiple professors tell him how good he was specifically at character breakdown. He would eventually direct stage and television, including one of the highest rated episodes of *Cagney and Lacey*.[22]

Rosenzweig was also good at creative and combinative thinking, something that would play an important role in the making of the *Star Wars* radio dramas. Marc shares:

> For his senior thesis, Dad took an experimental theater course. The entire class each pitched their ideas for what the experimental theater class production would be. Dad was out late one night at a USC college party, and was racing to the class the next morning, driving late, and The Who's *Tommy* was on the radio. He got to class while various students were giving their ideas. My dad was sitting in the class hoping and praying that he wouldn't need to pitch until the following week because he hadn't prepared anything. And of course, the professor said, "Okay, Joel, what's your idea?" And on the spot, because my Dad was an idea man, a totally creative idea guy, said, "'Well, I want to do a stage production of The Who's *Tommy*. I want to introduce my generation,

through the music that they love, to musical theater that I have this great appreciation for because of my father. I want to introduce it to them through a rock opera, and music that we all love." The professor said, "It's just an album." My dad said,

"Well, there's a story there and we would put it on as a rock opera, as a musical." The professor told him to come back next week with the idea fully fleshed out. The class and the professor agreed that they were going to move forward with doing The Who's *Tommy* and that that was going to be the big production they did as a class for their senior thesis, and my dad would direct it.

The senior class president came into the rehearsals. I think he was maybe dating someone in the show or close friends with someone in the show or something like that. At the end of the rehearsal, he asked my Dad, "Would you be willing to do this not only as your senior thesis, but as the USC senior class show?" As the senior class show, it'd be put on in the largest auditorium on campus, which I believe at the time had only been sold out two or three times and that was for Martin Luther King, Jr., and John F. Kennedy. My dad, of course, says, yes. Doing it as a senior show also came with additional funding as well, which there wasn't much of originally since it was just supposed to be this class project. They ended up selling out all five of the performances. The show got a lot of press and a lot of excitement. My dad was 22 or 23 years old, graduating and super excited about the show. He started getting approached by producers, both in LA, who wanted to do the show professionally at some major theatres, and also by Broadway connected producers. Dad came to an agreement with The Who's manager at the time. As a 23 year old getting paid to direct professionally his own show, that was a great situation for him.[23]

Marc reveals an irony, however, about Joel Rosenzweig and his idea that created the rock opera theater genre, "His original vision was of getting his friends into musical theater and having them appreciate it the way he did through their music. He said what actually ended up happening was the opposite. Instead of introducing his friends to musical theater, he introduced the previous generations to The Who."[24]

After graduation, Rosenzweig's affection for USC brought him back occasionally to campus. Toscan continues,

A former graduate student of mine, Joel Rosenzweig stopped by. We met when he was a student and I knew that he was doing a stage adaptation of the rock musical *Tommy* on the USC campus, with all student performers and players in the orchestra. He asked me to be the faculty advisor because the Student Affairs Division of the University got very nervous about this production. That is how we really got to know each other. And it was a brilliant production. Over the following years, Joel periodically would stop in to say hello.

One day, Joel visited about a month or six weeks into my stewing about what we could do for NPR. We were chatting about what he was up to and his projects and so on, and then got around to what I was doing. I was explaining how I had this thing with NPR and that I knew we needed to create a scandal. But I

> couldn't find an idea. Without even missing a beat, he says, "Why don't you do *Star Wars*?" And it was an instant click. That was the thing that had legs. That was the thing that would be a scandal. How on Earth could we possibly take the most visual film in Hollywood history and turn it into a radio drama? And then if the story was well done, and the thing was produced as I thought radio drama should be, we'd be able to hold the audience for all 13 weeks and with luck, it would produce what Frank wanted.[25]

What no one else could see, Rosenzweig did. But there was another reason Rosenzweig's suggestion was taken seriously by Toscan and that was because of how brilliant his adaptation of *Tommy* had been. Toscan recalled, "His original staged version was absolutely brilliant. Joel really was a genius as a director."[26] That was brought home many months later when commercial producers took over Rosenzweig's concept for *Tommy*. "Joel invited me to opening night and from the first bars of the overture, it was obvious they'd totally destroyed his concept. They'd rescored it as though The Who had written an ordinary Broadway musical. I felt sorry for Joel, but it underscored for me what great production instincts he had."[27]

Unfortunately, Rosenzweig died at age sixty-six in 2014. At the time, Marc, now a writer and director, was studying at USC, the third-generation Rosenzweig to attend the school, when he learned the news. "Dad went in for what was supposed to be a routine surgery and he had some blockage in his arteries, and they were putting in stents. It's supposed to be something that happens all the time. He would be at the hospital for a day. He'd be able to teach again next week. He had the stents put in and they said it was a successful surgery. They sent him home. And that night he collapsed. I was in LA. I was a sophomore. I was doing my midterms, studying for those."[28]

Throughout his many accomplishments, Joel Rosenzweig was proud to have contributed something to *Star Wars*, though never interested in receiving credit for his contributions. Marc shares, "I think even though my dad wasn't involved in the *Star Wars* movie, I think he took pride in it because of it being the creation of a fellow USC student. He really believed in the USC community."[29]

Thanks to Rosenzweig, Toscan now had his scandal. The question was, would Frank Mankiewicz agree? Moreover, would George Lucas let NPR convert the biggest box office success of all time into a radio drama?

3

The Deal

During the summer of 1978, Richard Toscan met at a local New York deli with Frank Mankiewicz and John Bos, director of National Public Radio (NPR) Arts and Performance Programs. Over corned beef sandwiches, Toscan pitched the idea of a radio adaptation of *Star Wars*. Surprisingly, Mankiewicz himself required little convincing. The same would not be true of others at NPR, but Mankiewicz was sold almost instantly on the concept. Bos and Mankiewicz recognized that a *Star Wars* radio drama held within it the same kind of ratings and publicity possibilities as the radio drama that Orson Welles and John Houseman had achieved with their own adaptation of a popular science fiction tale, *The War of the Worlds*. Time was running out for NPR to make the splash necessary to generate the funding needed to achieve Mankiewicz's goals. Bos and Mankiewicz knew a good—if risky—idea when they heard it.

Mankiewicz explained his reasoning: "*Star Wars* not only provides us with an opportunity to make use of the latest technological developments to produce radio drama, it is also a major step forward in involving a broad range of American talent at every level. This series should provide a stimulus for drawing new people to public radio—both as listeners and participants."[1] Speaking to *The New York Times*, Bos recalled, "How do you get a young audience back to radio except for the 'Top 40'? We wanted to borrow the allegiance to *Star Wars* of young people and this gives us a chance to demonstrate state-of-the-art radio—the best available technology."[2] But Mankiewicz knew he would have to convince others at NPR among the executive staff and board, some of whom did not like what was perceived as his radical ideas in the first place. How would they react to sinking a sizeable amount of precious resources into something as mainstream as *Star Wars* when public radio was meant to be educational?

But whether NPR executives were on board or not with the plan would be of little consequence if Toscan could not secure the rights first from George Lucas. Toscan remembers the challenge:

> There was a period of about three months or so where the first question was, how best to approach Lucas and Lucasfilm. I was talking with a young lawyer colleague of mine about Lucasfilm and *Star Wars*, and the problem of how to make contact with Lucas. He says, "Oh, I went to business school at USC with the business manager at Lucasfilm, I can get you a meeting there." So the two of us went out and met with the Lucasfilm team. I pitched the idea of *Star Wars* for radio. Would Lucasfilm give the rights at some reasonable amount? You know, the usual public radio sob story because we didn't have a lot of money. Would they consider such a thing?[3]

A few weeks after his August 1978 meeting with Lucasfilm, Toscan was contacted with the good news that the company was interested. The negotiations would be tricky due to the lack of resources available to NPR and the fact that, according to Toscan, "We didn't at that point really know what George Lucas' attitude was toward this whole thing or what getting the rights would really mean."[4]

By this time, as Mankiewicz was working on convincing executives at NPR about the wisdom of the plan in addition to his other responsibilities, Toscan's NPR contact became Samuel C.O. Holt, a pioneering academic and radio executive. In 1967, at the request of the newly formed Corporation for Public Broadcasting, he conducted a study about the feasibility and process of developing public radio, which became the blueprint for how NPR was created. Holt was the coordinator of programming for the Public Broadcasting Service (PBS), playing a role in creating shows such as *Masterpiece Theatre* and *The Electric Company*. It was Holt who hired both chef Julia Child and Fred Rogers of *Mister Rogers' Neighborhood*. At the time of the development of the *Star Wars* radio drama, Holt was the senior vice president of programing for NPR and was the primary advisor to Mankiewicz.

As the day drew closer for the lawyers from Lucasfilm and NPR to begin negotiations, Holt called Toscan. "Holt said, 'I know this is going to be hard, but I think we need to change lawyers. I think we need someone with really substantial experience in entertainment law and rights and so on. Is that okay with you? We'll pay the guy who made the first introduction.' This is kind of how Hollywood operates so it was not out of the blue that such a thing would happen," observes Toscan.[5] To negotiate, NPR brought in lawyer Thomas G. Gherardi, senior partner with Dean, Snowden and Gherardi, a boutique Washington, D.C., law firm with major clients, who had experience with such contracts. Everyone at NPR was amazed at the deal Gherardi secured and that Lucasfilm offered. It was nothing short of an extraordinary act of philanthropy on Lucas' part at a time when any *Star Wars* licensing was pure gold.

Lucasfilm would grant NPR the rights to the radio version of *Star*

Wars and supply the original sound effects and story for the sum of $1. That act of generosity also had an influence on the separate negotiations that were needed to secure the rights to John Williams's award-winning musical score as performed by the London Symphony Orchestra, owned by 20th Century–Fox. Toscan reminiscences, "I said to Tom Gherardi that I would also like to have the rights to the music. I didn't fully realize how important that was going to be." Toscan knew he had to have the original music to make the radio dramas the way he thought they needed to be done. "If I had the London Symphony score, then Ben Burtt's sound effects would have to be used throughout to match that level of sound. It was a sort of guarantee that I'd be able to get this new sound for radio drama out of the final mixes Tom Voegeli would do."[6] Toscan explained, "Could Gherardi get us the rights to the John Williams score? Lucasfilm controlled the rights to *Star Wars* proper, but 20th Century–Fox controlled the music. So Tom went to 20th Century–Fox, and how he did this, I don't know. But he ended up getting a deal where we got the rights for $1 per episode. $13 which was 13 times what we had to pay Lucasfilm for the story and sound effects rights!"[7] In other words, for the sum total of $14, NPR had the rights to do the *Star Wars* radio drama, featuring the original sound effects and music used in the film.

There were many reasons for this generosity. First and foremost, there was George Lucas. There was much about this project that would likely appeal to him. Lucas was a radio kid, part of that technological swing generation between the Golden Age of Radio and the Golden Age of TV. When he was born in 1944, radio was still popular, and television was getting ready to become ubiquitous. Lucas shared with journalist Jimmy Carter, "Well, I grew up with radio. We didn't get a television until I was 10 years old so mostly up to that period I spent my nights listening to the radio and radio dramas were very big then and it had a very big influence on my life."[8] Sound was essential to Lucas and his films, and he understood that it was music that carried emotion and sound effects that grounded visual special effects in reality. As an experimental artist, the idea of seeing if NPR could rise to the challenge of turning his visually relevant film into an audio-only experience would have been an exciting prospect. Lucas had fought against incredible odds to bring *Star Wars* to the screen and Toscan said, "That likely played a part in his agreeing to let us do it. It's easy to forget now that every major Hollywood studio he brought the script to passed on it. The consensus was, 'Nobody wants to see sci-fi anymore.' It was only after Alan Ladd at 20th Century–Fox agreed to take a second look, that Lucas' vision finally got a greenlight for production."[9]

The University of Southern California (USC) connection, and its role as the *Star Wars* radio hub, too, cannot be overemphasized. Lucas wanted to do something to give back to the school that had given him so much, and with the university's radio station, KUSC-FM, being the primary player and producer of the radio drama, giving the rights for only $1 could be one such act of gratitude. Vice president of Lucasfilm, himself a former USC graduate, John J. Moohr, said to *The Los Angeles Times*, "We were pleased to participate because it's a new medium for the product, also a contribution to the university. We think that radio can be a positive and complementary medium to film."[10]

Another reason Lucasfilm's generosity was something of the heart was that the radio drama would be free and accessible in a way that a movie playing in theaters would not have been. This was before the eras of home videos and streaming services, and before audio descriptions for the visually impaired were available in theaters. For shut-ins, those with vision challenges, and those without extra financial resources, the radio dramas were a way for everyone to enjoy the adventures of Luke Skywalker and his compatriots. In fact, it was this philanthropic aspect of the radio dramas that appealed to many of the performers. Mark Hamill, who would reprise his film role of Luke for the radio version, spoke of this idea in June 1981 to *Starlog* magazine:

> It appealed to me because it wasn't money-oriented. It sprang purely from the desire to help revitalize interest in radio.... This is one way that we can pay back and do something for the fans. This will be free over radio. It's not only great for the kids who can't afford the $4 or $5 to see the movie, but also for shut-ins. There are shut-ins I get letters from who say they have heard the records and all that but have never seen the film.[11]

Perry King (Han Solo in the radio drama) shares Hamill's emotion: "All the people involved in the making of the *Star Wars* radio drama, from Lucas on down, they were all doing it for some other reason than commercial. That's what was so beautiful about it. You felt that all through it. We were all here for one reason. To do something we can hand to somebody else who loves it. Something of quality that will be valuable to other people."[12]

In addition to the rights, Lucasfilm supplied NPR with the original screenplay, the novelization to the film that was credited to George Lucas but really written by Alan Dean Foster, and permissions to use, if they wished, materials from Foster's *Splinter of the Mind's Eye*, the book sequel to *Star Wars* that started the expanded universe of stories. None of *Splinter* would factor its way into the radio dramas per se, but it is important because it demonstrates how few resources were available in 1978 and 1979 regarding *Star Wars* lore and background materials.

Toscan was given one other gift, that of a Lucasfilm contact who would help shape the radio dramas and who deserves much credit for starting the now-popular *Star Wars* fiction and nonfiction book lines: Carol Titelman. As executive producer for Lucasfilm on the radio drama, she would liaise with Toscan, the executive producer of the entire project. It was Titelman who would act as Lucas' spokesperson and decider of what could and could not be in the radio dramas so as to conform to the *Star Wars* universe, reflect the values of the company, and not tread on any possible story lines of the forthcoming film sequels.

Born Carol Wikarska on July 7, 1946, in New York, Titelman graduated from the University of California Berkeley and became a film critic and editor of the influential Women & Film Project. Initially hired as secretary to Charles Lippincott, the vice president of advertising, publicity, promotion and merchandising for Lucasfilm, who was responsible for the brilliant marketing strategy of introducing *Star Wars* directly to comic book and science fiction fans at 1976 and 1977 conventions, Titelman eventually became director of publications. Her responsibilities included managing the burgeoning book and media tie-ins for Lucasfilm. Titelman shepherded *Splinter of the Mind's Eye,* the Han Solo trilogy of books by Brian Daley, served as editor on *The Art of* Star Wars, annotated *The* Star Wars *Portfolio,* wrote the introduction to *The* Star Wars *Sketchbook*, and authored *The* Star Wars *Album.* Titelman died in 2019 of complications from Alzheimer's disease. Toscan remembers her with fondness:

> She was really interesting, heavily into baking. I remember, every time she would bake, it was something like 10 or 12 loaves of bread that weekend. I guess it was her therapy for getting away from her Hollywood job. She began her career as I remember designing backpacks. She was interested in hiking. Lucasfilm hired her as a secretary, when they were starting out. She was from a product development background because of her work with this outdoor company. I found her wonderful to deal with. Sort of no nonsense, yet always pleasant.[13]

Toscan thought of Titelman as "the guardian of the world of *Star Wars.*[14]

For her part, Titelman also enjoyed working with NPR on the project, "We developed things that would have been logical for the film without touching any of the original literary concept George (Lucas) created. It's easy to run into problems when you're developing something, especially when you're somewhat restricting, but we have no major problems working together at all."[15]

With Lucasfilm on board as the licensor, and with the rights secured from 20th Century–Fox for the music, Mankiewicz was working on getting support from the NPR side. To do *Star Wars* right, it was estimated that the costs would be somewhere between $235,000 to $250,000 even with Lucasfilm and 20th Century–Fox basically giving the rights for next to nothing. This would make *Star Wars* the most expensive radio drama ever produced. Mankiewicz felt it was worth it, arguing to NPR that the series would not only likely improve ratings and provide visibility to the network, but it could help advertise NPR's new satellite technology, something they hoped would be ready by the time the radio dramas premiered. Using the technologically sophisticated galaxy far, far away to showcase modern NPR technology was the perfect synergy. Mankiewicz got most of NPR's agreement, if begrudgingly, although in some instances, some local stations refused to air the drama because it was not, in their view, simpatico with the mission of public radio. One of the reasons that the NPR board of directors agreed to *Star Wars* was because they had already asked Mankiewicz to secure the British Broadcasting Corporation (BBC) as co-producers on this radio drama venture. It was felt that whatever NPR lacked in expertise and experience could be made up by the BBC's participation.

The partnership had begun strongly, with Toscan and BBC executives Richard Imison and Aubrey Singer generating ideas before *Star Wars* was chosen. Singer expressed his hopes to journalist Dick Kleiner in 1979, "It is our first, and we hope certainly not our last, coproduction with your NPR. Secondly, we plan to put this on Radio 1; that is our 'pop' network with a younger audience, and it never before has had drama. And, third, we are simply delighted to have a property like *Star Wars*."[16]

The following quote is attributed to Alfred Hitchcock: "To make a great film, you need three things—the script, the script, and the script." Without a workable script, all the best laid plans of mouse droids and humans would not make the *Star Wars* radio dramas successful. It was the struggle to find a writer for the radio drama that put that originally good working relationship between NPR and the BBC in crisis. According to Toscan:

> The BBC was going to provide a writer. I can't remember the writer's name, but he was a respected BBC writer who had worked in science fiction a lot for them. He knew how to do multiple episodes. He had been writing for radio for at least 20 years. No slouch, very bright writer. The contract that NPR agreed to was a standard BBC contract for writers. By this time my wife Sharon and I are living in a condominium in Malibu and I'm stewing around, waiting for the first script and I keep calling. I need to look at the script and bring it to Lucasfilm for approval. One day, several months later, this fat package arrives in the mail, and it's the first seven scripts because his contract said that when he completed the seventh script, he would get paid his full fee. He had been sitting there, writing all seven scripts in order to make his entire fee on this thing. From his point of view, it was a good decision, I'd have to say.[17]

The problem was, the scripts were unusable. Toscan said:

> I start reading it. It is a well written radio script. Yet, it wasn't *Star Wars*. The characters were in there, Luke and Vader and Princess Leia Organa. Consistently, it's the world of *Dune* mostly, much more that and the world of Tolkien, than *Star Wars*. Though those had been influences on Lucas, he came up with a very different world. The scripts were not *Star Wars*. The question was, as for any producer, really, do you go back to the writer who has missed the boat, even though they are an accomplished writer, and attempt to edit it into something that will reflect the work you're adapting, or do you move on? My conclusion without talking to anybody about it was there was too much at stake to try to do that. I made copies of those seven scripts and trundled out over the mountain to Lucasfilm, handed them over to Carol Titelman, and said, "I don't think these are workable. But I need you to read them and tell me if I'm right about that." She told me, "Yeah, you are right. I can't approve these."[18]

Perhaps the fundamental problem was that the scripts lacked the unique vibe of *Star Wars*, something the team producing the radio dramas would come to think of as a kind of American energy. Although *Star Wars* owed strong inspirational debts to the films of Akira Kurosawa, most especially 1958's *The Hidden Fortress*, there were also influences, direct and indirect, of American war pictures, Westerns, *The Wizard of Oz*, and other American art forms. It had a kind of pow-zap entropy familiar to readers of American comic books and viewers of Saturday afternoon cartoons and movie serials. The result of Toscan and Titelman's realization that the BBC's best was not able to produce a usable script threatened the continuation of the project.

Toscan wrote to Imison and Holt saying that the writer would not work and was being fired. "That letter led to an immense explosion out of the BBC offices in London and at NPR in Washington," Toscan revealed. "For Richard and Sam, my letter was saying that *Star Wars* can't be done for radio. For Imison, the thinking was if you don't use our writer, the BBC is out of it. We are not going to pay for it."[19] A meeting was scheduled for a few days later in Los Angeles for Toscan, Imison, and Holt to discuss the future, if any, of the project. It was not looking good. Sound designer Tom Voegeli concurs:

> Everyone got nervous because originally the BBC was the co-producer and the BBC, because it was the BBC, they wanted to modify the scripts to make it different. They sent trial scripts that did not conform to the world of *Star Wars*. I mean, they were the world of *Star Wars*, but they were very, very different. When the BBC withdrew, it was a really difficult situation because the Director General of the BBC had come to a press conference to announce *Star Wars* for radio, yet the BBC couldn't be involved in a co-production that it didn't have ultimate control over. And of course, they didn't give them control on these radio dramas. So it almost blew up at that point.[20]

Toscan continued with this idea:

> The day after getting that feedback, and knowing the whole project was at risk of blowing up, I decided not to go into the office. Instead, I sat at my wicker table in Malibu, with my tiny electric typewriter, and using the screenplay and novelization, I wrote a 30-minute episode, the opening episode, as a pilot for what *Star Wars* should be. I lifted the dialogue directly from the screenplay and novel for the most part but putting it into audio terms. I duplicated two copies besides my own original and expressed mailed it to Imison and Holt. I didn't put my name on it, because after the blowup I thought they might dismiss the script if they knew I'd written it. I wrote a note that said I wanted them to look at this script, that it was by "a young writer associated with Lucasfilm." I was young. I was a writer. I was associated with Lucasfilm. And so it wasn't a complete lie, but it was a typical Hollywood distortion. A few days later, I got Imison at the airport. Sam was there. Imison said of the script that I sent him, "I hadn't read this script until I got on the plane. I guess it was reading it on the plane, but I could feel the energy in it and understand your point about the other scripts. And yes, this could work."[21]

This vote of confidence was the result of Imison being sensitive to cultural distinctions. Despite this understanding, Imison shared bad news. The BBC was not going to put any money into the project as a co-producer. They would listen to it once finished and perhaps decide if they wished to pay for the rights to air it. Although the BBC was no longer a direct and participating partner, Imison had blessed the project, which was enough to satisfy Holt that it should continue. Toscan's script had calmed corporate nerves and proved it was indeed possible to write a *Star Wars* radio adaptation.

Toscan revealed, "The whole point of my pilot was to prove it could be done. Unfortunately, Richard and Sam liked the script too much. Now they were eager to meet this anonymous writer."[22] Holt wanted the writer of the script to be the writer for the entire radio drama. It was now time for some candor, and Toscan confessed he was the writer. Holt said, "Maybe you should write the series?" to which Toscan thought for only a moment and then decided, "I think as producer, it's better for me to have somebody else write the series rather than trying to wear both hats."[23]

The clock was ticking. Everything was nesting together—the rights, the budget, NPR's support—but there was no script. Was there perhaps a writer Lucasfilm could suggest? There was. Enter Brian Daley.

4

The Brian Daley Solution

"I'm a guy with a hot ship and places to go."[1] With these words, Han Solo describes himself, with his usual swagger, in the book *Han Solo at Stars' End*. Without the braggadocio, the description could easily also describe the life of the novel's author and radio dramas' scriptwriter Brian Daley.

It is not hyperbole to call Brian Daley the heart of the *Star Wars* radio dramas. Via his words, listeners learned more about Luke Skywalker's alienated youth, Princess Leia Organa's mercy missions, and Han Solo's transformation from rogue to hero. Daley gave C-3PO as much purpose as humor and Chewbacca as much moral courage as mere sidekick-ery. He showed fans corners of the universe that were not shown in the film. From Leia's relationship with her father on Alderaan, to her bravery while being tortured by Darth Vader, to understanding exactly how Luke was able to pilot an X-wing expertly despite never having flown one before, Daley expanded each of the *Star Wars* movies in organic, believable, and character-enhancing ways. The original *Star Wars* film has only about twenty-seven minutes of actual dialogue during its two hours and one minute running time. By contrast, Daley would need to generate five hours and fifty-six minutes' worth of material for the radio drama. Brian would fill in those details using some extraordinary Lucasfilm resources and, most especially, his own imagination. For Brian was not only a talented writer—he also was a *Star Wars* fan. Brian's contributions and life, which would end entwined intimately with the *Return of the Jedi* audio drama, are worthy of remembrance.

On December 22, 1947, Englewood, New Jersey, was bracing for a snowstorm that would have made even a Tauntaun skittish on the planet Hoth. The headlines in *The Record* newspaper advised, "Cold Weather Here, Chief Gives Warning." While travelers braced for the worst, Brian Charles Daley was born at Englewood Hospital to father Charles and mother Myra Ann Daley. The blizzard was so bad that it kept Brian and his mom at the hospital until after Christmas. To bring cheer to the stranded

Brian and his mother, nurses sang "Away in a Manger." The holiday favorite would become, ever after, son and mother's song.

Daley grew up on Gerson Lane in Rockleigh, New Jersey. His older brother by six years was David; his younger sister by six years shared the same first name as their mother, Myra. The Daley family worked hard, with his father and mother working full-time to make ends meet. Charles was a natural-born salesman, selling everything from automobiles to encyclopedias, and Myra Ann was a stenographer and cook at St. Joseph's Village, which was a local orphanage across from their home, and in summers for a day camp.

Daley's appreciation for books began when his mother Myra Ann gave him a copy of *The Black Stallion* during the summer after second grade. As a result, he started reading anything he could get his hands on, especially *Flash Gordon* comics and the writings of Jack Kirby, Poul Anderson, Isaac Asimov, Arthur C. Clarke, and eventually William Gaddis, Thomas Pynchon, Jack Vance, and two authors who would have influences on Brian's later Han Solo novels, Robert Heinlein and Lester del Rey. "I looked to [Heinlein's] books as a model when I started doing the Han Solo books," said Daley in an interview with *Star Wars Galaxy Magazine*.[2] It would be Lester del Rey's wife Judy-Lynn who would give Daley his first book contract. Some of these influences for Daley, *Flash Gordon* most particularly, were also inspirations for George Lucas, which is one reason Daley was able to navigate the worlds created by Lucas so easily.

Daley's sister Myra remembers, "Brian collected Marvel Comics. We probably had every comic that came out. Even when he was in Vietnam, he had a list of the ones that my mother had to go and buy every month. There were thousands of them. His favorite TV shows were *Captain Video* and *Flash Gordon*."[3] Mowing lawns, dog walking, and babysitting were some of the ways that Daley supported his comic fandom. His comic collection was so large that it became a draw for kids in the tight-knit community, who spent time at the Daleys' sharing comics and reading Brian's issues.

Daley became enamored of science fiction, reading, and writing. While his siblings and other kids were out playing, Brian was inside writing. "My oldest brother David and I were much more active," Myra shares, "Where Brian would always go to his Royal typewriter and be typing away all the time. David used to joke that while we were outside with other kids playing, Brian was inside reading about kids like us who were outside playing."[4]

This early love affair with science fiction is described by Daley's best friend James Luceno, who would eventually make his own significant contributions to the *Star Wars* universe as the author of *The New Jedi Order: Agents of Chaos I: Hero's Trial*, *The New Jedi Order: Agents of Chaos II: Jedi Eclipse*,

Darth Maul: Saboteur, Cloak of Deception, Labyrinth of Evil, Dark Lord: The Rise of Darth Vader, Millennium Falcon, Tarkin, and *Catalyst: A Rogue One Novel,* among other short stories, comics, and *Star Wars* reference texts. "I was a science fiction fan, but not in the way Brian was. Brian was a fan of science fiction from the get-go. I mean, he was a collector of comics, he had read everything that had been published in science fiction. He was a wealth of information. He had a really amazing memory, not just for books he read, but he could just quote from movies and from Shakespeare."[5]

Brian Daley had his eyes on the stars from a young age. "We did not have a lot of extra money to spend on entertainment and we didn't have air-conditioning," Myra explained. "At night, Dad would get us outside and spread a blanket on the lawn to show us the stars. And then he told us about them. I don't know how Dad knew anything about stars. It was great because Rockleigh was a rural town and at that time there was no sky-glow so the star gazing was amazing and that became our evening entertainment. I think that really had a big influence on Brian and his interest in space."[6] Daley would dedicate his book *To Waters' End: Book Four of GammaLAW,* "In memory of my father, Charles Joseph Daley, and of meteor watching on warm August nights."

Mother Myra Ann's influence was more down to earth. Myra Ann gave Brian a love of music, as she had been a radio singer when she was younger. Brian would harmonize and sing with her. When Brian was in Vietnam, his mother sent him a box of kazoos, so he started a kazoo band with his buddies there. Not merely inspiring Brian's love of reading and writing, Myra Ann instilled in her children the value of education. Daley's sister Myra reminisces, "When we were young, my mother was big on reading. She actually taught me to read before I went to kindergarten. That was just her thing. We must have got all the awards for perfect attendance at school because we were never allowed to stay home. 'You get up and go to school. The taxpayers are paying for your education so don't waste their money lying in bed.'"[7] As a symbol of his love and affection for his mother, Daley would dedicate his fantasy book *The Starfollowers of Coramonde* in part "for Myra A. Daley, who knew."

A good student, Daley attended Nathan Hale Elementary School and the Northern Valley Regional High School at Old Tappan. His yearbook described Brian as an avid reader, with a clever humor who loved folk music. As a budding writer, Daley was the only male in his high school typing class, which helped account for his proficiency as a typist when he became an author and his admirably neat manuscripts. His science teacher Mr. Petrus started Daley's fascination with science and technology, and Daley was part of a group of science-minded friends who nicknamed themselves The Egg Heads.

Another influence on Daley was famous journalist Edgar Snow who lived in the town. "Our father used to drop us at Edgar's house on weekends," Myra explains. "He had a big library and he would talk to us about him being the first American journalist permitted in China. He wrote the classic 1937 book *Red Star Over China*. Brian really enjoyed listening to him. He was a great guy and his wife was a soap opera star."[8]

Myra remembered that Brian and David were, through it all, the best big brothers, albeit a little overprotective.

> I used to cry to my mother to find me another babysitter because they were so overprotective. They would bring me to the town swimming pool. Back then we wore huge orange life preservers like you would use on a ship. They were gigantic. Brian would make me wear my life preserver from the time we left our house until the time we got home. I had to wear it when I was having lunch with the other kids, which was embarrassing. Brian helped me sell Girl Scout cookies. He would let me sit on the handlebars of his bike and take me door to door. I was the only Girl Scout in my little town, so I had the market cornered on sales. When the *Babes in Toyland* movie came out Brian took my friend and me on a bus many towns away to see it. He sat alone in the back row of the movie theater with his head down because the entire audience was little girls. Just another reason I loved my brother.[9]

While he wanted to go to college, finances delayed that dream. The solution for Daley was to join the U.S. Army. It was an idea his mother approved of, Myra recalled. "My mother Myra Ann's father was an English soldier killed in World War I at the Somme Offensive when my mother was four years old. He left my grandmother with two young children and this affected her for her entire life. Eventually, her mother married an American soldier and moved to the United States. My mother insisted that both of my brothers complete their military obligation before they marry."[10]

"He signed up at 17," Brian's partner Lucia St. Clair Robson shared, "He was in Vietnam at 18. He could go to school on the GI bill and he wanted that college education because his family couldn't afford to send him. He was always very, very loyal to the Army."[11] Being underage at time of his enlistment, Daley needed parental permission, which inspired him to frequently joke that "my mother had to sign a permission slip so I could join the Army after high school because I was not yet 18."[12] While at Fort Dix, Daley would need to learn how to use his right hand to fire weapons because he was left-handed. It was during a year-long tour of duty in Vietnam with the 11th Armored Cavalry Blackhorse Regiment that Daley was affected by the conditions of Vietnamese children in a local orphanage, perhaps because of the time his mother spent working at the orphanage near his Rockleigh home and because he knew, from his mother, what it meant for a child to lose a parent due to war. "He would go to the orphanage and entertain the children. He was very talented musically. He could sing harmonies, but he did not play an instrument,"[13] recollected Robson. After the war, Daley continued to send money to that orphanage for many years.

By 1967, he had earned a rank of specialist 5, somewhat equivalent to a sergeant. His mother wrote to him on July 1, 1967, and she told him that she was watching the news and saw his regiment featured at exactly the moment the phone had rung, with someone asking for Brian. "Well, there went the good resolve not to get emotional," Myra wrote to Brian. "Anyway, here's the message which you probably have already received."[14] Myra shared that the phone call was about Brian being transferred on September 24 to Berlin, Germany, as an Army security analyst. Myra then went on, in the way only a concerned parent could, to counsel Brian that family friends had cautioned her, "it's always cold in Germany, so maybe it would be too big a change for you." Myra ends the letter with, "Be careful now, and God bless you."[15]

Thinking of that time, Brian's sister Myra shared:

> We had a Welcome Home from Vietnam party for Brian at my brother David's house. Cousin Dan Daley announced at the end of the party that he would be leaving for Vietnam at the same time Brian was leaving to be stationed in Germany. Dan was killed in action while on a combat mission. Brian was told of his cousin while he was in Germany. Brian was so angry and began to plan to go back to Vietnam. The Army said no because they needed him for work in Germany. My uncle told Brian that my mother suffered badly from the stress of Brian's first tour in Vietnam and begged him not to return.[16]

Although Germany was purportedly safer than the active hot war in Vietnam, Daley was there during the anxious days of the Warsaw Pact's invasion of Czechoslovakia in August 1968. One of Daley's responsibilities in the service was writing war zone reports, which continued to develop his writing skills. As with many Vietnam vets, Daley forged relationships with his comrades that endured past his service time. He returned to New Jersey and to his home during August 1969. According to sister Myra:

> Brian was a sleepwalker when he was a kid. He would perform while sleepwalking, acting out all kinds of comic book stuff. When he came back from Vietnam, he was staying at Mom's for a while. In our town, they used to have a fire whistle that was very loud. One time, the fire whistle was activated in the middle of the night. Brian came running out of his bedroom, yelling. It was frightening. My mother asked what he was doing, but he was back mentally in a war zone. He was trying to shove her, to protect her from artillery. I was crying. I just wanted Mom to get down and to make sense out of whatever was happening. "He doesn't know who we are." We couldn't reason with him. He was in another world. I believe it was post-traumatic stress disorder. The fire whistle triggered his reaction.[17]

With the G.I. Bill providing tuition, Brian wanted to start college. Myra and Brian both took their SAT tests at the same time despite her being six years younger. In keeping with Brian's motto of "anything worth doing is worth overdoing," he got a perfect score on his verbal and a near-perfect score on his math portions of the test. Brian was a preparer, studying diligently for the exam, typing Latin words and all the checklists. A few weeks after the tests, a high school counselor called Myra to his office, wondering, "You know, what is going on here? You are the better student academically, and your brother has been out of school four years, and yet he does better than you?" Myra answered, "I'm in high school. I can get by on 125 words. Brian was an Army Security Analyst writing war reports every day. He has been writing every day since third grade."[18]

The fact that Brian earned a perfect score on the verbal portion of the SAT exam exemplified his intellect. Daley had a knack for language and spoke Spanish. Robson described Brian as "brilliant, good looking and kind of unaware that he was that way. He just had a voracious appetite for information. He understood everything. He was an encyclopedia. I don't know how he did it, but he knew so much information. He had so much information in his head. I was astonished by how easy he made it look. Not just the military, but machines and everything. He knew how things worked."[19] One of the reasons that the *Star Wars* radio dramas had an authenticity about them was that Daley understood how the real military functioned and knew how to communicate that kind of detail.

Brian studied media at Jersey City State College from 1970 until 1974, graduating magna cum laude. His classes focused primarily on writing and media, including a creative writing class where Brian wrote poems. He learned how to make amateur films and began his first novels, one a serious treatment of the experiences of returning veterans, the other a more fantastical adventure, *The Coramonde Campaign*, the story of Sergeant Gil MacDonald and his armored personnel carrier crew being magically transported from a fight in the Vietnamese war zone to a magical land. It was around this time that Daley met James Luceno.

> My wife and Brian's girlfriend at the time were waitressing in New Jersey. Brian had just finished *Doomfarers* and I had just finished an early draft of my book *Headhunters*. We met in New Jersey while he was still in school at the time. He was doing some acting, in fact, he was playing the Chief in *One Flew Over the Cuckoo's Nest* at that time, and so we each read each other's novels and we became fast friends. It was one of those relationships where we liked each other right from the start. He was a bit wild in those days. Maybe I was, too. He was the life of many parties. He spoke like he wrote. He was very funny. Very, very fast. Just a pleasure to hang out with.[20]

While shopping the book around to publishers, going to school, and after graduation in 1974, Daley earned money at whatever was available to help make ends meet, such as working as a bartender, waiter, dock worker, a Medicare specialist who created a special program to help returning veterans, and a UPS truck cleaner. He was proud to have graduated from Jersey City State College, frequently wearing for years a red shirt with the school's logo.

Daley would return to Rockleigh to vote because that was his legal residence. Myra laughed, "Mom wanted him to vote there, and it was a lot more fun to vote in a town of about 30 or 40 voters where every vote truly counted. Every year Brian would come out of the voting booth and ask for a pen. When anyone asked why, he said, 'Yeah, I'm writing in myself, because I don't trust anyone on the ballot.' My mother hated that line, 'Oh, Brian, why do you have to do that and cause a big ruckus?.'"[21]

The years 1976 and 1977 would change Daley's life, both as an author and as a science fiction fan. Ballantine Books had started a new imprint during 1976 by Lester del Rey and run by his wife, editor-in-chief Judy-Lynn del Rey. Specializing in science fiction and fantasy, Del Rey's first book was fortuitously *The Sword of Shannara* by Terry Brooks. Del Rey associate editor Owen Lock had read Daley's *The Coramonde Campaign* manuscript, by now retitled *The Doomfarers*, which he found in the slush pile—jargon for the pile of unsolicited manuscripts sent to publishers. Lock thought *Doomfarers* had promise and he liked that it was, joked Daley, the most neatly typed of the group. With editing and rewriting, Lock thought it could be worthy of publication. Judy-Lynn del Rey was skeptical, having previously rejected the novel in February 1975. At that time, she wrote to Daley's representative that he was a promising writer, but there were too many glitches with his book. She encouraged Daley to submit more, but added that he should clean his typewriter keys because she had difficult distinguishing an e from an o because of the ink.[22]

To his credit, though, Daley took the notes that del Rey had sent on the novel and instead of despondency, there was revision. Daley appreciated that as a new writer, he could learn from more experienced editors and writers. Del Rey agreed to publish Daley's book upon reading the new version and with Lock's recommendation. On July 6, 1976, Daley received a call with the news that he had sold his first novel and that Ballantine wanted him to create a sequel. While lecturing at his alma mater, Daley revealed, "If I could draw a line right through my life, before and after, it would be that day, that minute, that phone call when I found out I was actually going to be paid to write."[23] The next day, Judy-Lynn del Rey wrote a letter to Daley welcoming him to Ballantine and telling him that she was delighted to be publishing the book. She praised his professionalism reworking the novel and rightly predicted the book would be the first of many Daley and del Rey would produce.[24]

With that, Daley would begin a long association with Del Rey and a genuine friendship with Lock who discovered many science fiction authors working today, giving them their first breaks in publishing as well as advice. In August 1976, Lester del Rey decided to rename Daley's book to what he considered a more fantasy-friendly combination of the author's previous titles. The now renamed *The Doomfarers of Coramonde* would become the first of nearly fifty novels published by Daley. Luceno reflects, "I think Brian really comes to life in his own books. You really have to read *Doomfarers* and *A Tapestry of Magics* and his other books to really get a sense of what an amazing writer he was. He can write a character that someone else created, but his own characters are extraordinary."[25]

Before *Doomfarers* was even published, Daley had begun work on a sequel. However, Daley experienced what he called his sophomore slump, receiving a seven-page letter from Lester del Rey outlining some of the improvements needed.[26] Daley took the advice to heart, improving on what he considered the other half of *Doomfarers*, rather than a sequel, much the same way George Lucas conceived of his trilogy of films as being one story. Originally, Daley proposed various monikers for the book, *The Sword, The Firmament,* was his first idea. Then, later Daley recommended either *The Trailingsword, A Sword Among the Stars*, or *The Starfollowers of Coramonde*, with the latter being the name that del Rey accepted.

Daley's *Coramonde* duology was received with critical and sales success. Two of those who wrote congratulations to Daley would themselves become *Star Wars* authors in addition to successful writers in their own right. On March 25, 1977, Del Rey colleague Terry Brooks wrote Daley that he enjoyed *The Doomfarers of Coramonde* and jokingly chastised him for sitting around instead of working on the sequel, adding his encouragement and words of inspiration.[27] Brooks would go on to write the novelization of *Star Wars: Episode I: The Phantom Menace* in 1999 among his own numerous bestsellers. Kevin J. Anderson, a reviewer for *The Madison Review of Books*, wrote to Daley on August 15, 1980, about *The Starfollowers of Coramonde,* sharing how much he liked the book and praising Daley for his research.[28] Anderson eventually authored or co-authored more than sixty *Star Wars* comics, books, and short stories from 1994 until 2005.

The Doomfarers of Coramonde was published in 1977 as part of Del Rey's first group of books. It was, of course, also the year that *Star Wars* premiered. It was the science fiction movie experience that Daley had been waiting for his entire life. Daley and Luceno went to see the film,

> We saw *Star Wars* together at the Paramus Theatre on Route 4. That helped bond us. The film was on Brian's radar. But I just remember sitting in the parking lot and drinking something that Brian had brought along and just going to the movie and just having our minds blown by the film. Especially Brian, he was never the same after *Star Wars*. I think for Brian, it was because he had such a vivid imagination. Like I said, he'd been immersed in science fiction for so long that to see sort of the images that he had in his head up on the screen was overwhelming for him. He just took to it immediately, which I think went a long way to making him one of the best writers who ever contributed to *Star Wars*. It was his universe. He just was right at home in that universe from the very start.[29]

Of his experience seeing *Star Wars*, Daley said he was, in his own words, "flabbergasted," and he told Lucia later, when recalling that day, that he left the theater transformed. He was most affected by both Luke Skywalker and Han Solo as characters and the designs and visuals of the droids and starships. Daley told Bob Woods of *Star Wars Galaxy Magazine*, "I have a real affinity for Luke. As a teenager and a science fiction fan, I shared his dream that there's a bigger world out there. They called him Wormie. They knew he wasn't going to stay there with them, and they resented it. I wanted Luke to be like a lot of science fiction fans. He knows there's something bigger out there, and that sometimes he doesn't fit in."[30]

On the other hand, Han Solo was the only character who faced a serious moral choice in the first *Star Wars* film, and Daley found the character fascinating. Plus, Daley had a lot in common with Solo. Although more humble than Solo, Daley also had a wry sense of humor, a joie de vivre, a military background, a charming personality, an adventurous spirit, and a love of fast vehicles. Luceno recalls, "He had a 1974 Stingray Corvette, kind of a classic he was very fond of. He had a lot of talents really. He had a terrific voice. He was pretty skillful at karate. He could play the spoons better than just about anybody I knew. He had a really good sense of rhythm. I think Brian could have gone in a lot of directions. Could have been an actor, probably even musician if he wanted."[31] Daley even had his own Chewbacca, a collie named Laddie who had one blue eye and one brown eye. A bologna sandwich and a soda or beer satiated Daley, who was, like Solo, a realist and satisfied with simple pleasures. Daley would sign his *Star Wars* books sometimes, "From the Wook, the Crook, and me" showing his affinity for Chewbacca and the pirate Solo.

Star Wars radio dramas director John Madden commented on Daley's affection for the galaxy created by Lucas, "I speak with enormous affection and admiration for Brian. He was sort of the original geek about this material, but in a way that far transcended that slightly reductive term. There was literally nothing he didn't know about the original material."[32]

By this time, Del Rey had been one of the few companies, with Marvel Comics and Kenner Products, which had agreed to take on *Star Wars* as a license before the film became the year's mega success and all-time box office champion. Robson noted, "Judy-Lynn del Rey had a personality as big as all outdoors. Judy told us the story of how this guy Charles Lippincott, George Lucas' publicity supervisor, just came in and they got some cockamamie story about something called a Death Star. They want to publish a book to go along with this movie. Judy was not originally that impressed apparently. But it worked out."[33] Worked out, indeed. The original *Star Wars* novelization, featuring a cover by Ralph McQuarrie and published on November 12, 1976, six months before the film premiered, sold out of its 125,000 first edition copies by February 1977.[34] The novelization would sell another 3.5 million copies in the next months.

The success of Alan Dean Foster's *Splinter of the Mind's Eye*, the first expanded universe novel, released during March 1978 as a hardcover and the next month as a paperback, was immediate. The book was on *The New York Times* Paperback Best Sellers list from April 23, 1978, until July 9, 1978. Both Del Rey and Carol Titelman at Lucasfilm wanted more. Naturally, Daley—due to his talent and his fandom—was one of the authors considered. Daley told Alex Newborn of *The Star Wars Collector* in 1995 that "Judy-Lynn said, 'Pick me somebody from *Star Wars* and write a proposal for a character novel about them.' The keys to the candy store.... At that time, Jack Chalker was preparing to write about Solo, and Leigh Brackett was scheduled to take on at least one Princess Leia novel. But all that changed very quickly, since Jack decided to finish the series he was working on and Leigh passed away. Solo was the obvious choice because he undergoes a moral transformation in the course of the movie. Everybody else starts out either good or bad, and stays that way."[35]

Writing his first work-for-hire novel, Brian observed, "I was a little worried because I would need Lucas' approval to some extent," but, "it was a chance to study Solo's character before he undergoes the changes in *Star Wars*."[36] There were several limitations that Daley had to deal with when writing the Han Solo novel. First, only Han and Chewbacca could be featured. No Empire, either. Despite these, Daley "was absolutely thrilled," said Luceno.

> And it was real work for him, because it was a quick turnaround on those books. If I remember correctly, he wrote one of them in a place that I was renting in New York, while I was traveling. I think it might have been the second book in the series. He was thrilled to be part of *Star Wars*, as you can imagine, especially being one of the first invited into that franchise. His first draft he was incorporating a lot of things from the film, then he found out he couldn't do this, he couldn't do that. He wasn't allowed to use this character or that

> character. But, he had gone out to Lucasfilm and he had a lot of archive material. So Brian had a lot to draw, but it was still a really tough and a quick turnaround. But he was great. He was terrific at that sort of thing. He could sit down and just write 20 pages in an afternoon.[37]

Robson still has the typewriter that Daley used to write what eventually became a successful three book series, April 1979's *Han Solo at Stars' End*, which Daley wrote in only six weeks; October 1979's *Han Solo's Revenge*; and August 1980's *Han Solo and the Lost Legacy.*

Han Solo at Stars' End tells the story of Han and Chewbacca about two years before the events of the first *Star Wars* film as they seek the help of a technician named Doc who can repair the *Millennium Falcon* after a smuggling run goes bad. More importantly, Doc can secure them the needed waiver documentation to operate in the Corporate Sector Authority (CSA) territory, even if not quite legally. The CSA is a government that exists in regions not controlled by the Galactic Empire and in an area of space that Han believes presents lucrative possibilities. Doc's daughter Jessa informs Han and Chewie that Doc is missing, but that she and her team can repair the *Falcon*. If Han is willing to rescue a group stranded on Orron III, he can also use their data center to get the waiver he desires.

To help, Jessa provides Han and Chewbacca with two droids that will accompany them throughout the three novels. BLX-5, known as Bollux for short, is a labor droid that many dismiss as useless. As is a trend with Solo's character, he tends to find value in those whom others reject, and Bollux becomes an important part of the team. Daley likened Bollux to a working-class longshoreman. The other droid is the information retrieval box known as Blue Max, which depends on Bollux for transportation, residing in the more mobile droid's chest. Daley named the droid after a Volkswagen Beetle he once owned that he called the Blue Max. For fans in Great Britain, though, they would know the pair as Zollux and Blue Max because the word bollux is a slang term.

A *New York Times* bestseller, *Han Solo at Stars' End* featured a cover by artist Wayne Douglas Barlowe, who had previously done the illustrations for the May 1978 *Star Wars: A Pop-Up Book* and would contribute the art for the unique flip-style *Star Wars: The Empire Strikes Back Mix or Match Storybook*. Fans of the first novel by Daley would only have to wait about five months for the release of the sequel, *Han Solo's Revenge*, featuring a cover by Dean Ellis, with designs by Ann Silver. That book finds Han and Chewie engaging in a quite usual side hustle. As cargo runs have slowed, Han and Chewie are accepting goods in exchange for showing the Kamarian Badlanders holodocumentaries outside the *Millennium Falcon*. The Badlanders can't get enough of the movie *Varn, World of Water.* Han makes the mistake of changing the show to the musical *Love Is Waiting*. As a riot begins, he realizes that the holofilm has taken on religious significance to the Kamarians.

He and Chewie escape, trying to find any kind of work available. Desperate, they accept a cargo mission only to learn that they are being asked to transport slaves. Han teams with a CSA auditor named Fiolla to try and stop the slavers because it is the only way for Han to be paid. But readers know that perhaps the real reason is that Han and Chewbacca know that slavery is an evil and must be stopped. *Han Solo's Revenge* constitutes the first time that the *Star Wars* galaxy addresses slavery, something that would become a recurring theme, especially for the character of Anakin Skywalker. Daley believed that the novel helped demonstrate just how much of a moral conscience Chewbacca had.

Carol Titelman and Lucasfilm were impressed by Daley's rapidity, creativity, and comprehensive understanding of the *Star Wars* universe with his first two novels. According to a note from Del Rey, Titelman asked only for a few revisions, more of an emphasis on Han's concern for Chewie in *Han Solo's Revenge*, and the avoidance of colloquialisms that were too Earth referential.

The last of the Brian Daley Han Solo books, *Han Solo and the Lost Legacy*, was written before the premiere of *The Empire Strikes Back*, but was not sold in stores until a few months after, making it a perfect companion piece to the 1980 summer of *Star Wars* fun. Cover artist William Schmidt gave form to the crystal masthead of Xim the Despot in a story which Daley wrote that feels like it would be home in either the *Star Wars* or *Indiana Jones* universes. The setting for the novel is in the Tion Hegemony, a name which would factor in the radio adaptation character Lord Tion. Han and Chewie are reunited with their smuggler friend Badure and begin a quest to unearth the fabled *Queen of Ranroon*, a lost ship that contains the treasures and robot warrior army of the once-powerful Xim the Despot. Meanwhile, Han also has to deal with Gallandro, the famed gunslinger he humiliated in the previous novel. In this novel, Han and Chewie part ways with Bollux and Blue Max and set a course for Jabba the Hutt, who Solo hopes will sponsor them in a Kessel spice run, setting up the events of the first *Star Wars* film.

Daley's Solo and Chewbacca trilogy would have profound effects on him personally, to the *Star Wars* franchise generally, and to the radio dramas specifically. Personally, it was because of the Han Solo books that Brian met his partner for the fourteen years before his death, Lucia St. Clair Robson.

Daley was asked by Owen Lock to go to Balticon 13, a science fiction convention held during April 13–15, 1979, at the Hunt Valley Inn in Hunt Valley, Maryland. Daley was reticent because he never sought the spotlight and rarely liked speaking in public or giving interviews, a sign of his humility. He would rather have been in New Jersey writing. Attending the convention was Robson, a Maryland librarian. On Friday the thirteenth, a day that Brian and Lucia would consider lucky despite its connotation, and on a lark, Robson decided to go to the panel about the Han Solo novel. Daley was sitting next to Arlene Lock, Owen's wife, waiting for his panel to start. Robson sat in the row behind him. He turned and started chatting, asking if she had read *Han Solo at Stars' End* which had released a few days earlier. Robson told the truth. No, she did not read it and was not a fan of media tie-in novels. Arlene turned around and told Robson, laughing, that Daley was actually the author. Robson was embarrassed, but Daley thought it was funny. He asked Lucia out following the panel and they remained together for the rest of his life.

"I was a librarian so it was a match made in heaven," Robson recalls. "I always loved books. My mother taught me the bus route to downtown West Palm Beach where the library was. The children's part was on the second floor. From then on, every Saturday, I would go by myself where the library was by the lake, check out books, bring them home and then spend the rest of the week reading. I was so smitten and impressed that Brian was published. He was a gentleman. He opened doors for me. He always walked on the street side when we walked down the sidewalk. He would walk on the street side so that if a car splashed it would hit him and not me. He was just aware. He was a guy who was very much aware of what was going on around."[38] Daley also encouraged Robson to write, and it was through the insistence of Owen Lock that she did, becoming a best-selling historical writer. "I wouldn't be a writer without Brian. I can't even imagine what my life would have been. He just added so much."[39]

Robson used to say to Daley, "I was just so lucky to meet you." But in an almost Solo-esque fashion, he would say, "It wasn't luck. It was kismet."[40] Daley dedicated his book *Requiem for a Ruler of Worlds*, "To Lucia, with love, thanks, and admiration."

The books would have a profound influence on *Star Wars* as much as on Daley. Out of his imagination would derive much that is familiar to fans of the saga. Examples include:

- Daley invented the Z-95 Headhunters, which makes its first appearance in *Han Solo at Stars' End* and would appear later in the mobile game *Star Wars: Commander*. Daley described the Z-95 that Han and Jessa's team use against the CSA in the novel as "a good little ship, legendary for the amount of punishment it soaks up."[41]
- Long before the *Millennium Falcon* gets the dreaded "scratch" on the ship during the obstacle-ridden access to the second Death

Star's reactor core in *Return of the Jedi*, losing its deflector dish, Daley had almost the exact same scene in the inaugural pages of *Han Solo at Stars' End*. As the *Falcon* tries to escape a CSA warship, Daley, writes, "There was a slight jar, and the shriek of metal torn away as easily as paper. The long-range sensors winked out; the dish had been ripped off the upper hull by a protrusion of rock. Then the needle's eye was threaded sideways, and the Falcon was through the mountains. Perspiration beading his face, dampening his light brown hair, Han pounded Chewbacca. 'What'd I tell you? Inspiration's my specialty.'"[42] The moment, developed independently from Lawrence Kasdan's script for *Empire*, also beats the film to the punch of having the *Falcon* escape its pursuers by turning on its side and eking through dual rock formations. That Daley used the same stunt as the movie makers demonstrates how much he understood the character.

- The shipyards of Fondor, which would later play a role in the video game *Star Wars: Battlefront II* and numerous books, including Daley's best friend Luceno's novel *Tarkin*, was a Daley creation. Bollux reveals that he was activated at the great starship yards of Fondor.
- In a mixture of coincidence and fortune telling, Daley foreshadows the debate that will occur nearly two decades later among fans as to who shot first, Han Solo or Greedo, in Chalmun's Spaceport Cantina, which erupted because of the changes wrought by the 1990s special editions of the films. In *Han Solo at Stars' End*, Solo brags, "I happen to like to shoot first, Rekkon. As opposed to shooting second."[43] Another sign of how intimately Daley understood the character.
- From October 6, 1980, until February 8, 1981, *Han Solo at Stars' End* was adapted by editor Archie Goodwin and artist Alfredo Alcala for the daily newspaper comic strip produced by *The Los Angeles Times Syndicate*.
- Swoops or swoop bikes were another Daley innovation. Han and Fiolla use swoops to escape in *Han Solo's Revenge*. Swoops would make appearances in *Star Wars: A New Hope Special Edition*, *Shadows of the Empire*, and most especially, be the transportation of choice by Enfys Nest and her Cloud Riders in the movie *Solo: A Star Wars Story*. Swoops would feature in several episodes of *The Clone Wars* animated show and its original film. The speeder bikes of *Return of the Jedi* are close cousins of the swoops.
- To escape the planet Bonadan and their slavery pursuers, Han and Fiolla take a starcruiser named the *Lady of Mindor*. The ship is

reminiscent of the function and purpose of the galactic starcruiser *Halcyon*, which was featured at the Disney *Star Wars Galaxy's Edge* theme park.

- The idea that there is a common language, known now as Galactic Basic Standard, is first named by Daley. He calls the language "Standard" in *Han Solo at Stars' End*, then changes it to "Basic" in *Han Solo's Revenge.*
- Fans of Gamorreans know the vibro-ax which the guards frequently utilize. It was in *Han Solo's Revenge* where the weapon was first mentioned. *Return of the Jedi*, *The Mandalorian*, and *The Book of Boba Fett* would all feature Daley's invention.
- *Han Solo and the Lost Legacy* brings to life and names an idea that Daley learned while researching Lucasfilm materials. While it is George Lucas who created the idea that Chewbacca owed a debt of gratitude to Solo for saving him from slavers, it was Daley who first named and first explored the concept of a Wookiee Life-Debt or Honor Family. Life-Debts would play a role in *The Phantom Menace,* and Chewbacca's Life-Debt is transferred from Han to Leia in *The Empire Strikes Back* when Solo asks Chewbacca to take care of the Princess.
- "They don't give out the Corellian Bloodstripe for perfect attendance," says Badure in *Han Solo and the Lost Legacy.*[44] Costume designer John Mollo had added stripes to Han Solo's costume for added texture and a militaristic vibe. Daley gave the stripes meaning and purpose, revealing that they were earned for acts of extraordinary bravery.
- The crystal masthead of Xim the Despot, which is featured on the cover of *Han Solo and the Lost Legacy* and plays an important role in the book, can be seen as one of the treasures owned by villain Dryden Vos in the movie *Solo: A Star Wars Story*, which features Han and Chewbacca helping to free slaves at the spice mines of Kessel.
- Daley's books were the foundational materials for the 1993 book *Han Solo and the Corporate Sector Sourcebook* by West End Games for their *Star Wars: The Role Playing Game.*
- When author Ann C. Crispin wrote her 1997–1998 trilogy of Han Solo novels, which detail his biography until the moment that the movies begin, Daley's work was always an inspiration. The third book, *Rebel Dawn*, includes an interlude that summarizes the events of Daley's books. Crispin described her interactions with Lucasfilm regarding how experienced at romance Han should be: "When I discussed my conclusions with the Lucasfilm licensing

reviewer, she agreed with me that Han had had a number of girlfriends before he met Leia. (Brian Daley had invented several of them.) So, while I may have pushed the envelope a bit, I didn't originate the idea that Han was a man of the universe."[45]

- Jason Fry, author of nearly fifty *Star Wars* books, including the novelization to *The Last Jedi,* wrote a tribute to Daley and *Han Solo at Stars' End* on the official *Star Wars* website. "I have loved this book three-quarters to death over who knows how many readings. I read it as a kid, as a teenager, then consulted it innumerable times as an adult and a *Star Wars* author."[46]
- "I grew up on Brian Daley's Han Solo and L. Neil Smith's Lando Calrissian book trilogies," Marc Guggenheim, writer of the *Han Solo & Chewbacca* comic series from Marvel Comics that began in 2022, told Kellie Lacey of *Comic Books Resources*. "So, from my (ahem) certain point of view, these corners of the franchise have always been fodder for wonderful stories."[47]
- The Corpo of the Preox-Morlana Corporate Zone, who are featured in the Disney+ *Andor* series, is evocative of the CSA introduced by Daley as a substitute for the Empire.
- The April 5, 2023, episode of *The Mandalorian* Disney+ streaming series, "Guns for Hire" featured a scene at a droid bar. One of the patrons has more than a passing resemblance to Bollux.

With time running out for Richard Toscan to find a writer for the *Star Wars* radio dramas, the solution was not to be found in Hollywood or at the BBC, but rather right there at Lucasfilm itself. "I thought we needed a writer out of Lucasfilm who understood the world of the film, where they didn't have to do a lot of catch up on what it was all about," Richard Toscan recollects. "I had a meeting with Carol Titelman. I asked if it was possible she had a screenwriter that we could work with on this. Within a week, she asked me to come out to Lucasfilm and she gave me the *Han Solo* novels by Brian Daley. She said, 'Here's somebody I think you should look at because I think he might be very good for this job.' I read them and thought this guy knows how to do this, he knows how to write dialogue. He's got a real sense of the world."[48]

So with that, Daley was to make his own kind of hyperspace jump, from novelist to script writer. And he was about to take millions of fans along with him for the ride.

5

The Winds That Shook the Stars

The Script, the Director, and the Sound Engineer

In November 1979, Brian Daley received a phone call from Carol Titelman. Could he come out to Lucasfilm to discuss a new project idea? At the time, Lucasfilm was located at 3855 Lankershim Boulevard, in Universal City, California, in a building that was known colloquially as The Egg Company, sometimes known as The Egg Factory, because of its previous status as an egg warehouse. Titelman explained the situation to Daley. It would be a writer-for-hire situation like the Han Solo books. Daley would have more freedom than the Han Solo books owing to the fact that the original film would need to be expanded to thirteen half-hour episodes, but would always be within some parameters defined by Lucasfilm. At least this time Daley would be permitted to use concepts like the Force, the Empire, and all the characters and situations verboten to him while writing the books.

The scripts needed to be done so fast it would make the six months he had to write *Han Solo at Stars' End* feel luxurious. Plus, Titelman knew about the significant problems there would be converting the film to radio. "The biggest challenge we faced was re-creating the visuals into something for radio," Titelman later told the *Daily News*, "I guess the audience will be the best judge of how we did."[1] Would Brian be interested in scripting the radio adaptation of *Star Wars*? Without hesitation, yet realistic about the situation, Daley agreed. He was about to contribute directly to the film that had changed his life, and Daley couldn't be happier.

The magic number of thirteen episodes is one of the holdovers of the influence of the British Broadcasting Corporation (BBC) on the project. Director John Madden explained, "13 is a quarter of a year. A lot of the seminal BBC television series, for example, like *Brideshead Revisited*, or *The Jewel in the Crown*, were in 13 parts."[2] But Frank Mankiewicz also knew he needed a long season of episodes to have the potential for a real effect on National Public Radio's (NPR's) audience numbers. To Daley, the number of episodes was a good omen. Thirteen was his lucky number ever since meeting Lucia St. Clair Robson at Balticon 13 on a Friday the thirteenth.

What Han Solo actor Perry King recalls most about Daley is that sense of happiness.

> What I remember so well about Brian was his joy, his enthusiasm. He was so happy to be doing this. So proud and excited to be part of it. He was just filled with a kind of pure, innocent openness. He had a big beaming smile and he was shaking hands with everybody. And it just struck me that he was having his greatest dream realized and he knew it. And he was valuing it and appreciating it. That's what I mainly remember about Brian. He was a sweet guy that was so happy about what was happening. As we all were, really, because we all felt like we were doing something wonderful.[3]

While never having written a professional script before, and certainly not a radio script of this magnitude, Daley did have an understanding of the medium. As with George Lucas, born three years earlier than Daley, Brian listened to radio dramas as part of the radio–TV swing generation. "I just remember being a kid and coming in on the end of radio on the first TV coming into our home, so I sort of had experience with that," Daley told NPR's Derek McGinty in 1993.[4] During college, Daley was both formally educated in classes on radio production and worked at the school's radio station WBOX. Lucia St. Clair Robson believed:

> Radio was right up Brian's alley, I think. He thought it was great because he had always listened to radio. We grew up at a time when there were radio dramas. We didn't have TVs when we were kids so radio dramas were it. "Who knows what evil lurks in the hearts of men? *The Shadow* knows." I was riveted. I had a little radio and a room to myself, the smallest room in the house. My father who was in World War II, made me earphones. He fixed the radio so that I could wear earphones and not disturb anybody. I listened to so many radio dramas, with the sound effects and all of that. Brian was the same.[5]

Leaving New Jersey for California about a month before Christmas, Daley sought out his cousin, film and television editor LaReine Johnston, whose mother Adriana was the half-sister of Daley's mother Myra Ann. Although the two knew of each other through their parents, Daley had never met Johnston face to face. The two got on like cousins who grew up together despite never having met, thanks to Daley's personality. Johnston recalled, "Brian was the kind of guy that engaged with you immediately. Everyone felt very much at ease with him. Whether you were a stranger, he would engage with you like an old friend. He had that kind of personality. The great thing talking to Brian was that he looked right at you when you talked with him. He was a good natured guy."[6] Johnston believed this was an asset to Daley as a writer. "He was a disciplined writer. He also engaged people and wanted to listen and hear their experiences. Whether he was working as a social worker back in New Jersey or as a writer, he was always engaged. Maybe that's how writers get their ideas for their characters, from their interactions and experiences."[7]

During the first few weeks in Los Angeles as he began to have preliminary meetings about the *Star Wars* radio series, Daley stayed with Johnston until he found an apartment of his own where he could write. Johnston was already connected to the Hollywood community, having edited films such as the 1978 romance *Moment by Moment* starring Lily Tomlin and John Travolta. The cousins would pal around, attending Hollywood parties and haunting the famous Patys Restaurant in Toluca Lake, a favorite of many famous faces which had connections to *Star Wars*, including Carrie Fisher's mother Debbie Reynolds and future Jabba the Hutt radio drama voice performer Ed Asner. They went to see *Star Trek: The Motion Picture* at the Grauman's Chinese Theatre on opening day, December 7, 1979, at Daley's request. Daley was a fan of the original *Star Trek* series, although not as much as *Star Wars*. Johnston reflected that Daley "enjoyed those kind of experiences with fans because he loved science fiction."[8]

In the pre–Internet, pre-email era, Daley thought it wise to move to North Hollywood where he temporarily rented an efficiency apartment so he could better coordinate with Lucasfilm. Daley went to work immediately by first researching the materials that Lucasfilm provided him so he could expand the story with verisimilitude. In addition to the novelization, *Splinter of a Mind's Eye*, various drafts of the movie scripts, and preproduction materials, Daley was given something rather unique. During July and August 1977, Titelman had recorded and transcribed interviews with George Lucas as he pretended to be the characters he created for *Star Wars*. As Princess Leia, C-3PO, and Han Solo, Lucas answered questions about origins and experiences. Today, these documents are priceless, as they provide a window into what Lucas thought about the characters during the very summer the film was released. Much of what Lucas said about his characters would indeed become part of the sequels, while other ideas would be abandoned. For Daley, these transcripts represented Lucas' thoughts and feelings that would allow him to better understand the backstory of the characters, environments, and history of the *Star Wars* galaxy.

According to Lucas acting as Princess Leia, she had two brothers who were much younger than her. Luke's father's name is revealed to be Aniken, spelled differently from the final version. Lucas confirms that yes, women could be Stormtroopers,[9] an idea that would eventually get expression in some of the comics and on film in *The Force Awakens* with Captain Phasma. Much of the material with the Leia interview would find its way into Daley's script, especially the second episode, "Points of Origin," which details Leia's mercy mission to the planet Ralltiir and outwitting the Imperial Lord Tion while secretly receiving information about the Death Star from a Rebel spy. Tion, voiced by actor John Considine, was meant to be of the same family and political alliance as the Tion Hegemony from Daley's *Han Solo and the Lost Legacy.* "Points of Origin" also gave listeners the first scenes ever of Leia on Alderaan with her father, who is characterized much as described by Lucas in his interview with Titelman. The episode helps humanize the loss of Alderaan that was not possible in the quicker-paced film.

As Han Solo, Lucas revealed that while the *Millennium Falcon* was built on the planet Corell, a gas giant, Han himself is from the planet Saberhing. His parents were gypsies, and he was eventually orphaned and raised by Wookiees between the ages of seven and twelve before going to the Space Academy. This idea was almost included in *Revenge of the Sith* which originally featured a scene with a young Han Solo helping Yoda on Kashyyyk. One of Han's previous occupations had been herding Coldppeda, twenty-three-foot-tall animals that look like a mix between a giraffe and a lizard.[10]

During the interviews, Lucas shared that C-3PO was originally estimated to be 112 years old, made on the planet Affa. While eventually reversed by the time of *Revenge of the Sith*, Lucas as C-3PO claims he has never had his memory erased, but believes that R2-D2 had experienced many memory erasures.[11] Threepio shares with Titelman why it is that Chewbacca never received a medal. It was because medals have little meaning for Wookiees. Rather, Chewbacca was honored at a ceremony on Kashyyyk by his own family and friends because his victory was perceived as bringing honor to all Wookiees. Thus, these comments were the root for *The Star Wars Holiday Special* that followed during 1978.[12]

The reason for the uncertainty Threepio has about Artoo is revealed by Lucas during the interview to be because the droids only recently met before the events of *Star Wars*. Interestingly, early promotional material for the radio drama promised that listeners would learn about the first meeting of Threepio and Artoo. For example, *The Washington Star* newspaper foretold that "Among the new material is an episode in which Princess Leia travels to Alderaan where she meets her father prior to embarking on a daring mission that ends in a confrontation with Darth Vader. In other new episodes, listeners will hear how R2-D2 and C-3PO met, as well as more detailed stories on various conflicts within the Empire."[13] Daley was actually asked to avoid depicting the first meeting because Lucas would likely deal with that in some future film, which is exactly what occurred nearly twenty years later with *The Phantom Menace.*

These Lucas-in-character interviews were valuable to Daley as he started writing. "I read through them to see what he thought about the universe, and to see how he invented as he went along, what choices would he take when he had a creative decision, to flesh the universe out."[14] In addition to his own love and understanding of the film and the materials and guidance from Lucasfilm, Daley also had Richard Toscan to help who knew that "all Brian was going to need was some minor coaching on radio drama technique. I made another copy of the pilot script I'd written, and I sent him a copy of that and a group of blank format pages that had numbers down the left side, which was the standard US audio drama format at the time to use if they were helpful for writing of the script."[15] Toscan's *Star Wars* pilot was an important herald of the scripts that would eventually be created. "It was a radio script written as a screenplay with lots of short scenes, tight dialogue, and using sound to tell us what and where the action was," Toscan recalled. "Very different from what was then traditional US radio drama. That's where the 'energy' came from that Richard Imison felt while reading the pilot on his flight to Los Angeles. And there was no narrator."[16]

Daley paused long enough to enjoy the 1979 Lucasfilm Christmas party at The Egg Company. His cousin Johnston was there, too, and remembered it as a fun party where Daley would meet George Lucas and Harrison Ford for the first time. "People would come up to him because they knew him at the office."[17] For Johnston, her cousin was someone who did not give up his "boyish dreams, but rather got to live them out through his writing."[18] That does not mean creating the radio drama was easy, but writing and thinking fast were never problems for Daley. As Robson described, "If he had to write, he was like clocking in at a factory. Brian remembered everything. I'm the librarian. I've got to have a system. He'd write quickly right from his own imagination."[19] Ironically, Brian Daley, a science fiction writer, rarely used a computer and resisted using them even after they became the tool of choice for most writers. He preferred the clackity-clack of a manual Royal typewriter, even with looming deadlines. Meanwhile, Robson, a historical novelist, used the latest word processors.

Daley would finish a script and bring it to Toscan first, who would then make recommendations that Daley would implement, and then the script would be brought to The Egg Company building. At first, until the team of Daley, Toscan, Titelman, and Lucasfilm story editor Lindsay Smith found their groove, the process was arduous timewise. Soon, the team gelled, and they were reviewing three scripts at a time for edits. "The work process was that he would write his draft of the script and send it to me to edit," Toscan described.

> The first scripts he wrote were very nice, but they were overwritten in terms of dialogue. We were being told too much that we didn't need to know. And there wasn't enough room left for score and sound effects in it, so they needed to be spare in their writing. I would take a black magic marker and go through and probably cut maybe 10% of the dialogue, maybe in some sections of the script 20%, something like that, but a relatively small amount. Not rewriting it, though. We didn't need unnecessary exposition or direct references to location. Daley's attitude I remember in one conversation was, "I miss what's not there, but you're the boss." He was cool about the needed changes. I kept my role to that editing process through the 13 scripts. I didn't tinker with the structure of the scripts, he had that nailed. I would get each of these scripts and would bring them out to Carol to read and she would approve them in terms of what the information was in them.[20]

Sometimes the changes requested included the names of episodes. Originally, episode 10, "The Luke Skywalker Initiative," was called "The *Millennium Falcon* Irregulars." With the title of episode 6, "The Millennium Falcon Deal" being similar, it was thought wise to create a new moniker.

Because of Toscan's belief that radio dramas were more like movies than stage plays and that the sound effects could communicate as much, or more, than dialogue, the decision was made to limit the narration of the radio dramas to an introductory summary and an ending preview or tease of what was to come in the next episode. For a novelist, the removal of the narrator element was quite an adjustment. In his introduction to Star Wars: *The National Public Radio Dramatization* script books released by Del Rey in 1994, Daley wrote that without narration, "I felt like the prizefighter in the old joke who, told by the ref that there would be no biting, gouging, or kicking, says, 'There goes all my best punches.'"[21] But Daley adapted so proficiently, that Toscan revealed that Daley's scripts became the heart of the radio drama, "I was really happy to see the original material that Brian added that he made up himself and I knew then I'd made the right decision in hiring him."[22]

Daley enjoyed the opportunity to resurrect deleted scenes and create new ones. "In expanding George Lucas' creation to thirteen half-hour episodes, we who worked on the project got to revive 'lost scenes' from the screenplay and explore quirky corners of the story; in some ways the dramatization was akin to Tom Stoppard's play *Rosencrantz and Guildenstern Are Dead*, which shows what was happening elsewhere during Shakespeare's *Hamlet*."[23] Moments like Han, Chewie, Luke, Ben, and the droids needing to hide in the cramped, secret cargo holds of the *Millennium*

Falcon provided a dramatic moment worthy of further exploration, giving Daley a chance to showcase the characters and their apprehensions. Immediately, listeners of the *Star Wars* radio drama knew they were getting something different, yet familiar. The first episode, "A Wind to Shake the Stars," has no material seen in the original theatrical release of the first *Star Wars* film. Instead, Luke Skywalker's life on Tatooine is explored, featuring new moments from Daley's imagination and elements filmed but discarded with Luke's friends. Daley felt it important to have episodes 1 and 2, be moments that occurred before the film begins so as to really learn who Luke and Leia were, each getting a thorough focus.

About Luke and "A Wind to Shake the Stars," Daley told NPR's Derek McGinty in 1993,

> We see him interacting with his friends. And I think the most important part—and this was suggested by material that was cut from the script or from the movie itself, because Lucas, of course had to edit that movie down—we see that he is to a great extent, he's a misfit. Not that he is socially unviable, or that he is not a capable fellow, but he is restless. He feels like he is a little different. And in short, I mean, he is like a lot of teenagers who think that there is something that is calling them. There is something they want to do. And it is not the same as what everyone else is doing.[24]

Early during scripting, Daley was also let in on a secret that few knew outside of Lucas, Mark Hamill, director Irvin Kershner, screenwriter Lawrence Kasdan, and a limited group of trusted others: Darth Vader was Luke's father. "I knew going into it what the relationship between Luke and his father, as we find out, Darth Vader, would be at the end of *Empire*," Daley said. He was told because they did not want him, in his expansion of *Star Wars*, to deal with Luke's father. "I had had that explained to me by Carol Titelman at Lucasfilm, but I couldn't go into it too much. I wasn't allowed to give away any of this. It was a great secret to be sprung, 'I am your father.' Really, I think building in some premonition of that on Luke's part, some prescient experience, would have been fun to do in the first series, but you couldn't do that."[25] In addition to Luke's parentage, Daley could not use the character of Jabba the Hutt because of Lucasfilm's plans to use that vile gangster in the third film, which was then in the very early preproduction stages. Instead, Daley created the character Heater to act as a substitution.

In addition to making suggestions to Daley on story edits, Toscan was trying to find a director and sound designer. Because of the importance of the sound engineering, whoever was selected would, de facto, be acting as the editor of the radio drama as they assembled the material together. Toscan would turn to the experienced hands behind *Earplay*. "John Madden and Tom Voegeli had the reputation as audio creators. They knew how to work with major stars, with major performers, they knew how to get them, make them comfortable, and so on. Tom understood engineering. By the time Tom and John were hired, Brian had already written a couple of scripts. John then started meeting with Brian to lay out the thirteen increments of the story and what they would focus on how the plots would work. It was all Brian's work, but John was coaching him along the way."[26] Madden recalls working with Daley as an easy process, "It was a very, very good collaboration. We saw eye to eye on almost everything. And I'm sure that we did some adaptation or some compression or some rewriting as we went."[27] Daley's only proviso was that he wanted to be able to return to the East Coast for the St. Patrick's Day Parade, an important tradition for the fun-loving Daley. He met his goal, finishing the first draft of all thirteen episodes during mid–March 1980.

Considering his experiences on *Earplay*, Madden understood the potential and the power of a radio series adapted from *Star Wars* to create compelling and unique drama:

> There's something counterintuitive about it from a strictly sort of austere first principles radio drama production standpoint, which is that, famously in radio, what one always says, you don't really need anything, you just start with an empty space. And all you need to do is to put enough information in there that the audience, the people who are hearing what you're doing, what you're saying, provide the landscape themselves. They don't need any more than a simple hint or suggestion that will give you what you need. You can distill the world into something very simple. So that, you know, a door opening and closing can have an enormous significance in the right way, without any other context.
>
> During *Star Wars*, it felt as if what we were doing was taking worlds themselves indicated by sound effects essentially. What would happen is this would immediately key a landscape, because obviously, anybody listening to the radio drama adaptations, would by definition, have seen the films. I mean, there may be some people who've come at it the other way around, but I can't really imagine that as possible. So that what you were doing was, even though Brian would be writing scenes and we talk about adding scenes which obviously we had to because we had to amplify the original version, the actual story is in the film itself. We had an obligation to render those scenes. If you were writing these from scratch, you'd never do that. Because how could we possibly convey a battle? But part of the excitement of doing *Star Wars* was that you could do that. With a few well-chosen lines and a few well-chosen sounds, that picture was already in people's heads. *Star Wars* is a funny kind of backwards version of what radio drama could be.[28]

In radio, the image lives in the imagination of the listener.

Madden, like many working on the radio dramas, had been affected by *Star Wars*, "I remember seeing the film incredibly vividly. Because it was the first time I can remember a film you both wanted to see and then immediately wanted to see again."[29] Madden is proud of his association with *Star Wars*, "Whenever I am doing interviews for a movie or something, people always ask about the radio trilogy because it appears on my IMDB page. It is quite extraordinary the amount of interest there is."[30] Madden would prove to be the right choice of director, especially because he was able to both collaborate with seasoned radio veterans like Anthony Daniels and yet also help those new to the medium, which was a majority of the actors.

"John Madden is a good director. He was very warm and supportive to me," Perry King said:

> I directed a film not too long ago called *The Divide* that was a project I'd worked on for years. I was preparing to direct it as well as act in it. I read everything I could find on directing.... I found a quotation from Clint Eastwood who said, "When I'm directing, I tried to be the director I want to have when I'm acting." I thought, "Oh, my God, that's great. I know who that person is. The director I want to have." The director I want to work with is the director who says, "Great print, let's go on" or, if they don't like it, "Let's do another one." John Madden was definitely that kind of director who took what you had to offer. He was very aware of what you could bring to it. He let you bring it to it. And he didn't ask for something you couldn't deliver.[31]

Daley, too, praised Madden, "Not only did he know the movie, its locale, and its back-story well, but he made sure that his actors did. If a performer taking on a major role was unfamiliar with the picture, John would explain things thoroughly to that person before proceeding with the recording session."[32]

Voegeli understood not only the technological challenges—and there would be many considering the need to match the pioneering sound quality of the *Star Wars* film—but also the philosophical and artistic requirements of radio dramas. "The question we faced was how do you transfer what was admittedly a strongly visual experience to radio?" Voegeli wondered, calling back to that which Toscan believed had made the radio dramas a creative scandal or attention-getter in the first place.

> There are scenes in the movie that just will not work on radio. The cantina scene, for example, is one of the most inventive moments ever in American films. The old story that with radio you can create an even greater creature in your imagination than can be done on the screen is sometimes baloney. You just couldn't do the cantina scene on radio as well as it was done on film, and some of the battle scenes don't work as well because it's hard to move from shot to shot to shot. I would argue that because radio is a different medium, however, there are scenes that work better on it than film—usually, they are the more quiet scenes. Radio works very well at the intimate level.

The quintessential radio moment is when you're listening to the thoughts in someone's head.[33]

As Lucas and his team had done for film, that is creating a new process of filmmaking, so, too, had Madden and Voegeli done for their previous radio projects. Radio dramatists of the 1970s "were working on radio drama here the way it had always been done, complete with coconut halves sound effects representing horses," Madden explained.

> Sound effects literally were being produced in a sort of isolation within a studio. All sorts of techniques that just seemed antediluvian to me. During *Earplay*, Tom was coming out of a recording studio called Sound 80 in Minneapolis, which was actually a music recording studio. Essentially, we assembled the productions using 16 track tape, which was the sort of frontline, state of the art production tool that you use for producing music albums. We were using multiple tracks simultaneously and that kind of thing. We commissioned *The Water Engine*, a drama by David Mamet. We started using different techniques on that because we had the means to allow us to do that rather than the simple fade in and fade out, which is what radio drama in the UK was using, and still does, you know, constantly. The particular task that *Star Wars* represented we were ready to deal with because we were using those techniques anyway. We were equipped to approach that particular challenge.[34]

Toscan knew the importance of the sound effects and music and what an important role Voegeli would play in the production and postproduction of the radio dramas. Toscan expressed this to the *Austin, Texas Villager* in 1981, "Most people overlook the fact that the incredible visual effects created for the film were accompanied by the equally impressive sound effects created by Academy Award winner Ben Burtt."[35] Voegeli would become custodian of those effects for the radio drama. With best friend and creative partner Voegeli on sound and editing, Madden was able to promise, with confidence, "You may think you've seen the movie, but wait till you hear it."[36]

With the behind-the-scenes team now in place, from Daley at his typewriter to Voegeli at his sound mixing board, the radio drama was ready to move to its next important phase, assembling the cast of performers who would be crucial to making the radio dramas believable and relatable. This would be no easy task, as many actors, despite their years of experience on stage or film, were not familiar with the style and conventions of radio acting. To find the right actors, Madden turned to an old friend, Mary Lylah "Mel" Sahr, whom Daley described as "the Heroine who, in cliff-hangers galore, rescued NPR's *Star Wars* and *Empire* from the Forces of Chaos."[37]

6

Purest Acting

Working on the *Star Wars* radio drama was a reunion of sorts for the *Earplay* team, not only for John Madden and Tom Voegeli, but for Mel Sahr also. "Mel used to work on *Earplay* with us. That's how we knew her. She had moved out to LA from Minnesota by this time. She just seemed a perfect person to kind of handle that side of it," shared Madden.[1] "That side of it" was actually two sides. Sahr would do double duty on all three *Star Wars* radio dramas, responsible for casting along with Madden during preproduction and as a production coordinator, acting as a creative problem solver during recording sessions.

Sahr and Madden had to assemble a large cast and fast. The first question was how many, if any, of the original film actors would be willing to reprise their roles for the radio drama? Madden reveals that "there was a while in which we were understandably holding out to see what members of the original cast might be persuaded, just for the sheer interest of it, to come do it."[2]

Mark Hamill and Harrison Ford had first learned there would be a radio drama while filming *The Empire Strikes Back* at Elstree Studios near London. Alan Arnold, author of *Once Upon a Galaxy: A Journal of the Making of* Star Wars: The Empire Strikes Back, records that Hamill said, "I want to play my part on radio. I'd play it for fun. I don't want some other guy playing Luke." Harrison Ford agreed: "Until something like this happens you don't realize how possessive you've become about the character you're playing."[3] At the beginning, Toscan, Madden, and Sahr were able to secure Hamill, Ford, Carrie Fisher, and Anthony Daniels, who all agreed to the radio drama. Unfortunately, as the radio drama continued to be delayed because of the scripting crisis, Ford would have to bow out of the project because of his commitment to play Indiana Jones in *Raiders of the Lost Ark*, which began filming on June 23, 1980, at a time near the radio drama recording. With Ford out, Fisher also decided to decline.

Not only would the supporting roles of Darth Vader and Obi-Wan Kenobi be recast, along with many other characters, but the main protagonists Han and Leia would, too. This meant that Sahr had quite the challenge. "We didn't want to find sound-alikes," Toscan told journalist Judson Klinger in 1981, "We didn't want somebody who was going to mimic what Harrison Ford or Alec Guinness had done in the movie. But we had to accept the fact that *Star Wars* is almost an American myth now, so we had to at least *suggest* the original characters."[4] Luckily, though, Hamill and Daniels were available. The final cast assembled would be a mix of original *Star Wars* actors and actors from stage, screen, television, and even acting classes.

Mark Hamill (Luke Skywalker)

Mark Hamill had been acting for nearly a decade before *Star Wars*. Guest-starring roles on *Room 222*, *The Partridge Family*, *The Magician*, *One Day at a Time*, and in the pilot episode of *Eight Is Enough* as oldest son David Bradford demonstrated his range in everything from drama to comedy. His early voice acting was in the animated version of *I Dream of Jeannie*, *The New Scooby-Doo Movies*, and a 1977 *Star Wars*-inspired skit co-starring Carrie Fisher for WLS-AM 890.

Hamill took the role of Luke on the radio drama as both a protective measure, to ensure that Luke was portrayed consistent with the film, and as a creative experience. Considering the long hours of the marathon thirteen-day recording sessions, Hamill basically volunteered his time to the project, earning minimum union scale of less than $200 per day.[5] "It's not the money. We're all getting just scale. But from an ego standpoint, I really didn't like the idea of somebody else doing my part. And in my generation, we missed out on so much: on live television and on radio."[6] Born in 1951, Hamill, by his own recollection, never really knew a time before TV. "This is a labor of love.... It's an opportunity for me to work in a medium that has been denied me simply because of my age. I really wanted to be involved in the radio series from the minute I heard about it."[7]

"I really did it for the fun, and it turned out to be more fun than I expected," Hamill shared.[8] Hamill may have been born too late for radio, but he didn't show it. From the start, he displayed a natural talent for voice and radio work. Madden said, "Mark Hamill was absolutely a natural. He was a brilliant radio actor."[9] Voegeli had a similar evaluation: "Mark Hamill was great at holding himself in a scene which was another really important technique of radio drama. It is interjections that are not in the script. It has to be completely natural, but its improvised reactions. Mark was superb at that. He is a great actor."[10] For Ann Sachs, the actor who played Leia, Mark was "such a sweetheart. Such a dear guy. I was just sort of daunted because he had been in the movie. I didn't know what it was going to be like, but about two minutes after meeting him, it was like we had been in summer stock together. There was just a real connection. It was wonderful."[11]

That is not say there were no challenges for Hamill. He compared doing the film to the radio drama by saying, "It's also a bit like doing a show in New York and then doing a revival of it somewhere else with a different cast. Because Perry is *not* trying to do Harrison Ford."[12]

Anthony Daniels (C-3PO)

One familiar face among the group of actors for Hamill was Anthony Daniels. The radio drama recording would be a kind of graduating class reunion for the pair, each of whom had recently been doing press for the newly released *The Empire Strikes Back*. "Of course, Mark was there for the first two [radio dramas]," Daniels observed. "That was lovely because he was always very easy to interact with. And he knew the part."[13]

Before *Star Wars*, Daniels had been one of only two graduate acting students to earn that year's prestigious Carleton Hobbs Bursary Award granting him a contract with the BBC's Radio Repertory Company. While initially reserved about the possibility of playing C-3PO, partially because he was busy appearing on stage at the time in *Rosencrantz and Guildenstern Are Dead*, Daniels changed his mind when he first saw *Star Wars* artist Ralph McQuarrie's rendition of the droid. So C-3PO was born of Lucas' imagination, McQuarrie's vision, and the sculpting work of Liz Moore, who had been responsible for creating the Star Child of *2001: A Space Odyssey*. Daniels reveals in his 2020 autobiography *I Am C-3PO: The Inside Story*, "Liz had created something magical. Lovely in repose, yet blank enough for me to add life and emotion. Threepio was beautiful."[14] Moore also sculpted the iconic Stormtrooper helmets.

On August 16, 1976, nearly five months since the start of filming on *Star Wars*, Liz Moore died as a result of a car accident. Daniels wrote in his book, "A senseless loss beyond words. It fills me with a real sadness that she died before ever seeing her creation come alive on film—to become such a beloved and iconic figure around the planet. We all leave this world eventually. Artists can only hope to retain a kind of immortality in the work they leave behind. The Star Child. Threepio. They are immortal. I will always remember Liz as a most beautiful and kind and creative soul."[15] What Lucas, McQuarrie, and Moore formulated, Daniels personified and brought to life. His previous experiences acting, with mime, with voice, and on stage, combined to create a singular performance.

Because of the circumstances of acting on film within the confines of a costume under challenging conditions and acting, most frequently, against a nonspeaking R2-D2, there would be some parallels to radio acting for Daniels. In 1976, Daniels explained:

> I had just come off a West End play where I was talking to another actor all evening and he was talking dialogue back to me. Not with *Star Wars*. Very quickly, I had to improvise, because most of the time Artoo was either a box sitting there or it was radio controlled or occasionally Kenny Baker was in there. But, basically it was a blue and silver box. I had to improvise in my head that this was a real friend. That this was my companion and I hadn't thought to do that. I thought about normal relationships between characters or actors. The communication is there automatically. I say this. The other actor replies. Okay, now I can respond. With Artoo, it was zero. I mean, zero.... I thought, well, I am totally on my own. So I developed and would write out lines for Artoo, guessing or inferring from the line before and after. It's a bit of a brain teaser. I got totally used to pausing in between my lines. It became second nature. I only got paid for one character [Daniels laughs at the joke]. Then, of course, when I heard Ben Burtt's audio incarnation of Artoo—wow. He slid it in as though it was there all the time. So, people just assumed it was. But the same thing happened with the radio production, using Brian's extant material and his ability to create phrases.[16]

Daniels's previous radio acting gave him a kind of experience that was valuable to not only his performance but to those of other actors. "Radio really does stimulate the brain cells," Daniels knew from years of audio and voice acting.

> With film, half of it is done for you because if the director wants to come into close-up to emphasize something, you don't have a choice. In the theater, you can look over there, or over there, or up. The actors are directed in film, but so is the audience because they are manipulated. With *Star Wars* that occurs to a huge extent by sound, particularly the music of John Williams.... Music, as we know, is key to all sorts of emotions. It is international. And [with *Star Wars*], it is totally riveted onto the story. It only takes a few bars, a couple of notes, to know Darth Vader is right behind you. We were all brainwashed in this wonderful way. And of course, I've seen the films when I'm working on them without that sound.[17]

As a result of the radio drama, Daniels and Brian Daley formed a connection with each other that would lead to not only creative collaborations but a genuine friendship and respect. Of Daniels, Daley wrote, "Anthony Daniels, who plays See-Threepio, has played tremendously varied roles on the stages of London's West End; he's a multitalented fellow who also writes children's musicals for the BBC. He brought with him fidelity not only to his role, but to the personality and character of the golden droid's sidekick, Artoo-Detoo. Tony made sure nothing in the series contradicted or demeaned the strange but warm friendship between the two, or made them ridiculous rather than amusing."[18] C-3PO was Daley's favorite character to write because, "I like the character and the surprising virtues he can muster, and in part because I admire Tony Daniels' talent and dedication to his craft."[19]

The feeling was mutual. When Daniels first met Daley at the recording sessions:

> I had the scripts in advance, so I was really ready to like him. I felt his love of Threepio.... So there I was meeting this guy for the first time, and he was very good looking, very charismatic, and quiet. Should have been an actor. Without being immodest, I think, he had confidence in what he had done.... Brian had a way of going, "Well, yeah, Threepio has qualities of which he is very involved in the story, but he is kind of stuck to the side." Threepio has been this kind of spokesperson, kind of like Enobarbus to Antony and Cleopatra. If he appeared a coward, he actually wasn't. He was self-saving, but also self-sacrificing. So there's a bunch of paradoxes. And Brian, I tend to want to say because of his educational background, his literary background, or just his ability to write, helped him to explore that, and therefore gave me a lot to do.[20]

Lucia St. Clair Robson shared an example of their bond:

> Anthony Daniels has so much affection for Brian. I know that because I met Tony a number of years after Brian died. They took a *Star Wars* concert on a road tour with Tony Daniels as the emcee. It stopped in Baltimore. I heard about it and I went to Tony Daniels' website to see about getting tickets. He called and said he would have a ticket for me. He said, "During intermission, tell the usher that you want to come backstage." So I spent the intermission with Tony in his dressing room down in the bowels of the theater there and we talked about Brian. That's how much he wanted to meet me, because I was connected with Brian. He is a wonderful person and actor.[21]

When Daniels agreed to reprise his role of C-3PO, it enhanced the project. Madden called Hamill and Daniels "a kind of magnetic north for everybody working on the radio dramas."[22] Not only had Daniels long been Threepio, and Threepio him, but his participation in any *Star Wars* project always adds a legitimacy and rectitude. In turn, the radio dramas were rewarding acting experiences for Daniels. Speaking to *Fantasy Empire* magazine in 1984, Daniels said, "One of the reasons Mark Hamill and I do the radio shows, by the way, is because, well, first of all, I love radio. I think it's far better than film or TV. It's much more stimulating, it really allows the audience to use their minds. Then, Mark Hamill, George Lucas, and myself, really believe in giving something back, because you don't have to pay to listen to the radio. Anybody can tune in free and listen to *Star Wars*."[23]

Daley's script gave Threepio not only more to do, but also articulated the reasons Threepio was doing them for the audience. His scripts could take their time to tell their tale. "The pacing of those stories was a delight," Daniels shared. "Even now, things are much more fast paced and not necessarily always to good degree."[24]

Perry King (Han Solo)

Perry King was both *almost* Han Solo and *actually* Han Solo. His association with the character began in 1976 when he auditioned for the role in the film. Reflecting on the experience of meeting George Lucas, King recalled asking:

> "So, what's the movie? What movie are you doing? Tell me about it." He said, "Well, I'm making a movie for kids from eight to 80" or something like that, which then became a very famous line. I remember being impressed by that line. I remember thinking that is a really interesting idea, a movie that appeals to everyone so that the kid in me can enjoy it, you know, as well as real kids. Then, we did the screen test. I did it with Charlie Martin Smith, a wonderful actor. But I'd never met him before. I was playing Han and Charlie was playing Luke. And Lucas had set it up so that instead of moving the camera, to get singles on each of us, he moved the actors. I remember that really threw me off balance. It really confused me because you get comfortable with something.... But the answer for Lucas was you hire actors good enough that they can handle that, which he did. He's very smart.[25]

When the footage of his test was to be included in a recent documentary, Lucasfilm sent King a copy for his approval to include. He joked, very much in Han Solo–style, "After I saw it, I thought, 'No wonder I didn't get it!'"[26]

Although his father wanted him to consider being a doctor, King knew he had wanted to act ever since appearing in school plays. He received his drama degree from Yale University and was a student of John Houseman at the Juilliard School. By the time of his *Star Wars* audition, King was already an accomplished stage, miniseries, and film actor. Perhaps his best-known role then was as David "Chico" Tyrell in the 1974 film *The Lords of Flatbush*. King recollected, "I did a film with Sylvester Stallone and Henry Winkler. We were totally unknown at that point.... Henry Winkler and I came out on the same plane. I remember it took us like five hours to get from LAX to Beverly Hills because we didn't know where we were going or what we were doing. We spent a lot of time together in the first few weeks, just keeping ourselves going.... Stallone impressed me so much. He's a genius."[27]

The second time around for Han, King didn't have to audition: "I had done some radio with NPR before. It was given to me. It was like a gift."[28] King knew he had to make the role his own. "I knew what Harrison Ford had done with the role. Because his performance is just magnificent. He just understood it so perfectly. It's iconic, that performance. I mean, he's a good film actor, but he's never done anything better than that first Han Solo. He was riveting.... I didn't attempt to do anything like a Harrison Ford version of it. Because I knew I would only fail.... So I just approached it my own way and let my version of Han Solo come out."[29]

Because more time could be spent on each character in the radio drama, King's Solo gets a chance to move from archetype to fully realized personality. The fun he had playing the role was apparent, even to his co-stars. Ann Sachs shared, "Oh, my goodness, Perry. Perry is such a heartthrob. He just is. I met him and I thought, 'Oh my God!' It was just terrific. The thing is that he was so not full of himself the way so many handsome heartthrobs are. He was just really down to earth, saying 'Okay, let's look at this and break it down here.' He was such a joy to work with that. I was very impressed. I thought, 'How could anybody that handsome and that charming be so talented too?' I thought there *is* justice in the world."[30]

King summarized his fifty-year acting career when he stated, "I'm one of the luckiest actors I know because I've made a living at it for half a century. How could you ask for more than that? Making a living doing something you love to do?"[31]

Ann Sachs (Leia Organa)

Ann Sachs had the calling to act from the time she was six years old. "I was actually in first grade. We were doing a little play, which was *Hansel and Gretel*. I played the witch, and I scared the little girl who played Gretel. Literally scared her off the stage. She ran off the stage and I thought, 'Hey that works. It was great fun!' So, that was my first kind of little taste of acting that I remember."[32]

Sachs graduated from the Drama Department at Carnegie Institute of Technology, which is now Carnegie Mellon University. Stage acting would be her first passion, and she began acting professionally in 1967. Ann made her Broadway debut in *Dracula* playing Lucy Seward with co-star Frank Langella. The play ran for three years, from October 1977 until January 1980, earning five Drama Desk Award nominations and winning two Tony Awards. Her husband, Tony Award winner Roger Morgan, designed the lighting for *Dracula*. Critic William B. Collins praised Sachs's performance, writing, "Ann Sachs is an affected delight both in her ingénue flapper moments and as the hotcha girl moving in on her boyfriend (Alan Coates)."[33]

Sachs met John Madden while she was playing Rosalind in *As You Like It* for the Yale Repertory Theatre in April 1979. "I was doing a play or two at Yale in the drama department there, and I met John. We really got along well and it was terrific."[34] When Fisher bowed out of the NPR *Star Wars* adaptation, and knowing the importance of the character to both the film and the radio drama, Madden thought immediately of Sachs. Her stage experience playing everything from comedy to drama would be valuable when playing the Princess and Senator from Alderaan.

Brock Peters (Darth Vader)

Writing in 1994, Daley shared with readers what Mel Sahr told him was her biggest casting apprehension, "filling Vader's jackboots."[35] With James Earl Jones unavailable due to his obligations to the TV show *Paris*, another actor would be required. Who, though, could play the sinister Dark Lord of the Sith when David Prowse's and James Earl Jones's combined performances had made Vader the most recognizable screen villain of all time? Daley continued, "But then, she had called Brock Peters, whose credits include the marvelously poignant movie *The L-Shaped Room* as well as several *Star Trek* movies. As soon as Mel heard Brock's deep, dynamic tones on the other end of the line, she told me, 'I thought, 'Here's my Darth.' The search was over.'"[36]

Peters, whose real name was George Fisher, was born on July 2, 1927, in New York City. Like Sachs, he knew at an early age that acting was his passion. Encouraged by his agent, he changed his name, choosing to reverse the name of a childhood friend. By the 1950s, he was starring in roles that would become iconic, especially his turn as Tom Robinson in the 1962 version of *To Kill a Mockingbird*. Peters would be nominated for a Tony Award for his performance in the 1973 Broadway play, *Lost in the Stars*. No stranger to science fiction, Peters has guest starred on *The Bionic Woman* and *Battlestar Galactica*. He has a singular distinction of playing a father in two of the biggest science fiction franchises of all time, as Luke and Leia's father in the *Star Wars* radio dramas and as Captain Benjamin Sisko's father on *Star Trek: Deep Space Nine*.

Many of the scenes Peters plays in the radio dramas are with Ann Sachs. Similarly to how Carrie Fisher spoke on many occasions of what a gentleman Peter Cushing was during filming despite playing the reprehensible villain Grand Moff Tarkin, Sachs, too, had great affinity for Peters as a person and actor: "What a wonderful guy! What a loss. He was elegant.

He was such an elegant fellow even in his everyday interaction with you. His voice was extraordinary. I loved working with him. Absolutely loved it and I miss him."[37]

Peters passed away in 2005. When reflecting on Peters, King mentioned how much in awe he was of him. "I remember feeling really happy to be in the company of all those people. Very lucky."[38]

Bernard Behrens (Obi-Wan Kenobi)

Known as Bunny to his friends, Bernard Behrens was born in London on September 28, 1926. He knew he wanted to be an actor since the age of seven when he, because of his poverty, would sneak into movie theaters without paying, entranced by the performances of the actors. Despite his experiences as a child refugee during World War II, Behrens never abandoned his dreams of acting. He would become a fixture on stage at the Bristol Old Vic and the Stratford Festival. A reliable character actor, Behrens could be seen on television shows as diverse as *Great Performances*, *The Bionic Woman*, and *Starsky and Hutch* before the radio dramas.

Unlike nearly all the other actors, Behrens had not yet had the chance to see *Star Wars* before being offered the role by Sahr and Madden. Before recording, Behrens thought perhaps at first he should see the film, but then changed his mind. "I didn't want to become patterned after Alec Guinness," Behrens told Alan Brender of *Starlog* in 1981. "What I did before starting work on the show was to read the book. Still, not having seen the movie, I did have some difficulties—especially since Mark Hamill and Anthony Daniels had a sort of style I wasn't able to capture right away. I messed up one day, and we had to retape that. It worked much better the second time. The director, John Madden, is an incredible man. He worked wonders with all of us."[39]

Despite that rocky start, Behrens would reprise his role of Obi-Wan Kenobi in the trilogy of *Star Wars* radio dramas. He would be nominated four times for The Academy of Canadian Cinema & Television's Gemini Award for his acting, winning twice. Behrens passed away in 2012.

Kale Browne (Biggs Darklighter)

Biggs Darklighter looms large in the *Star Wars* radio drama. While film audiences knew Biggs only as a confusing figure in the 1977 film, someone who Luke mentions at the start of the film and then seems to care about at the end when he dies during the Battle of Yavin, no real explanation or context was given. Only by reading the novelization or comic book adaptation would fans learn about the deleted scenes with Biggs as Luke's best friend back on Tatooine. The radio drama gives Biggs his fullest due. Most interesting are the conversations between Biggs, Luke, and Han that occur in episode 12, "The Case for Rebellion." These scenes add an important element to *Star Wars*—underlining that Luke has two role model figures in the older Biggs and Han, and hence, two very different influences. While Han tries to convince Luke not to volunteer for the Rebellion, Biggs works with Luke on a simulator to give him the necessary practice before he pilots his X-wing. Daley's script captures the contrast:

> **HAN:** Biggs, the hometown hero, eh? Luke talked about you. You're on the team, too?
> **BIGGS:** Yes. And you?
> **HAN:** Not a chance. Me and my friend have places to go and things to do.
> **BIGGS:** So do we.[40]

Although Han will redeem himself as all rogue-heroes must, it is Biggs who provides Luke the moral compass he needs peer-to-peer. "He's the reason that Luke joins the resistance," explained actor Kale Browne. "He's like the older brother that Luke has never had."[41]

To play the role of Biggs, Sahr and Madden chose Browne, asking him to play the role without the need for an audition. "I always thought I got into acting when I was in college, I fell in love with this girl who was in love with an actor and I thought, 'Well, hell, I can do that.' ... But you know, it was very funny actually," recalled Browne:

> I went to a Catholic high school for a couple of years. And then all of a sudden in junior year of high school, I wake up one day, and I've been switched to the public school. I thought it was because my dad was out of work or something. I wasn't quite sure. But a couple years ago, my mom finally breaks it to me. She said, "Oh, no, no, no. You came home from doing a play when you were a sophomore at Catholic high school and you announced you wanted to be an actor. Well, hell, I'm not paying for that." She wasn't going to spring for private school at 25 bucks a month.... The truth of the matter is, I never really wanted to do anything else.[42]

Kale has an interesting connection to George Lucas via Marin County, California, where Skywalker Ranch is located:

> I went to school at this little tiny junior college in Northern California, The College of Marin. There was Robin Williams, Kathleen Quinlan, David Ogden Stiers, Bart Braverman and myself. I mean a whole pile of people who kept working in the business who became professional actors. I always have been fascinated with synchronicity like when you've got these pockets of people that

> you would not expect to know each other, have grown up together, and they all started out together.... I was living in Marin County there. I had gone to Hawaii, and I get a call from a guy that I'd done this little college film for and he was a casting director in San Francisco. He was casting a funny little film and I went over and auditioned for it. I didn't get the part I read for but they said, stick around. And of course, that was *American Graffiti*. So, I had a brush with Lucas prior [to the radio dramas].[43]

Browne had always been a science fiction fan, and of *Star Wars* in particular. "Sci-fi has always been a favorite of mine.... I thought it was incredible. And beautifully done. You know that for the time the effects were phenomenal.... I grew up in Marin County, so when I saw Boba Fett's spaceship, I thought that looks just like the streetlights [that are common in California]. That's exactly what they did. Somebody went out and said we need a strange shape for the guy with the rocket pack.... I love that stuff!."[44]

By the time Sahr was casting the radio drama, Browne had made an impression working on night-time soaps and on stage. He would eventually become a stalwart daytime actor, playing Michael Hudson on *Another World* amidst runs on *Days of Our Lives, One Life to Live*, and more film and television roles. Because of his love of science fiction and appreciation for radio, Browne remembered fondly working on *Star Wars*: "Radio forces you to pay attention. You engage the mind. It is not all done for you. So you're imagining as you're listening, but they take that time. With television these days, the way it has become, it's like so fast and so furious, that it just strips your gears of even having to imagine anything. You don't have time to catch up. I mean, radio is as close to a book as you are going to get."[45] The one thing, though, he joked, "I wish I kept that damn script. It was like two inches thick!."[46]

Ken Hiller (Narrator)

Daley had an idea that would have brought the *Star Wars* radio dramas to a poetic full circle with its progenitor, the 1938 broadcast of *The War of the Worlds*. One of the public relations writers attending the recordings of *Star Wars* during June 1980, had been the biographer of Orson Welles. Daley suggested to Mel Sahr that Welles would be the perfect narrator for the *Star Wars* radio dramas. Toscan recalled, "It wasn't lost on anybody that Welles had been the narrator for his notorious production of *War of the Worlds*."[47] While Sahr liked the idea, there were concerns by others that Welles would both cost too much and have a deleterious effect on production because of his rather perfectionist personality. Daley told Alex

Newborn in 1995, "The series narrator did a great job, but Mother of God would I have loved to hear Welles have a go at what I'd written."[48]

The series narrator who did that great job was a Minneapolis stalwart that Tom Voegeli had known, Ken Hiller. After serving in the U.S. Air Force, Hiller moved to Hawaii where his bass and baritone voice was perfectly suited to being a disc jockey. Local hosting duties and a role in *Hawaii Five-O* followed. In 1971, Hiller moved back to the mainland and would do voiceover work on hundreds of radio and television commercials. He was the perfect and experienced choice as the narrator for the *Star Wars* radio dramas.

Voegeli recalled, "The narrator reviews where we are in the story and then at the end there's a little bit of a recap of the story or a teaser for what's coming up. One of the things that made the production hard was that, particularly for battle scenes, there was not a narrator to rely on to say, 'Then Luke and Han rode off on a Tauntaun.' That narrator function wasn't there. It had to be in the script and in the acting. So that made them hard to do for everybody. Ken Hiller was a local Minneapolis voiceover talent. Great voice."[49]

In addition to the *Star Wars* radio drama trilogy, Hiller would return to the galaxy as narrator on the video game and novella-inspired audio dramas, *Dark Forces: Solider for the Empire*, *Dark Forces: Rebel Agent*, and *Dark Forces: Jedi Knight*. Hiller passed away in 2016.

Toscan recalls the narrator voice as being a particular concern for Lucasfilm. "I think because we had Mark, Tony, and at that point Carrie and Harrison lined up for the cast, Carol probably assumed she didn't need to get actively involved in casting approvals."[50] But the narrator voice was a different story. "I still remember my reaction to the prologue of the film when I first saw it. That title crawl that nobody had ever done before put you on notice: 'Hold onto your seat! You're in for the ride of your life!' That opening crawl was so much a part of the initial impact of the film and we needed an audio version of it. When I played the Hiller demo for Carol, she was pleased that Mel had found the right performer to capture the vocal equivalent of that amazing opening crawl of the film."[51]

Sahr and Madden's ability to recognize good actors was sometimes prescient. Some of the actors they tapped for the radio dramas would go on to affecting careers later. For example, Adam Arkin who played Fixer eventually became a star on *Chicago Hope*. Thomas Hill, performer of Uncle Owen, created one of the 1980s most quirky sitcom characters in Jim Dixon on *Newhart*. Future *Designing Women* star and Emmy Award nominee Meshach Taylor was the voice of rebel pilot Wedge Antilles. Grand Moff Tarkin actor Keene Curtis had made his film debut in the 1948 Orson

Welles adaptation of *Macbeth.* He would be remembered for his recurring role as John Allen Hill, the owner of Melville's Restaurant on *Cheers.*

Tony Award winner David Alan Grier, a pioneering comedian best known to TV audiences for his work on *In Living Color,* was earning his master's degree in fine arts from Yale University at the time. One of his teachers had been John Madden. Grier voiced various characters, including X-wing pilots and Stormtroopers, in the radio drama. In an interview with *Sidewalks,* Grier spoke about what it meant to him as a financially challenged student to get asked by Madden to join the troupe of actors while he was on summer break in Los Angeles: "He told me that he was doing a radio version of *Star Wars,* like a serialized radio version. And he called me up and asked me do I want to do this. Now the best thing about this is that I think I worked maybe four days and I got like nine hundred dollars. And I could not be happier. I was like, 'Are you kidding me?' Nine hundred dollars! It was awesome."[52] Sahr and Madden had an eye for talent, giving some of today's most successful actors one of their first chances. They would also be able to convince already popular actors to join the radio dramas. That, however, is a tale for future chapters.

With the task of assembling the actors complete, Toscan faced one last hurdle, a major one threatening to upend the carefully assembled project. As Toscan recalled, "Mark's Luke was the hero of the story. No question about that. But Tony's C-3PO was the anchor that would keep us tied to the film through one of its two most iconic characters. So Tony was critical to making this work now that we were down to only two actors from the film."[53] Sahr had arranged for Daniels to fly from London to Los Angeles and for him to stay at the Chateau Marmont, the legendary film industry hotel in West Hollywood.

Several days prior to the start of recording, Toscan drove to the airport to meet Daniels, not realizing what was coming, "As we left LAX and merged onto the freeway, Tony said 'Are Harrison and Carrie here yet?' I suddenly realized he didn't know we'd lost Harrison to the *Raiders* shooting schedule only weeks before and Carrie hadn't wanted to stay without Harrison. What was awful about this was that Tony had been wooed with the idea of joining all of them in the radio project. I explained what had happened, that Spielberg had moved up filming of *Raiders* and of course about Carrie, though without her linkage to Harrison."[54] Realizing that Daniels had been misled, albeit unintentionally, Toscan "tried to reassure him that he'd enjoy working again with Mark and the new cast. By the time I checked him into the hotel, he was a bit more comfortable. Standing there at the front desk while he handed over his passport, neither of us could have imagined how important the *Star Wars* radio series would become for Tony and his friendship with Brian Daley."[55]

Tom Voegeli arranged for recording to occur at Westlake Recording Studios in West Hollywood. Music artists and producers such as Quincy Jones, Missy Elliott, Donna Summer, Giorgio Moroder, and Justin Timberlake have recorded there. But in late June 1980, for thirteen days, it would become home to a galaxy at war.

7

The Nexus

Tom Voegeli knew the special requirements that the recording of the *Star Wars* radio drama would entail. A recording studio that had isolation booths was a must for actors such as Anthony Daniels and Brock Peters, whose voices would need to be isolated to make the effects Voegeli would add later on more effective. Preferably this would be a recording studio where the isolation booths would permit Daniels and Peters to see the other actors, even if they were not in the same room as them. This would also be a studio with enough space to permit both the large number of actors some scenes required and to utilize the omnidirectional microphones that would capture sound as it, and their voices, moved. For example, during recording of the cantina scene, more than twenty actors were grouped around three microphones, with Daniels isolated in a booth. In short, Voegeli needed a rather revolutionary location to record a revolutionary radio drama.

He found the right location at West Hollywood's Westlake Recording Studios, itself a new studio, founded in the early 1970s by Glenn Phoenix and Tom Hidley. Among Hidley's achievements was helping to pioneer car stereo systems during the 1950s with Earl William Muntz and helping to standardize recording facility designs for which Westlake would be the model of choice by those that followed. Chris Stone of the Record Plant studios told *Billboard* in 1979, "What originally made California studios unique was Tom Hidley. Hidley developed many of the innovative acoustical designs that you see in studios today.... For example, virtually all California studios utilize a UREI 1176 limiter and you won't find that in London or the East. It's helped make the California sound warmer and its absence makes the sound harsh."[1] The UREI 1176, designed by Bill Putnam, was a limiter compressor that helped usher in a new era of solid-state recording technology rather than the vacuum tube era common before the 1960s and 1970s. Hidley helped make it a part of nearly every studio.

By standardizing rooms and technology at the same recording studio, and across different studios in general, the recording industry was transformed from a world where recordings had to be done live, with all musicians and singers gathered together, to one where the music, and even each individual instrument, could be recorded separately at different times and locations and then assembled to create a gestalt composition. These innovations, led in part by Hidley, would create what became known as the unique, clear "California Sound."[2] So popular were the designs of Hidley's Westlake Recording Studio that soon much of the industry wanted their own "Westlake rooms." By the 1970s, nearly 40 percent of all session work done in the United States was in California.[3]

Voegeli found what he needed at Westlake. "I picked the studio out of past experience. It was an absolutely first-rate studio. We needed isolation booths to record. We needed at least two booths separate from the main studio mostly to record actors as pilots, to give a radiophonic effect with squelches. Oh my God, the amount of squelches I put in those productions. I remember that and how many times C-3PO's motors had to be figured out. A lot of what I'm proudest of is all the texture, all the little stuff in the mix."[4] Those isolation booths would also be used by Stormtroopers. The original idea was to try recording the actors playing the Empire's troops using painters' masks to mimic them being behind a helmet. However, that experiment did not work, and isolation booths became the best solution. Voegeli would have to work his magic in postproduction.

As the recording sessions began, Voegeli would work closely with Madden and the actors so that he could record the elements needed to match Daley's script. Actor movements were similar to what occurs on stage so that the microphone could record natural movements more authentically depending on if a character was entering or leaving a space or standing still. Madden created an environment for the actors that encouraged creativity within the confines of those technological requirements. One reality of radio is that the ear is a kind of truth detector. It knows when something does not sound right, much the same way the eye can detect computer-generated effects as artificial in modern films. As an illustration, if Luke is supposed to be speaking to Han on his left and Leia on his right, the ear can actually detect, if recorded properly, the difference in voice quality and location depending on which character Luke is addressing. Madden would sometimes direct with his eyes closed so that he would simulate the listener experience, because "the listener, although he may be unconscious of it, knows whether the actor is actually running or just standing in place and breathing heavily in time. The ear is the best detective."[5] As Voegeli warned, "You can have all the best sound effects in the world, but if the actor's voices don't match those sound effects, it doesn't work, particularly in what we called *effort*."[6]

Where the directing catchphrase "faster and more intense" is attributed to George Lucas, Madden had his own shorthand with radio actors to help compensate for the deprivation of visuals. It became known as *effort*. Actors were directed to put more energy with their voice into the scene to indicate movement. Mark Hamill defined the process of *effort* for *Entertainment Tonight* in 1982, "So much more of it has to be indicated. You know, if I put on a jacket in the movie, I put on a jacket. Here it is, 'Let me just get this jacket on. Yeah. Button up.' It is taking stage with your voice really. We talk to ourselves a lot more in the radio adaptation!"[7]

Ann Sachs agrees with Hamill's analogy: "Yes, which was wonderful. It was such a relief. Because I think that, for me, this particular show was the first time that I've ever done something that was just radio. It was a relief because I felt as if I was on stage. I could just let it rip."[8] That comfort while recording, Sachs attributed to the atmosphere created by Madden. "We all realized that John really knew what he was doing when he brought us in. He was going to make it work optimally. What a good director. I was always able to see the person that I was doing the scene with. I was always very comfortable. John has a way of just making you comfortable wherever you are."[9]

Effort sometimes made for funny visuals in the studio as actors contorted face and body to get the necessary emotional quality through the microphone and to specify what needed to be indicated using only their voices. "You can't worry about how foolish you look, because people won't see that. What matters is how your voice comes over the air," said Hamill.[10] *Effort* was the essential ingredient for Madden helping actors unfamiliar with radio learn how to communicate their performance without the benefits of visuals. Madden explained, "You just need to make it as real as you can. It also gave a different acoustical quality. You might as well create something that actually helps you do that, and certainly helped the actors. I mean, the *Star Wars* radio dramas were challenging in that way because they were so much more dialogue dependent than the film."[11]

Beyond expressing *effort*, each of the actors faced experiences while recording that were unique to their specific character. Unlike Harrison Ford, who had Chewbacca actor Peter Mayhew on set to play against, Perry King would never have his Wookiee companion next to him during recording, as the character of Chewie would be added later by Voegeli using Ben Burtt's sound effects library. For King, the answer to making his relationship with Chewbacca believable was going back to childhood. It was about balancing the *effort* against the *effortless*.

> I worked with James Mason, who was, of all the wonderful actors and people I've gotten to work with, the most wonderful. One of the many things he said to me that I've never forgotten was, "What we're paid to do is to believe that

> what's happening is really happening and has never happened before. It's that simple. It's not easy, but it's simple." It transformed my acting. I used to have all these notes that I'd go over before every scene. He said, "You should throw those notes away. They're just getting in your way. You don't need them. You've already thought of them. If they need to be there, they'll be there. Just believe it. Believe that what's happening is really happening. It's there."
>
> When my youngest daughter was about four or five, she had this little set of toy figures of knights and damsels and a castle. She would sit on the floor, play with them, and say, "Oh, Sir Knight. Oh, please come save me from the dragon!" I used to interrupt her and watch her. I'd say, "Hannah, do you want some lunch? Are you hungry?" And she would look up, "Oh, no, no, I'm not hungry at all. I'm fine, thanks Dad." She could go right back into it. So she'd be in a fantasy world. She'd go out and then she'd come back in effortlessly. I thought I should be able to do that. I'm a professional. Why should I take all this time to go to prepare, and do all this angst-ridden stuff to get ready to play something? It should be just like that for me, just that effortless, I should be able to step out and step in.
>
> The best for me was Chewbacca. That was my favorite part of doing the radio shows. I loved that Chewie became totally a real living creature to me. Still is, like a friend of mine that I hadn't seen for years. I'd be alone in the studio when we did those scenes. And I'd have a mic and I'd say, "So, Chewie, what do you think? Should we go that way? Or should we go this way?" Pause, pause, pause. "All right, Chewie, I think you're right about that. Let's go." I had to hear him in my head. And that's the best place to hear things. You know, he was very real to me. You'd be in a soundstage area with mics. So if I'm doing a scene with me and Chewie only, I'm the only one in the room in front of a microphone.
>
> Now, does it matter if Chewbacca is speaking to me in his language or in English, or, really, not at all? It doesn't make any difference. I still hear what he says because I am pretending. I hear it in a way I can understand it because Han could speak Wookiee and understand it. [Han could say,] "You know, hell, Chewbacca and I are so close, I didn't really need an answer for him. I could look in his eyes and that is all I need." When I did those scenes, Chewie was very much with me. I'm not kidding you when I say that I consider Chewbacca one of my good friends in life.[12]

Another challenge was the inevitable comparison to Ford that some fans would make. For King, this was never really a problem because he never tried to compete:

> Harrison Ford had done such a magnificent job of it. He invented it. It's his. You can't mess with it. On radio, it is more doable for another actor to play the role. I think that's why I made the choice not to go back and see the movie again. I didn't want to remember what Harrison Ford did because I can't do it. And I'm not going to try.... [Playing Han] was not so much a second chance at the role for me as a first opportunity to do something really significant on radio, with voice, a different kind of venue for acting. I mean, acting is so much

> fun. And you can do it in lots of different ways. It's always like playing games, and in this case, it was a really strong chance to work just vocally. I love that. I love the fact that you could show up for work and it doesn't make any difference what you look like. When you're a film actor or stage actor, you're always trying to look your best and you want to look like the part. The visual side of acting is such a big deal and so crushing to actresses, but also for actors, too. It's not talked about much but actors have the same problem with having to look good these days. Young actors, I feel so sorry for them. You always got to look like a bodybuilder now. Who wants to waste your time doing that? But with radio, you show up, your voice is there.... It doesn't make any difference what you look like. I don't think I've ever enjoyed anything, as an actor, so much as doing that show. Doing voice work is joyful.[13]

For Ann Sachs, perhaps the most efficacious scene for her was the one that is most frequently discussed by fans of the radio drama: the disturbing Darth Vader–Leia torture scene that Daley had expanded for episode 8, "Death Star's Transit." The original film hinted expertly, through the use of clever editing and music, the pain and suffering that Leia would endure for the cause. But it never showed it directly. The radio drama would.

In the August 1, 1975, version of the script *The Star Wars: From the Adventures of the Starkiller*, George Lucas had scripted the rescue of Princess Leia differently than how it was filmed. It is Han and Chewbacca in this version who break Leia out of her cell. They were shocked by Leia's appearance, bloodied with yellow eyes, and disfigured. Leia was hanging upside down. Chewbacca would carry her through the next scenes of the film until she recovered. Carrie Fisher spoke about this never-filmed moment to *Rolling Stone* in 1980: "I was hanging upside down with yellow eyes, like in *The Exorcist*. They shoulda just gotten Linda Blair for it. Some form of radar torture was done to me and I was in a beam, bruised and beaten up, suspended in midair. The reason it was cut from the film was because I was unconscious and the Wookie [*sic*] would have had to carry me for, like, the next fifteen minutes."[14]

Daley knew that it would not be possible to recreate that moment on radio, so instead, he focused on the equally distressing psychological aspects of the torture Leia endured. Radio drama audiences would learn that the torture droid that accompanies Vader in the film gives Leia a mind control drug that was physically painful and mentally damaging, creating hallucinations and confusion that Vader uses to intimidate Leia. Daley said of the scene, "While the motion picture doesn't depict the encounter, I took it as a chance to show Vader and Leia clashing will-to-will. It was a nightmarish confrontation, and it got us our one and only letter of complaint—but since the *Star Wars* radio drama drew a lot of mail, I don't think that response was too damning."[15]

In a moment revelatory to how much Daley had his pulse on the spirit of *Star Wars*, Vader invokes Leia's father during the torture, named in the radio dramas as Prestor Organa, rather than Bail as eventually determined by Lucas. Daley wrote:

> **VADER:** Yes! Your fault! Tell us where the tapes are or all those Rebel deaths will be your fault!
> **LEIA:** Please ... leave me alone.
> **VADER:** Your father commands you tell us!
> **LEIA:** Father ... father?
> **VADER:** Yes. He orders you to tell us! Don't you want to obey him? Don't you wish to please your father?[16]

The performances by Brock Peters and Sachs are chilling, easily one of the best of the series. It is a painful moment to experience for the audience, yet one which declares the bravery of Leia. One would think that such a sustained scene would require a great deal of rehearsal and preparation. But rehearsals can be as much a detriment as a help. They can save money and time, but they lose spontaneity. Madden explained:

> You don't really need to rehearse in radio any more than you need to rehearse. Strangely, depending on the material, it is the same with film for the same reason, which is that you're sort of capturing lightning in a bottle. If you are rehearsing for a stage play, you have this kind of moment that is very analogous to the radio play where we have a read-through and everybody simply sits around a table and reads. You just read from the script. Read cold. And it's very interesting, because they just get a very instinctive reaction, the actor relating to the words in front of them. Actually, the piece comes alive in that circumstance.
>
> If you're doing a play, you then find very quickly that you have to start investigating every choice you're making, and experimenting and pulling things in different ways, and trying different approaches in order to get to the truth of what's being said. The reason for that on stage is that your body needs to relearn its instinctive response. Because with a play, it has to do it through repetition, which is not true of the radio play and not true of film either. With a play, you need to be able to recall something the next day that you just performed, which requires teaching the brain and the instincts to go back to that primitive level where you read it in the first place. In radio drama, you would do kind of a read through.[17]

Sachs appreciated that ability to bring naturalness to the role of Leia, especially for the torture scene. "I just jumped in. That's always the easiest way for me because you never know what's going to come out of you or what's going to come at you. I always find that it's better, especially in a really highly emotional scene like that, to just jump in. That's what I did."[18] After the tough recording session, Brock Peters came out of his isolation booth and hugged Sachs.

One of those affected by the scene was Sachs's son, Samuel Sachs Morgan. This was something that Ann learned during the interview for this book. Mother and son had this genuinely moving, sweet exchange about the scene during the interview:

> Samuel Sachs Morgan: It traumatized me as a kid. I remember listening because we were in the car on the way up to up to the Adirondacks. I had my little Walkman and was listening in the car on the drive up there. I remember being so terrified during the torture scene because it really felt so real. I was just terrified. I had to stop listening. I think I might have been crying. It really, really, really affected me as your kid. And I wish I could remember how old I was. I mean, probably younger than I maybe should have been listening to it. It was a testament to the performance. I mean everything about it felt so real—obviously, when you're hearing your mother being tortured by Darth Vader.
>
> Ann Sachs: Well, that's what I love about acting is that it came so easily to me. It was second nature and whether it was a scene that was just sort of sitting around talking, or whether it was being attacked, or whether it was a passionate love scene, I thought, "Oh, my God. What kind of a gift is this to give a person to be able to go through all of these emotional conditions and get paid for it?" This is how I make my living and it is just amazing. I'm so sorry that it was so traumatic for you.
>
> Samuel Sachs Morgan: I don't hold it against you. It's such a clear memory. Wow. I had seen the *Star Wars* film before ever hearing of the radio drama. I also remember being excited in high school when you were in *Return of the Jedi* when you were going to record that. That was also when the prequels were coming out and then the re-releasing of the original films. That was such a huge thing for me and my friends in high school, going to the Ziegfeld Theatre in New York and waiting in these insanely long lines to buy tickets and seeing the films there, which was really amazing. So it was definitely a big part of my childhood for sure. There was definitely some sort of bragging rights of my mom being Princess Leia.
>
> Ann Sachs: Wow, you never let on. I knew he loved *Star Wars* and everything, but I thought it was just sort of ... bless your heart.[19]

Anthony Daniels understood the necessity of *effort* from his own radio experiences and because of his portrayal as C-3P0. It is not hyperbole to say that Daniels knows what it means to literally suffer for his art—physical pain from the costume and, perhaps worse, emotional pain of isolation from everyone else not acting behind a mask. Reflecting on playing Threepio, Daniels recalled those challenges he experienced filming the first movie.

> The emotional side was extraordinary, because I would spend in those original films, pretty much most of the day, all day, in the costume. That was really, really hard. Because not only was it physically awful, as I couldn't bend joints so they became kind of locked, which was very painful.... But also through my little eyes, I could see people joshing with each other. You know, sharing

> a cup of coffee, relaxing, whatever. Now I'm just kind of looking at them as an observer. Although people were very nice, and they would come up to me, they were never quite looking at me. People would talk to me slightly to one side, because you couldn't see my eyes. Most of my brain is saying, "Well, this is the job, I put my head in a ball of plastic. I sort of agreed to do it." But, I didn't quite know it was going to be like this. It was no secret there would be a mask and acting like that. But it was harder than I could possibly have imagined. Absolutely. I think more difficult than the team or George Lucas thought it would be. And that's nobody's fault. They tried to make this suit over six months. Nobody had ever done that before.... The emotional side got worse over the years. If you read my book, you'll see that when the film came out, basically, people pretended I wasn't there.[20]

While Daniels would be freed from the physical costume for the radio drama, there were still both physical and emotional challenges to the role. He would still be isolated physically from the other performers because of the need to isolate his voice. Because of the design of the Westlake studio, Daniels would be looking through glass from his isolation booth at others in the center of the larger room being able to interact with each other, much like his experiences while ensconced in the costume during the film, but instead of being hidden behind a Threepio mask, it was behind a glass partition.

> [With the radio series], the fascinating thing was that I, once again, had to be sectioned off from the other actors. Tom needed a separate voice track because whereas I do sound like C-3PO, it is actually better if the voice is slightly thinned, and a tiny kind of treatment or echo, or reverb, delay is added. Milliseconds, a tiny adjustment.... Because they needed the voice channel separating, I couldn't be in the same environment, same reverb of all the other actors who basically are humans, in the same room, at the same time, speaking in our human voices. So I would be in a booth, and mostly it was glass, I could actually see people, but again, rather like on the film set, I could see them relating to each other because they were on mics, very close to each other. Whereas I was hidden away with a mic of my own and a script. And that was kind of reliving slightly the original film.[21]

Just performing the voice of Threepio takes *effort*, even if Daniels is not in the costume:

> I could deliberately kind of loosen up after a session because *I* would become really tense in order to create *his* tension. There's really no way around it, I found. Believe me after a long day, either on the film set, or in the sound studio, I would lie in the hot tub. Really relaxed. Glass of wine, as well. But the other thing is that in addition to the tension of him being like that, and the pressures of working in a sound studio, is that very often, you cannot have the air conditioning system on when we're actually recording. You can have it on during rehearsal. When that red light goes on, that fast acceleration of fans suddenly stops.[22]

Daley, who was in the studio during the recordings, saw firsthand Daniels's full engagement as he played Threepio, finding it fascinating to watch. Daley wrote, "In order to get fully into character, he did spasmodic Threepio moves with his arms, upper torso, and head as he spoke, looking like a human marionette."[23] Said Toscan:

> Tony was a delight to work with, a real pro in the English acting tradition, but Mel also had to bring in a number of very young American actors to play Luke's buddies, Stormtroopers, crowd scenes, all of that. It's just typical that these U.S. performers of that age are full of energy, joshing around with each other in the studio whenever they get a chance. And all of this hijinks was much to Tony's restrained exasperation since John would have to calm them all down again before the next take could be done. Tony was out of that English performer tradition: It's a job. You come to work, you do your job, you go home. As time went on, he became a model for those performers, as did Ann and Brock.[24]

While it is unusual for a writer to be on set or in the studio, Daley was needed in the studio during the recording of *Star Wars*. It gave actors a rare chance to get to know the writer of the material they were performing. It was here that Daniels would come to know Daley as a friend and collaborator. Sachs, too, remembered first meeting Daley at the recording sessions. "When I met him I thought, 'Oh, wow. What a great guy.' He's just so relaxed about everything and just what a pleasure. There was none of this, 'I'm the writer. Watch it!' You get a range of personalities with writers. He was so refreshing. He was just a joy. I really loved working with him."[25]

Daley was there for several reasons. One was that he simply would not have missed it, being a fan himself, returning to LA from the East Coast specifically for the session. That it would last thirteen days had to be yet another omen for Daley and his favorite number. But Daley was not there only as a fan. He had work to do. Daley was needed to write extra wild lines, which he described as "peripheral, sometimes indistinguishable remarks and conversations you hear behind the primary characters in crowd scenes and such."[26] Usually left to extras and actors to extemporize, Daley worried that if listeners heard chatter like, "Let's do lunch, I'll have my Ugnaught call your Ugnaught," it could break the magic and believability of the radio dramas.[27] Daley learned from Madden the "two-minute rule," which was the idea that background dialogue and sound effects could be recycled, but only after two minutes; otherwise, the audience would know or recognize the reuse.

Daley was also there to deal with any writing adaptations needed. A few weeks prior to the Westlake sessions, Daley had been provided copies of the *Star Wars* radio production scripts by Mel Sahr, who had on May 14,

1980, shared with Daley her hopes that the production versions had value when John Madden called to consult if edits or additions were needed. Sahr added enthusiastic congratulations, telling Daley that she really liked the scripts.[28] An example of the kinds of changes Daley made was when Madden wanted extra words added to some dialogue so as to permit characters to interrupt each other, creating more natural-sounding conversations. For Madden, "Radio is a much more flexible and spontaneous form. So much of it was just about the energy, just guessing the energies so that the scene suddenly comes alive. Brian was very good at writing that. Rhythm is your major tool in terms of when you accelerate and when you decelerate. It is the silences, and how long pauses are, and how you shift and evolve the mood to the important moments. It is how you create foreboding."[29]

James Luceno was able to accompany Daley to some of the recordings for *The Empire Strikes Back* sessions and recalled, "I watched Brian work, writing wild lines. When they were recording and some line of dialogue wasn't working, Brian would come up with an alternative, you know, in a matter of a few minutes. So that was really a pleasure to see him come up with these lines that would astound Mark Hamill or Perry King or the other people involved in the recording."[30] Some of the script changes revolved around Threepio specifically.

Daniels explained, "Basically Threepio is on sustained breath because he doesn't breathe. Now in editing of course, certainly in radio, you can edit that pause and join the two words together. I love that kind of thing. Threepio is basically a lung full of air and then he talks in a very upright and very concerned manner, which eventually becomes quite difficult to do. It is fine for the odd lines that you get in a movie and the dubbing theatre. But with the radio dramas, Threepio had lines that were chunks and I remember becoming quite exhausted."[31] Daniels joked, "You know, it was surprising I didn't have a heart attack, especially during the more exciting scenes. So be careful what you wish for. Brian wrote all this stuff. I had to say it. Playing Threepio is a very tense experience, because of that breathing thing. That's the way I created him. God knows why! Many times I thought, 'Why didn't I use a different voice?"[32] Threepio's dialogue would therefore need to be reworked to accommodate the reality that while C-3PO did not need to breathe, Daniels did.

Despite these challenges, Daniels thought that the radio dramas were "never easy, but it was huge fun."[33] Part of the fun was the participatory nature of radio drama between actor and audience, where the listeners get to imagine the scene in their minds, guided by the music, sound effects, and performance. This was especially the situation with C-3PO whose expressionless face has always invited the audience to interpret. Perhaps this is why Daniels's voice and C-3PO have become synonymous with *Star Wars*.

> I always think of Liz Moore who created this face. Beautiful in repose, but blank enough that by putting timing or gesture, speed, energy, whatever, you, the audience can read [into the performance]. You're predisposed to that because he's a likable character. So you want to understand him.... I think audiences did some of the work there. But the intensity of the voice had to be more intense than the normal character because he doesn't have eyes that smile or a mouth that moves [as an unmasked character does]. So basically, what I'm admitting to is that I was overreacting horribly (laughs). And Brian loved it! (laughs).[34]

Sachs enjoyed acting with Daniels because of both his experience and his personality, "Working with Anthony Daniels was just wonderful. He was such a terrific actor and easygoing, and just a real pleasure. Very funny."[35] Executive producer Richard Toscan was at the recording sessions, and he found Daniels's understanding of his character an asset to the production. "The performers made a number of minor tweaks, especially Anthony Daniels because he had a real sense of rhythm of C-3PO and he was coming from England and had done radio work. He was, of all the performers, the most up to speed and knew what radio was about. Working with Brian and John, sometimes in the process of recording, Daniels would make suggestions for altering lines and whatever. Technically, I was there to approve those kind of changes. You know, really nothing needed approval because Tony Daniels was always right."[36]

As a testament to Daley's writing, very little beyond these kinds of practical changes needed to be made. Toscan elaborated, "Other than the normal other changes that are made, because John realizes that there's a line that doesn't have to be there, or it gets tangled up on the performer's tongue and can't get unscrambled, nothing that was of any real significance had to be edited while recording."[37] There is one change, however, that has stayed with Toscan's memories:

> Brian had a line that I missed when editing the scripts where Han Solo says in response to something, when they're on the *Millennium Falcon,* "I just drive the bus." It was funny, a good joke. They recorded the line and I thought, wait a minute. I went out and called Carol Titelman and I said, "Can Solo say this?" And she said, "No, not part of the world." I told them the line had to go and we have to redo that scene. John liked it, thought it was really funny. Perry King loved it. Brian was heartbroken. But the change had to be made.[38]

Ironically, a similar line Daley wrote for *Han Solo at Stars' End*, had met with Lucasfilm approval. In the novel, Han is debating the merits of getting involved in social causes and why he avoids the practice with Rekkon. Solo says, "Rekkon, you'd better take it easy; you've got me and

Chewie confused with somebody else. We're just driving the bus. We're not the Jedi Knights, or Freedom's Sons."

For Mark Hamill, the *Star Wars* radio drama required some artistic muscle memory. At the time that *Star Wars* was recording at Westlake, *The Empire Strikes Back* was breaking box office records and proving, importantly to the future of the franchise, that the original film was no fluke of popular culture. Principal photography for the film had taken place from March 5, until September 24, 1979. In the film, Hamill played a more mature Luke, embattled and embroiled with physical, psychological, and philosophical tests. Returning to the role of a younger, more naïve Luke Skywalker for the radio drama was a departure from what he had filmed on *Empire*. "Thank God it was radio. I'm not a teenager anymore," Hamill told *Starlog* magazine. "And I had to go back to that sort of 'Golly' kind of scooter guy. This was something I worked so hard to change in *Empire*."[39]

Daley was impressed by what Hamill was able to achieve. "In the radio series," Daley would write, "Mark showed unfailing energy and dedication to his craft and his role.... I have a personal story that shows how generous he could be. While being interviewed on New York TV to promote *Amadeus*, in which he was starring on Broadway, Mark fielded a question about the *Star Wars* series. He kindly mentioned my name—very generously, since it was a brief interview and the idea, after all, was to talk about his play. My mother had tuned in and got quite a charge out of it."[40]

A challenge common to all radio actors since the inception of the medium is understanding how to turn pages of the script so that the rustle of papers is not recorded by the microphone. King shared his strategy:

> A technical requirement of radio acting is turning pages silently. That takes you about five minutes to learn how to do that. Once you've got that down, and you put your pages out in such a way, and you learn how to move them with two fingers, they won't sound. One of my favorite tricks is you spritz it lightly so that the pages are slightly wet. All you have got to do then is the joyful part, which is figure out what you're going to do with the lines. How are you going to play this? That's the joy of acting, the fantasy.[41]

Despite the modern technology and the pedagogical and philosophical beliefs that Toscan and Madden had about how best to do modern radio, one thing had not changed from the days of Orson Welles and *The War of the Worlds*. Radio was a chance for actors to play roles in a creatively different medium than stage or film, requiring collaboration and imagination. Kale Browne, who played Biggs, recalled:

> We did it like an old radio show. We all stood in the same room around a bunch of mics. It was terrific.... The fact is, as an actor, when you get paid to do what you would do for free, you feel like the luckiest guy in the world. So when

> somebody says, "Pretend there's a dinosaur coming at you and go like this," you see the dinosaur and you do the thing.... Because it's just pretend time and especially with radio, it's all in your head anyway. It was a lot of fun.... The people that I worked with mainly were Perry and Mark. It was a pretty tight, small group of people. I became friends with Mark and we stayed in touch for quite some time after that.[42]

Toscan remembered the recording sessions at Westlake with fondness, "It was a wonderfully smooth process—surprisingly so for such a complex project—thanks to John's leadership in the studio and Mel's behind-the-scenes management of those incredibly complicated logistics. Any issues I had with performances had been handled quietly by John with his first-rate coaching skills and in a way that kept everything on track. On the last day, after it was a wrap, we all celebrated by signing the first copies of that marvelous C-3PO poster. Everyone had made new friends. It was a perfect way to end the Hollywood part of it."[43]

With the sessions at Westlake complete after thirteen arduous, marathon days, Tom Voegeli had the raw materials to begin to build the radio drama. For him, *Star Wars* was really just beginning.

8

Sound Advice

When not recording Jedi and droids, Tom Voegeli earned his living during the 1980s as a sound designer, engineer, and producer for Minnesota Public Radio (MPR). He would be returning to St. Paul and to the MPR Maud Moon Weyerhaeuser Recording Studio, named for the patron of the arts whose family was famous in the lumber industry. The twenty-four-track, state-of-the-art facility, of which Voegeli joked "This little room is sort of like a Lucasfilm Audio Spinoff,"[1] provided him the best location from which to edit the raw materials gathered at the recording sessions in Los Angeles into the complicated mix of voice, sound effects, and music. In essence, Voegeli was not only sound designer and postproduction supervisor, he was also the editor.

But before returning to Minnesota, Voegeli had one important errand to run in California. The sound effects of Ben Burtt would literally, as in the case of the voices of R2-D2 or Chewbacca, or more figuratively, as with the lasers and starships, be characters themselves in the radio dramas. Voegeli tells the tale of his first meeting with Burtt:

> I was very impressed by the sound. Until *Star Wars*, lasers had been done by synthesizers. Ben was really interested in making the sound effects out of natural sound. I went out there to Lucasfilm to get sound effects. And I think Ben was nervous as hell. I mean, management had made this deal with this bozo, me, who was going to come in and copy his best sound effects. And they were his. Ben felt very proprietary about them, which I would have, too. He had a studio at The Egg Company. He was working on *Raiders of the Lost Ark* at this time dubbing all his best sound effects. Ben asked me, "The opening of the Ark. Can you guess what it is? What is the origin of that?" And I got close with my answer, but I didn't really guess what it was.
>
> He took me into The Egg Company bathroom and slid the lid off the cover on the toilet. That's what it was, a toilet lid! He was great to let me have access to his sound effects. I tried to be very sensitive to that. These were the days when it was reel to reel. I flew home with the reels in a suitcase that I bought an extra airplane seat for so that the reels never left my side. I actually bought a ticket for "Mr. Suitcase." I work in classical music mostly and cellists buy a

> ticket for their cello with the ticket made out for "Mr. Cello." So I was kind of used to that. I even strapped in the suitcase during the ride.[2]

Eventually, Voegeli would have to augment the radio dramas with some of his own creations because of the new scenes that Daley had added. About the situation, Voegeli said, "Ben was very forgiving. They liked it. That may be why they wanted me to do *Raiders of the Lost Ark: The Movie on Record*."[3] An innovation in its own right, and a kind of metaphorical younger sibling to the *Star Wars* radio drama, Voegeli's Raiders of the Lost Ark: *The Story on Record* summarized the George Lucas–produced and Steven Spielberg–directed film using no narration whatsoever, something unique in the medium, relying only on dialogue, sound effects, and music that Voegeli mixed together and edited. The 1981 record would earn Voegeli a Grammy Award for Best Spoken Word Album. As with the *Star Wars* radio drama, much of the work assembling the *Raiders* album would be done at MPR.

In the 1981 MPR-produced *The Making of* Star Wars *for Radio: A Fable for the Mind's Eye,* a documentary that preceded the radio drama, Ben Burtt revealed, "I feel that the successful sound in a motion picture is one which goes unnoticed. That is, the average person goes, attends the film, and they never doubt the fact that those objects and places in the film—there is no question—that there were just mics there on a set, right? Or that they existed in space or they existed on some planet, or something like that."[4] Sound effects done right, which for Burtt usually meant using some natural, organic, or real-world sound disguised, make the unreal real. That kind of artistic approach is why Burtt and John Williams deserve credit as the sources of much of the saga's emotional quality.

Burtt made his experience available to Voegeli when he had questions. Voegeli gave an example to journalist Gary Lycan, "He [Burtt] also advised me on the nomenclature. For example, the last rebel location in the film *Star Wars* was Massassi, but it was never mentioned in the movie. And it never appeared in the radio script. So when I first came across sound effects labeled 'Massassi,' I didn't know what they referred to. Ben made the translation for me."[5]

In addition to Burtt's sound effects, Voegeli also had the entirety of John Williams's score, including music unreleased at that time to consumers.

> You avoid footsteps when you can. Rule number one. You don't want to get locked into footsteps all over the place, because it's just a pain. But sometimes you have to have them and those are all dubbed in later. I worked with a sound guy who did what you would now call Foley sound. So that was his footsteps, typically, in a studio. There were lots of other live effects, you know, like the steel deck plates on the *Millennium Falcon*. Those were real. They were added

> later, but they were certainly real steel plates. So there are a fair amount of effects that were added to Ben's effects. In the film, they obviously have Foley artists, really great ones, at their disposal. We did the same techniques done in a slightly different way, because we didn't have the studios built for radio drama.[6]

As with the sound effects, the extra narrative created by Daley would necessitate the need for additional music cues that Voegeli composed. "I tried to avoid it, but we did a session here in Minneapolis with all the wind players. I don't think they're tremendously successful, but I needed more material."[7] However, Voegeli noted, "They gave me access to John Williams' music off the sound stage before it had been edited. That was hugely useful."[8]

Imagine, then, a small sound control room, filled with thousands of feet of tape. Some contained actor voices, with every take, both good and unusable. Some contained Burtt's effects. Some contained Williams's score. Some contained the original effects and music created by Voegeli. All of it had to be assembled, voice by voice, effect by effect, into a coherent whole. Journalist Jeff Strickler described the process of putting together the radio dramas, "Like a maestro leading an orchestra, Voegeli waves his hands over the board, adding or subtracting, highlighting or diminishing each element as he composes."[9]

For Voegeli, another metaphor is as applicable. To him, postproduction on *Star Wars* was like a jigsaw puzzle with the script as a roadmap or set of guidelines that defined what that puzzle should eventually look like. "The biggest part of the jigsaw puzzle is to work the music against the dialogue," Voegeli told Strickler.[10] It was a puzzle that would take him nearly six months to complete with work so detailed that sometimes it would take an entire day to mix a single minute of the radio drama to the quality he thought best. Because he had access to the original recordings as made, rather than how they were assembled for the film, Voegeli was able to start from scratch, deciding which lightsaber ignition sound evoked the most emotion for a scene, which growl of Chewbacca fit the moment, or which music cue should be used where.

In *The Making of* Star Wars *for Radio: A Fable for the Mind's Eye* radio documentary, Voegeli walks through his process using the scene of Luke fixing a moisture vaporator before getting distracted by a battle occurring in Tatooine's orbit. While filmed for the movie, it was never finished and did not make the theatrical edit. Voegeli, then, had only his experience to guide his selections. To assemble that scene for the radio drama, he started with the monophonic recording of Hamill's performance from Westlake that had been guided by Daley's script and Madden's direction as to when to leave pauses and when to increase volume. Then, Voegeli would add Luke's footsteps, the wind, the Treadwell droid voice and motorized effects, and the music—among other sound effects—to give the audience enough information to know where Luke was and to make the world of Tatooine real.[11]

Whatever the metaphor, be it Voegeli as composer or Voegeli as puzzle solver, the result was a rich, layered sound mix using the best technology available at the time. Sachs believed that the reason the torture scene, or really any scene, was effective was because Voegeli made it so during the editing process.[12]

Lest it is thought it was all work and no play, Voegeli had great fun mixed with the effort. For someone who loves sound so much, *Star Wars* was a dream project. Voegeli's favorite? "R2-D2 was incredibly fun to do because he is so freaking expressive. We had this big reel of his bleeps and blinks and raspberries."[13]

As 1980 ended and 1981 began, Voegeli delivered his final edit of the first episode he'd completed to Richard Toscan for Lucasfilm's approval. Toscan remembered, "Tom sent me the first episode he'd mixed on this huge 15" tape reel and I drove it over the mountain to Lucasfilm, sort of eying it lying there on the passenger seat. This was the culmination of two years of work by me, Tom, John Madden, everyone involved. The real test." Would Lucasfilm give NPR approval now to broadcast *Star Wars* for radio? While Titelman had approved pieces of the series, this would be her first hearing of an assembled episode as it would be broadcast. Toscan continued, "Carol and I went into one of their screening rooms with a technician who put the reel onto one of those massive tape machines we used in those days. The episode began and we just sat there not saying a word as it played. When it was over, she turned to me and said, 'I never thought it could work, but you did it.' I was stunned. But it drove home how really outlandish the idea was to put *Star Wars* on radio, even at Lucasfilm."[14]

Now, the biggest questions were about to be answered. Would radio audiences appreciate the radio drama enough to help NPR as Frank Mankiewicz needed? Would *Star Wars* become the creative scandal that captured the national imagination as Toscan hoped? Would fans accept the additions made by Brian Daley? In March 1981, the actors and creatives of the *Star Wars* radio drama, the leadership of NPR and Lucasfilm, and the press gathered at the Griffith Observatory in Los Angeles to begin to answer those exact questions.

9

Clear Receptions

With a cost totaling more than a quarter million dollars, National Public Radio (NPR) was not taking any chances. It wanted to make certain that the trumpet of the *Star Wars* radio drama could be heard loud and wide. The publicity campaign that Sam Holt supervised was nearly as involved as that for many motion pictures. Radio ads, a red-carpet premiere, and press interview junkets were among the strategies employed. *Fantastic Films* magazine featured a story on the radio dramas in the June 1981 issue, with a cover of the film characters around an NPR microphone by artist Scott Gustafson. "And Now, *Star Wars* on the Air" was the April 13, 1981, *Time* magazine Show Business Spotlight. Comic books featured illustrated advertisements. Timing *Star Wars* to premiere during an NPR fundraising campaign further capitalized on the radio drama's hoped-for ability to help NPR financially and with ratings.

The radio ads featured the voices of Mark Hamill, Anthony Daniels, and Ann Sachs introducing themselves and their characters and inviting listeners to join them on NPR. One of the ads, known as "Fair Compensation," features C-3PO and R2-D2 encouraging people to give money, yet bemoaning that, as droids, they do not expect to get a coffee mug or tote bag as a thank you for their generous donation. Anthony Daniels participated in a photography session on London streets while carrying a C-3PO cardboard standee interacting with motorists and riding the 137 trolleybus. The images would appear in newspapers and magazines to promote the British Broadcasting Corporation (BBC) Radio 1 premiere.

Local NPR stations did their part during the original broadcast and subsequent reruns. Many ran promotions with sponsors of the program whereby fans could go get their pictures taken with costumed *Star Wars* characters and get autographs from Darth Vader or Jawas. In Illinois, Appletree Stereo, a then popular store on Lincoln Highway in DeKalb, co-sponsored a promotional event with WNIU-FM 90.5, as did the Chicago Carson Pirie Scott department store with WBEZ-FM 91.5.

Several months before recording sessions were set to begin, NPR had contacted Richard Toscan because they decided promotional plans for the radio series needed a poster. "NPR asked me to see if Lucasfilm would be comfortable with a commissioned piece for the series using *Star Wars* characters. Carol Titelman agreed with the caveat that she have final approval of the artwork."[1] Celia Strain was hired to create the artwork, and a few months before the premiere, she unveiled what would become one of *Star Wars'* most unique and iconic posters outside of the theatrical versions. The 22" × 22.5" original acrylic art featured C-3PO by a microphone with headphones as T.I.E. Fighters buzzed around, set against a starry field. In February 1981, Toscan got the original mockup of the poster. He liked it, but there was something that seemed strange about the image and he could not determine exactly what concerned him. "I met with Carol, poster in hand, and after one quick look she said, 'No. C-3PO's torso is too short.' That's why it looked weird. The graphic designer redid it and Carol was comfortable with the second version we used for the series."[2]

The red-carpet premiere was held at the Griffith Observatory planetarium high above Los Angeles. Toscan has vivid memories of the main event that night. After brief welcoming comments, "The lights dimmed to completed darkness, our seats reclined back so we were enveloped by this dome with thousands of stars appearing, and then suddenly the John Williams score flooding out of this amazing sound system. It was magical. That's not a word I use often, but it really was magic."[3] As sample episodes from the radio drama played, a laser light show was presented on the eighty-five-foot ceiling. Attendees included Frank Mankiewicz, Wallace Smith, Toscan, Mark Hamill, Perry King, Ann Sachs, and Bernard Behrens. The press was invited, including their children. Among the crowd was a costumed Darth Vader and Boba Fett, courtesy of Lucasfilm. After the episodes played, Hamill addressed the crowd discussing the hopes that *Star Wars* could help reignite the radio drama format in the United States.

There was some debate and controversy about exactly what the nature of the sample episodes should be. Toscan noted:

> Somehow NPR ginned up this tremendous press coverage full of wonder, amazement, doubt, whatever, all the right stuff. Lots of really good publicity, tons of interviews. The only issue I had was that NPR wanted to use at the premiere, an episode that had almost no new information in it. I called Sam Holt and said you can't do this. The press is going to say, "Oh, it's just the film put on tape." I told Sam we have to premiere an episode that had new material. I said, and this a direct quote, "And if you don't use that episode, you and Frank are going to look like fools. That's my last word on this, you get to decide." I think that was the only other time I left a little blood on the floor while producing this other than firing the writer at the beginning.[4]

Holt and NPR saw the wisdom in Toscan's advice, and episodes with more original material, such as "A Wind to Shake the Stars," were selected. Despite the debate, all is well that ends well. "Within a week or two after the Griffith Park event," Toscan revealed, "They got this amazing response and tons of additional press."[5]

But there was still a dissident view of *Star Wars* among many NPR staff. "I was on the phone with this NPR guy about planning for their upcoming public radio conference and suggested a panel on the series," Toscan said. "He responded, 'Why would we want to do that? It's over-produced and under-acted.'"[6] Toscan was amused and secretly delighted with that response. "He confirmed we really had gotten close to what I was after in this new way of doing radio drama, deliberately doing something that was much closer to filmmaking than old-style radio drama production. We'd gone for a far more restrained acting style paired with elaborate use of sound effects and score, all of that being typical of feature film production. In a weird upside-down way, this guy had nailed it and hated the result. But he did leave me wondering if audiences would agree with him and bail out after our first episode."[7]

The radio drama would premiere beginning on March 1, 1981, as the flagship drama of the new *NPR Playhouse*, the successor of *Earplay*. It would closely be followed by a radio adaptation, originally produced by the BBC in 1978, of Douglas Adams's *The Hitchhiker's Guide to the Galaxy*. Each of 243 NPR stations that chose to add *Star Wars* to its programming customized the day and time to its audience demographics. Perhaps a sign of the creative scandal idea that Toscan and John Houseman designed the radio drama idea upon, a few local affiliates refused to air the program. An example was Tampa's WUSF-FM 89.7, whose programming director thought that the "majority of our listeners wouldn't be interested in *Star Wars*" and did not "feel that's how we want to get those new listeners," worried about the consistency of an audience first introduced to NPR via such unusual programming fare.[8] Many of those general managers and programming managers who made the choice to pass on *Star Wars*, including WUSF, changed course once the show's ratings started to be tabulated because *Star Wars* as a radio drama became for radio what *Star Wars* as a film became for movies: a revolutionary smash.

And not just in America. When the BBC pulled out of the project, Sam Holt got the Canadian and Australian equivalents of NPR to commit to broadcasting the series and contributing to the production costs. The Canadian Broadcasting Corporation first aired *Star Wars* that July and the Australian Broadcasting Corporation premiered it later the next year.

As critics and journalists listened to copies of the radio dramas supplied by NPR or after attending the gala premiere, reviews started appearing in newspapers, almost universally in praise of the production as something special. A sampling:

- *Woman's Day*: "It's a daring venture, considering how much of the movie's success depended on its astonishing visual effects. But the audio version works."[9]
- James Brown, *Los Angeles Times*: "*Star Wars* not only has taken radio drama one step beyond in terms of sound quality, but also has bridged the gap between the deceptively simple, 'Theater of the Mind' wonderment of radio's past with the technological wizardry of its present. The result is a fun, spine-tingling, mind-bending piece of escapist entertainment that doesn't miss the visuals one bit."[10]
- Vince Staten, *Evening Dispatch*: "The wait has been worth it.... *Star Wars* was such a visual film that it would seem foolish to translate it to radio. But the *National Public Radio* (NPR) producers have turned it into an exciting experience for the theater of the mind."[11]
- Gerald B. Jordan, *Kansas City Star.* "Chewbacca's growls become less a novelty and more his truest means of expression. Ben Kenobi takes on more noble characteristics than the scraggly hermit we saw onscreen. The music, of course, still is sensational."[12]
- Rick Malaspina, *Tribune*: "Do yourself a favor and forget you've got a TV set tonight ... the folks at KQED graciously provided me with a cassette of the last *Star Wars* episode. What they don't know is that they're never getting it back. It's wonderful stuff."[13]

More important, though, to NPR was the audience reaction. The statistics were revelatory, with the radio drama succeeding beyond expectations by a wide margin. Arbitron ratings showed that the radio drama averaged 750,000 listeners. Toscan helped put this into a modern perspective:

> From my point of view, the best thing that came out of it is NPR got to be a functioning organization. A few of my ideas of how radio drama should work turned out to be correct. A month ago, I tried to figure out what the listening audience was for the first radio drama series of *Star Wars* based on the way we talk about episodic podcast fiction today, on downloads, as opposed to more traditional audience numbers. During the first decade when that first season of *Star Wars* was repeatedly aired on a lot of NPR stations, I figured we probably had the equivalent of about 30 million downloads. Perhaps 80 million with the CD releases, all of the re-releases, and the original 750,000 audience numbers, which puts it in pretty credible company with the most successful podcasts of the new Golden Age of audio drama.[14]

The *Star Wars* radio dramas led to an increase of 40 percent more listeners for NPR that year than the year before, with a 135 percent increase in drama programming specifically. There were increases in ratings among all demographic groups. Eleven percent of the 750,000 listeners were twelve to seventeen years old, an increase of four times the norm. Usually NPR generated 35 percent of its audience from the twenty-five to thirty-nine age group. With *Star Wars*, 50 percent of those listening were that age. Ten thousand letters and fifty thousand phone calls were received, a problem for NPR, albeit a great problem to have, because they had the capacity to handle only about a fifth of that number.

Mankiewicz summarizes it, "*Star Wars* inspired a renaissance of interest in radio drama introducing a new generation of listeners to its special pleasures. Response to *Star Wars* exceeded our expectations. The series generated more than 50,000 letters and phone calls, and played a major role in our unprecedented 40 percent audience growth this past year."[15] The success of *Star Wars* could not have been timed better for NPR. That April, while episodes 5 and 6 were premiering on local affiliates, NPR was facing financial concerns. The 1980 budget for NPR was $21 million, of which $14 million was from the U.S. government. Now, Mankiewicz was dealing with the very real possibility of serious budget reductions from Congress, while at the same time battling perceptions that NPR was too East Coast and too elitist in its orientation.[16] *Star Wars* gave Mankiewicz the data necessary, exactly when needed, to demonstrate to both the U.S. Congress and to the NPR board of directors that extraordinary ratings successes were possible at NPR. Further, *Star* Wars clearly established that NPR programming had not only national, but also international, appeal, and that it was not elitist. *Star Wars* also permitted NPR to showcase its pioneering satellite delivery system and tout that it had the nation's first radio satellite network, even before commercial radio. Toscan believed that without the *Star Wars* radio drama, the forces wishing to diminish or eliminate NPR radio in favor of Public Broadcasting Service (PBS) television would have won out.

There were other, less statistical measures of success for the actors and creatives involved in the creation of the radio dramas. For Toscan, "The icing on the cake was when after Richard Imison and Aubrey Singer at the BBC heard the *Star Wars* radio dramas, they decided to make them the first radio drama ever aired on BBC Radio 1, which was the pop channel, and they also aired it on the World Service."[17]

For Madden, "It was a thrilling piece of work. I've worked with Tom a lot and he was a close friend and God knows, Brian was wonderful. There was a sort of very nice sense of being involved in something that meant a lot to all of us while we were doing it."[18]

For Hamill, it was getting letters "from young people who never used radio for anything other than background. It's like they discovered a new art form. Who could believe that small box could create such drama in their lives?"[19]

For Daley, it was the reward of writing in a different medium about something he loved. "Perhaps the greatest transition I've gone through is from writing books to writing dialogue that people are actually going to deliver."[20] Daley, too, was gratified that George Lucas was gracious enough to let him know personally that he liked the radio drama. On April 31, 1981, Lucas wrote to Daley in a hand-signed letter that Sid Ganis shared with him how well the radio drama was being received and that he thought it is wonderful. Lucas told Daley he did a terrific job.[21]

Lucia St. Clair Robson recalled, "People canceled appointments to stay home and listen. It was incredible. People made sure they were home when that came on."[22]

Episode 13, "Force and Counter Force," of the radio drama would be recognized with a 1982 Major Armstrong Award nomination. Sponsored by the Armstrong Memorial Research Foundation at Columbia University and the National Radio Broadcasters Association, the award is named for the developer of FM radio technology, Edwin Howard Armstrong. The nomination was a symbol of the creative use of the medium made by the *Star Wars* team.

Perhaps the most unusual and humorous reaction, though, was from a letter from listener Ira Zimmerman, who played the radio drama while working on a ranch, "With the opening theme up, over 200 eyes from a herd of cattle quickly turned my way. It was not long before I was joined by these nonhuman lifeforms lining up along the fence, listening. Judging by the movement of their tails, they seemed to enjoy it as much as I did."[23]

The uncertainties and questions that had plagued the production since its inception had been answered. *Star Wars* was a creative scandal that caught the imagination of the press. It was a rating success that NPR was able to utilize in salvation of its budget and relevance. It would run and rerun for years on NPR. Now, a new question emerged. Would the *Star Wars* radio drama be a one-time collaboration between NPR and Lucasfilm? Happily, to paraphrase Yoda, the answer to that question was *no, there is another.*

10

A Rebellion Reunites for *The Empire Strikes Back* on Radio

On April 20, 1982, in Washington, D.C., National Public Radio (NPR) and Lucasfilm announced the return of *Star Wars* to radio with an adaptation of *Star Wars: The Empire Strikes Back*. Buoyed by the success of its predecessor, Frank Mankiewicz said, "I am certain that an even more enthusiastic audience awaits *The Empire Strikes Back*."[1] George Lucas added, "NPR did a great job with the 13 *Star Wars* shows, and we're looking forward to working with them on the production of the *Empire* series."[2] As before, Lucasfilm donated the rights to KUSC for *Empire* at a cost of $1.

The film version had earned a bit over $401 million in total domestic and international dollars, earning the status of best-grossing film of 1980. The Washington, D.C., announcement promised the participation of all principal actors and most of the creative personnel who had made the *Star Wars* radio dramas. Some, however, would not be returning, chief among them, Carol Titelman and Richard Toscan.

In 1981, Lucasfilm had moved out of The Egg Company in Los Angeles to a new location in San Rafael, California, closer to special effects artists at Industrial Light & Magic (ILM) and Lucas himself. Some employees decided not to make the move with the rest of the company, one of whom was Titelman who moved to New York with her husband, Russ Titelman, where she continued to work as a writer. After a lifetime of contributions to the arts, Titelman would pass away on December 7, 2019. Supervising for Lucasfilm would be Michael Levett, vice president of ancillary activities, whose responsibilities included publishing and recording projects. Taking on the day-to-day script approvals and acting as liaison to Lucasfilm would be Anita Gross.

Toscan had decided early on that he would not return for the radio sequel:

> Lucasfilm did a screening for employees of *Empire*. The theater held about 600 people or some number like that. My wife Sharon and I were invited, because we were by then considered part of the Lucasfilm family. I wasn't sure what I thought about *Empire*, except my response was much different from my absolute amazement when I saw *Star Wars* the first time. So at the end of the show, obviously, when they do these screenings for employees, there's always wild applause because all your colleagues have been busting their butts for the last year working on this thing. We all got up out of our seats and slowly funneled out of the auditorium into the large lobby that's attached to it. It was surprisingly silent. In front of us was a boy who was probably, I'm guessing maybe seven or eight years old. During this silence, the kid looks up at his father, and in a loud voice says, "I liked the first one better." It was at that moment that I realized NPR should not do *Empire*.[3]

Toscan had a conversation with KUSC General Manager Wallace Smith:

> I called Wally, the next day or so and said, "I know you want *Empire*, but there are a couple of reasons why you should not. One, you won't get the bang you got out of the first series. It's not going to be a scandal anymore. You are not going to get the audience numbers you got the first time out. Second, because *Empire* is now out of the box many of the original people we worked with at Lucasfilm who got [profit] points in the first film, and George was super generous in handing out points to everybody, many of those people may be taking their points and going home. It appears as though Carol is going to do that. You are not going to have the leeway that we had on the first series in terms of the story you want to tell. You won't be given that freedom that we had. So don't do it." Of course, because NPR was bitten by the Hollywood bug by that time, they did it anyway. A year or so later, Wally stopped me on campus and said, "You were right." I never asked him why, but looking back and seeing the numbers NPR got out of *Empire*, I think we were both wrong in terms of audiences for NPR.[4]

It would take Toscan until the spring of 1983 to realize what Wally Smith had left unspoken (see Chapter 12).

For *Empire*, the executive producer would be John Bos, director of NPR arts and performance programs. He had been part of the team working on the original *Star Wars* radio drama and subsumed Toscan's responsibilities. Forever a believer in the power of the arts, Bos had previously worked for Baltimore's famed Center Stage performing arts theater and was the chair of the Performing Arts Division of the New York State Council of the Arts, supervising a $15 million grant budget to promote music, dance, and theater. Bos innovated a grant program for nonprofits as part of his belief in the importance of accessibility to the arts. The primarily free medium of NPR meshed with Bos's ideology. It had been Bos who arranged to have the British Broadcasting Corporation (BBC) production of *The Hitchhiker's Guide to the Galaxy* licensed to NPR. Brian

Daley wrote, "John saw *Star Wars* and the proposed *Empire* as a way to anchor a six-days-a-week fare of radio drama offerings."[5] Bos would later earn a Peabody Award for meritorious service to broadcasting.

Despite the loss of Toscan and Titelman, many of the original participants did return for *Empire*. All of the principal cast, including Mark Hamill, Anthony Daniels, Perry King, Ann Sachs, Brock Peters, Bernard Behrens, and narrator Ken Hiller, returned. Hamill said, "Radio drama goes to the heart of what an actor really does—it involves total concentration and imagination. Because of that, I think, I've tried things for the series that I would never attempt in front of a camera."[6] Returning, too, were John Madden, Tom Voegeli, Mel Sahr, and Brian Daley.

An important contrast, though, of *Star Wars* to *Empire* was that the recordings would take place not at the Westlake Recording Studio, and not even in California. Rather, the production was moved to New York. Madden requested the change of venue because of his directing and teaching schedule. A positive unintended consequence resulted. The move eased the burden on Sahr when casting the new roles for *Empire*. According to Daley, Sahr shared with him that in Los Angeles, "Some actors had passed on supporting roles in *Star Wars* because they were unwilling to commit to a daytime job. 'They wanted to sit by the phone, hoping they'd get called for a pilot.' New York was much the opposite. Actors appearing in various plays and shows had free time during the day. They were usually delighted to come into the studio, take a role or two or three, work with peers, and practice their craft."[7] Such was true for Sachs, who performed Leia Organa by day while recording *Empire* and then rehearsed as Mandy for the Jules Feiffer play *A Think Piece* with the Circle Repertory Company by night. The success and publicity of the first radio drama smoothed the way for many stage actors, some of whom were nationally known, to join the already impressive actors from the original.

Billy Dee Williams (Lando Calrissian)

Sahr scored a major triumph by getting Billy Dee Williams to reprise his role as Lando Calrissian, making *Empire* the only one of the radio drama trilogy to feature three of the actors from the films in their original characters. Williams would be returning to his hometown of New York for the radio drama, having been born there in 1937. He was already an established star and heartthrob before joining the *Star Wars* troupe of actors, most especially famous for his turn as the charming Louis McKay in the biopic *Lady Sings the Blues* about jazz icon Billie Holiday. The film was nominated for eight Academy Awards, winning five. Williams would win an NAACP

Image Award for his portrayal. Other memorable roles were as football great Gale Sayers in *Brian's Song* and even playing himself on *The Jeffersons.*

Williams told the audience at *Star Wars* Celebration Orlando 2017 during the "40 Years of *Star Wars*" panel that as a fan of *THX-1138*, Lucas' first film, "When I had the opportunity to work with George Lucas, I mean I thought that was like going straight to heaven."[8] For Williams, the code to understanding the Lando Calrissian character has two components, "The cape. And 'Calrissian.' An Armenian name. I-a-n. And I thought, wow, that's interesting. Let me play around with this whole idea, because I did not want to do a kind of stereotypical, clichéd kind of character. I wanted to bring something really special to it. Something bigger than life."[9]

There was a parallel for Williams when he agreed to the *Empire* radio drama as compared to when he agreed to the film. In both situations, he was joining an already established ensemble of actors and behind-the-scenes artists who had worked on an original piece of entertainment. At least for the radio drama, though, Williams had established a relationship with Hamill and Anthony Daniels from time together at Elstree Studios. Another commonality that Williams shared with Daniels was that both had previous radio experience. "I first did radio many, many years ago," Williams said in 1983. "That's one of the reasons why I wanted to do this. I was curious about radio today. And it's an honor to be part of the *Star Wars* phenomenon. I'll be in the archives forever."[10]

Williams was welcomed, too, by his new companions on the radio drama. Sachs was thrilled to be acting with Williams, "Oh, what a sweetheart he is. I remember his penetrating gaze. When I would look at him, he would look at me, as if we were onstage alone, doing the most intense scene. That was Billy Dee Williams and his way of operating and the way he interacted. I loved that about him. I just loved it. I thought, 'Oh, great. There's a connection there.' Very much his own style."[11]

Having Williams as another actor reprising his original role and bringing with him personal experiences of Lucas' vision was a boon to the radio actors. Perry King shared that Hamill, Daniels, and Williams "were constantly feeding us information that we really need, that they've discovered in working with George Lucas. For example, there is no doubt in their minds when a piece of dialogue is right or wrong. But, at the same time, they are taking us under their wing as members of the *Star Wars* family."[12]

John Lithgow (Yoda)

John Lithgow has earned two Golden Globe Awards, two Tony Awards, three Screen Actors Guild Awards, six Primetime Emmy Awards, and nominations for Academy Awards and Grammy Awards. Yet despite these accolades, he is very proud to have played Yoda in the *Empire* radio drama. He told Graham Norton in 2017 that "[i]t makes me cry every time I hear it."[13] How he became Yoda, and who else almost became Yoda, is an adventure of its own.

Frank Oz, the original puppeteer and voice actor of Yoda from the film, was in England at the time and unavailable to reprise his singular performance style for the radio drama. As the search for radio Yoda began, a rather unusual possibility emerged. What if Mark Hamill could play both Luke and Yoda? Hamill was then, and is now, a chameleon voice artist whose Yoda impression is very good. Plus, no one besides Oz spent as much time with the Yoda character as Hamill. Daley explained, "One odd but tempting solution came up when Mark demonstrated that he did a *great* Yoda. John Madden almost went for it despite the technical headaches of having Mark play both roles in many and protracted scenes with himself. Mark was ready to tackle it, a unique radio tour de force."[14] At a book signing in 2011, Lithgow confirmed Daley's anecdote, revealing that it was his understanding that Hamill really wanted to play Yoda.

But the logistics would be too much for a production that already had a limited budget and limited time. In fact, the *Empire* recording sessions were to begin on June 1, 1982, and yet no Yoda could be found as of May. Approximately six days before recording of *Empire* was to start, a celebratory dinner would serve not only good food but also a helping of good fortune. Voegeli continued the tale:

> John Madden was directing John Lithgow in a play by Christopher Durang named *Beyond Therapy*. We were all going out to dinner, and John was there, I was there, Lithgow was there, and a bunch of other actors. Lithgow was asking about *Star Wars* for radio. John shared that we were having trouble finding an actor to play Yoda. Then Lithgow launched into Yoda. I know I've heard Frank Oz interviewed that lots of people can do the voice of Yoda, but they can't do the soul of Yoda. Lithgow just nailed it. He was cast on the spot. He loved being cast as Yoda, for his kids and everything. The irony is that while his voice is perfect for the role, he is a much different size than Yoda, because he is a very tall guy.[15]

Lithgow attributed his ability to perform Yoda to the imitations that he did for his first son of the many Frank Oz characters on *Sesame Street*. It helped, too, that Lithgow was friends with Oz. For Lithgow, the real credit for Yoda must be given to Oz. "A good friend of mine, Frank Oz, created the voice of Yoda. When I was asked to participate in this adaptation, I thought of his wry characterization. While I couldn't begin to duplicate his performance, I've tried to remain faithful to his interpretation."[16]

Many colleagues were impressed by Lithgow's performance. Perry

King said, "When he first opened his mouth and Yoda came out, I remember thinking, 'Wow, good for you.' Who knew he had that in him? Who would have guessed?."[17] Daniels reflected on Lithgow, "This man is a superstar. There he is hunched up being Yoda in the weirdest places, you know, because the studios weren't built for that kind of thing. They were very small in general. And of course, John Lithgow is wonderful as Yoda."[18]

Paul Hecht (Emperor)

Paul Hecht was no stranger to performing in plays that were about lost scenes that riffed on a popular original piece, as the NPR *Star Wars* radio series endeavored to do. That is because Hecht made his name performing in the play *Rosencrantz and Guildenstern Are Dead,* which was a model for Daley on how to add scenes and expand the narrative of the radio dramas. The London-born actor would earn a Tony Award nomination for his performance as the Player. Prior to *Empire*, Hecht continued his Broadway acting and appeared on the television programs *Hawaii Five-O* and *Remington Steele*, eventually playing Charles Lowell on the sitcom *Kate & Allie*. Although Hecht appears briefly in the episode "Way of the Jedi" for the *Empire* radio drama, he would be featured in more episodes of the *Return of the Jedi* radio drama.

David Rasche (Admiral Piett), best known as Jack Trenton on the sitcoms *Nurses* and *Empty Nest*; Alan Rosenberg (Boba Fett), the future Screen Actors Guild president and *L.A. Law* and *Civil Wars* actor; and Jay O. Sanders (Imperial Pilot), *JFK* and Broadway performer, rounded out some of the supporting roles.

Daley would be more than a writer on *The Empire Strikes Back*. He would return to acting, something he had pursued during his younger days, and has a cameo in the *Empire* radio drama as a Stormtrooper. After the *Star Wars* radio drama, Daley was productive by starting negotiations soon on the novelization to the movie *Tron* and continuing work on his original novel, *A Tapestry of Magics,* that would eventually be released during January 1983. Daley was approached by NPR during autumn 1981 to script the *Star Wars* sequel, and he began story conferences with Bos, Gross, Madden, and Voegeli in November 1981. He would have the winter to write ten episodes, with *Empire* being shortened by three episodes to adjust for growing costs. The *Empire* budget would be set at $235,000, near that of the original *Star Wars* radio drama. Daley did most of his writing in Hensonville, a hamlet in Windham, Greene County, New York, to be near Madden. He described the process as, "I paced, worried, wrote and had a wonderful time. An excruciating writer's paradise!"[19]

Daley thought of *Star Wars* and *Empire* as more than "simply films—those marvelous, breakthrough special effects not-withstanding—they're a story, in the fine old sense of the word. They're about a universe in which human beings, aliens, and machines (who reflect much that is human) experience things common to all of us: love, vengeance, fear, and wonder."[20] Such a canvas gave him a great deal of material to work from, and as usual, Daley had to deal more with having too many good ideas, not a lack of them. "The films are rich with dramatic possibilities for radio," Daley detailed. "Story line origins, off-screen situations and facets of characters that deserve exploration. It sometimes seemed that there was barely enough time in which to set forth the story."[21]

Even though *Empire* would have fewer episodes than *Star Wars*, Daley still had much to add. The film version had a total of thirty-eight speaking roles and about forty minutes of dialogue during its two hour and four-minute running time. By contrast, Daley would write fifty-eight speaking roles for thirty-two actors and three hours of dialogue during the radio drama's four hour and twenty-two-minute running time.

Originally Daley had a different opening scene from what was eventually used for *Empire*. As planned in the November 1981 "script treatment," the radio drama would begin aboard an Imperial warship as Captain Needa discusses military strategy with an unnamed Imperial Officer. The probots were being sent to "worlds where resources salvaged from Yavin by the Rebels (vehicles, clothing, medicines, etc.) would be of optimal use." It was odd, Needa and the Imperial Officer debated, that Darth Vader would waste a probot searching the ice world of Hoth, as it would be impractical for the Rebels to flee a jungle world for an arctic one, as they would not have the resources to survive. The scene then fades immediately to a parallel meeting among Rebels on Hoth, where General Rieekan, Leia, and various personnel are discussing that very problem of survival.[22]

These scenes are indicative of the realism that pervades the *Empire* script whenever strategy is discussed, likely the result of Daley's own experiences in Vietnam and Germany. While the scenes would be scripted and included in altered forms in the radio drama, Daley felt the need to open the radio drama not with the Imperials, but with the Rebels. As recorded, Commander Narra and the Rebellion's Renegade Flight Squadron are escorting transport ships bringing needed supplies to Hoth, explaining how it is that the Rebellion is able to survive there. However, a dire situation occurs as T.I.E. Fighters swoop in and destroy the convoy. Later, listeners will learn that Narra's sacrifice led to Luke's promotion as squadron commander.

This exact kind of situation would recur in the film *Rogue One: A Star Wars Story* where the audience sees the original Red Five sacrifice himself during the Battle of Scarif days before Luke would be assigned that very same call sign. The additional new opening scene adds action, yes, but it also alerts the listener to the fact that without these kinds of supplies, the Rebels are likely doomed. By humanizing the Rebel pilots, Daley increases the emotional risks.

As with *Star Wars*, Daley was principally concerned about expanding scenes so as to either explain plot questions or to discover elements of the film's original story that were rife for more exploration. Option one gave Daley a chance to write narratively. The other option, a chance to write character. Sometimes, those two options came together in the same scene. For example, in the second and third episodes of the series, "The Coming Storm" and "A Question of Survival," not only is the plot element of exactly how Han and Luke survive the bitter cold of Hoth made explicit when it was only hinted at in the film, but the scene contains some of the best interplay between Han and Luke in any medium. The two speak as friends, joshing sometimes, honest at others. There are some priceless lines, such as Han telling his friend, "Look, I don't need you to depress me. I can depress myself," and Luke telling Han, "You were always terrible at rescues Han." It isn't all banter, though.

"A Question of Survival" features some of Daley's best writing, when Han opens the shelter as the rescue snowspeeders approach. The combination of Daley's words, Hamill and King's acting, Madden's direction, and Voegeli's sound design produces a moment that is both expressive and triumphant. Voegeli explained:

> Radio is pretty bad with the battles, right? Because you have to tell the listener where the mic is and move the mic. Unlike film, where you can cut back and forth between the cockpit and the command center, you can't do that with radio. There had to be enough of a sound difference, or dialogue in the script or something to say where we are. I think battle scenes are typically kind of the worst scenes in the whole thing. Not that we didn't work like hell on them. But the radio drama is good at scenes where Han has ridden out to find Luke, and takes Luke's lightsaber and cuts open the Tauntaun, then sticks Luke in it to warm him up. In the film, you see him setting up. The radio drama has a scene that follows which is something that Brian was allowed to add, you get that they're spending the night there until the next day and they know they're going to be saved. That to me is one of the best and that's an example of how radio is really good at the intimate stuff. Not the most boisterous loud, battle stuff, but at the intimate stuff.[23]

Perhaps the character that gets the most affection and consideration by Daley is his favorite to write for, C-3PO. The director of the film version of *Empire*, Irvin Kershner, shared in the Kevin Burns documentary *Empire of Dreams: The Story of the Star Wars Trilogy*, that one of his challenges was "I felt I needed humor in the picture, and yet I couldn't have gags."[24] Kershner was able to find much of that humor via the character of C-3PO. Although comic relief is an important and endearing function to serve in any narrative, it did come at a price to Threepio, who was not presented as multifaceted as he was in the first film. Daniels illustrated the problem:

> I should say, I regard Threepio as totally *other* than myself. I can speak about him in the third person as if he's in another room right now because we're going out to dinner, so he's getting ready (laughs). I can speak dispassionately and passionately about Threepio. I always thought he was slightly underrated as a character, particularly after *Episode V: The Empire Strikes Back* where the latest trick was to have him complain about everything, to give almost a redesigned view of like, "This is terrifying, I want to go home," which is a very un-brave thing to do. I think sometimes the writing in the movies got a bit lazy as we go, because Threepio is not easy to write for.[25]

Those character concerns began on the *Empire* movie. Daniels told *Starlog* in 1983, "This motivation was never explained in the film, where Threepio seems irrational and crotchety. In Brian's script, it comes across as complete loyalty, sensitivity, and rationality. I was really impressed with that fact."[26] Daley was able to keep the humor but give it a purpose. In "A Question of Survival," Luke gives Threepio a mission to protect Leia, which helps explain the droid's behavior.

> **THREEPIO:** And what about me, Master Luke?
> **LUKE:** I want you to stay here with the princess. If I don't see you here, I'll meet you at the fleet rendezvous point.[27]

Later, in the next episode, "Fire and Ice," Threepio and Artoo have an expanded good-bye scene of their own, where, in their constant *dolce e acido* relationship, Threepio wishes his friend the best while still managing to refer to him as "you silly little plumber."[28] Daley was directly inspired by a line by George Lucas, who in his July 23, 1977, interview with Carol Titelman while channeling C-3PO, said of Artoo that he is essentially a plumber.[29]

Threepio, while still maintaining his nervous energy in Daley's script so there is continuity with the film version, is also more likely to defend himself against Han Solo's sometimes dismissive attitude, adding more complication to their strained relationship. They both want the same thing. They both have the same mission to protect Leia. But their personalities don't mesh. In another expanded scene that takes place in the Bespin cell, Daley adds complexity to both the droid and the pirate as Threepio and Han discuss Solo's torture and Threepio's being blasted into literal parts in the episode "Dark Lord's Fury."

Han: Torture chambers. Take a tip from me, Threepio, don't ever get on Vader's bad side.
Threepio: That advice is rather tardy, Captain Solo!
Han: *(GROANS)* No argument there![30]

Throughout the script, Threepio displays the bravery that is sometime latent when considering his words. He tries to use his diplomatic skills to stop Han from being beaten by the Bespin guards, defending with words what his broken body cannot. C-3PO earns the respect of Lando, in "The Clash of Lightsabers," who tells the protocol droid, "You and your friend can ship with me anytime, Threepio."

Voegeli thought that of the three radio dramas adapting the films, *Empire* was the best, and a primary reason was Daley's writing in addition to the source material. "*Empire* is 10 times better radio. Brian Daley's scripts are better, which has to do with his learning a lot [about radio] and being more confident, consulting with the people who put it together. And the scripts are stronger because we used only 10 episodes. Broadcasts tend to work in increments of 13 because of 'quarters.' *Star Wars* had 13 episodes, so the script had to be extended; this time there's a little less fat."[31]

In March 1982, Daley delivered his final script to Bos and Gross for approvals. By the time the public was officially informed there would be an *Empire* radio drama at the April press event, the scripts were in good shape, casting had been mostly completed, and the production was ready to go. The team had learned a great deal during the tribulations experienced while pioneering the first radio drama.

One thing that would not change and could not be avoided was the speed with which the radio drama would have to be recorded. Madden, Voegeli, Bos, and the troupe of actors would have merely ten days for the Empire to strike back.

11

Our Own Little World

Recording at A&R

The statistics were revelatory. While the film crew making *The Empire Strikes Back* had seven months to complete principal photography, the radio drama would have ten days. Filming the Wampa creature attacking Luke and his escape took seven days, but only forty-five minutes to record for the radio version. Of the difference, Mark Hamill said, "It gets to be much more of a tedious chore to film something. Whereas when you're not doing coverage, and 50 million angles, it's very gratifying to be able to do a scene that took seven days in a couple of hours."[1]

While the movie version was filmed on two continents and three nations—Norway and England for principal photography and the United States for pick-ups and special effects—the radio drama version was recorded at a singular facility in New York and assembled in Minnesota by Tom Voegeli during postproduction. While the fastness of the radio recording could be seen as a detriment, art usually survives and perhaps thrives on such challenges. Sachs explained why the recording schedule was a blessing in disguise, "We're recording together for two weeks, and we do become a very close-knit unit. It pays off because the relationships come across."[2]

Recording in New York commenced on June 1, 1982, with the Wampa scenes and with Han saving Luke. The facility was the famed A&R Recording, Inc., studio, one of the largest and most sophisticated recording studios in the world, founded in 1958 by Jack Arnold and music producer Phil Ramone, hence the initials. Ramone produced artists such as Ray Charles, Aretha Franklin, B.B. King, Stevie Wonder, Frank Sinatra, and many other music giants and helped pioneer CDs and the original surround sound for motion pictures. As with Westlake, the National Public Radio (NPR) team required isolation booths with glass for Anthony Daniels and Brock Peters, among others. Brian Daley, who again participated in the radio drama recording sessions writing wild lines adding necessary dialogue, and making edits, described how important it was to have visible isolation booths for scenes such as when Luke Skywalker confronts Darth Vader. Hamill and Peters needed to see each other to maximize their performance, so Hamill was outside of Peters' booth, looking at him. "They could see each other, deliver lines, and make sounds to indicate physical exertion at just the right moments."[3]

Recording at A&R had another latent emotional effect on the actors. "It's rather strange sometimes, fighting a battle on the ice planet Hoth while, outside, New York City just goes along being itself," Daniels told *The New York Times* in 1982. "We create our own little world here in the studio. It's a shock to stroll outside at lunch and find yourself in a deli."[4] Hamill had a similar reaction, "It's incongruous, after a day of taping, to walk out and find you're in the middle of Seventh Avenue. If you're doing radio, and you're in New York City, you feel you should be playing the part. I'd like to be wearing a 40's suit and fedora, so I could stroll on over to Lindy's with Fred Allen."[5]

The expanded rescue scene and conversation between Han and Luke on Hoth was not only one of the first recorded for *Empire*, it is one of Perry King's favorites:

> I remember doing a scene where Mark and I are on Hoth. We are in an igloo-like thing that we created to protect ourselves on this ice planet. And we're standing there in front of the mics doing the scene and it just wasn't working. So John Madden and Mark and I just took whatever was around, coats and chairs and whatever we could find, and we built a little igloo-like enclosure. All three of us crowded into this enclosure and did the scene in there for the verisimilitude of that. It transformed it. The idea behind method acting is a really simple idea, but a beautiful one, which is, "If I believe, then you'll believe, so I have to believe."
>
> This is as opposed to the style of acting in the 18th and 19th centuries which was predominantly what is called *declamation acting* which was designed for huge stages with very dim lights and big theaters where you could barely be heard. Acting was all about projecting far back into the audience so that nobody would miss it.... The reason for that wasn't because they were bad actors, it was because that's what it took to reach through that terrible lighting and all the way back to the audience and get the idea across. But then you start having cameras that are recording people closer and closer, and that style becomes very false. So you had Konstantin Stanislavski at the turn of the last century creating this form of acting work, which is much more intimate. As soon as Mark and I got in this shelter, it just transformed the scene. John Madden was wonderful about that, helping us get there.[6]

For Hamill, recording the radio dramas turned out to be not all that different from some of the acting that was required of him during the filming of the movie version of *Empire*. For much of the film, it was Hamill on set acting against Des Webb in a Wampa costume, the Yoda puppet with Frank Oz invisible below a stage, Kenny Baker obscured as R2-D2, and David Prowse and Bob Anderson behind the Vader mask. In all those situations, it was frequently difficult to hear his fellow actors, and Hamill had to rely on his imagination, as he did on the radio dramas. "On a major portion of *Empire*, I work with an android who nobody understands, Artoo. It works like a Bob Newhart phone call. 'What's that you say, Mrs. Fetamine? You say you just made a left-hand turn?' It's the same thing: 'No, I'm feeling fine Artoo. Why do you ask? I'm sure Dagobah's perfectly safe for droids.'"[7]

If there was any pressure on Hamill, it was not visible to Daley, who discussed the fun and creative environment that the actors, Madden, and Voegeli had created. Speaking with Alex Newborn of *The Star Wars Collector* in 1995, Daley shared, "Almost everybody goofed around, especially Mark Hamill. When I referred to the medical droid at Hoth base, he ad-libbed a sitcom promo for *Medical Droid*. Something on the order of, 'This week, *Medical Droid* brings his boss Mr. Credenza home for dinner and delivers a laugh riot.'"[8]

Then there is the curious story of how bananas became droid fuel. Daley explained, "It became a ritual for Mel Sahr to make sure fresh bananas were available at the studio every morning for energy and because they kept Tony's stomach from rumbling in a way that, he said, might've resembled robotic grinding noises but would have given sound producer Tom Voegeli an ulcer."[9]

With recording wrapping on June 10, Voegeli would again become custodian, not necessarily of secret plans that could restore order to the galaxy, but rather of Ben Burtt's sound effect reels and John Williams's musical score. He would begin a process of postproduction that would rival the time period required for the motion picture because of its complexity.

Philosophically, Voegeli approached the sound mix with the same beliefs and strategies as for the first radio drama. "I built the sound for each scene in the radio series in a very similar way to how Ben would approach it for the film. The sounds aren't all sitting on one recording. I have to build them back up from his original development sound effects."[10] The challenges were much the same. The battle between Rebels and the Imperial Walkers required a crossfading and editing of nine pieces of music in addition to the dialogue and sound effects.

Practically, Voegeli had new technology at his disposal for *Empire* when he returned to St. Paul and to the Minnesota Public Radio (MPR) Maud Moon Weyerhaeuser Recording Studio, a 32-track 3M Digital Mastering System.

> I think the best technical work is on *Empire*. It was all assembled on the first build of a digital multitrack machine that we had in this country or we had in the world. That allowed me to do lots of pre-mixes without getting a degeneration loss or hiss of five generations down. I could finish a sequence of sound effects and then bounce it to a stereo pair and keep that. It was a very effective tool. I was thrilled to have it. We got a machine because I'm in Minnesota, and 3M was about to release the machine and actually tried to market it. Eventually, it didn't work and they stopped making the machine. But they loaned one of the machines to Minnesota Public Radio, because it is a nonprofit. The one disadvantage was the machine was like a space heater. I had to wear shorts and T-shirts with fans all around me in the studio.[11]

The film had a seven-month postproduction schedule. The radio drama would require five months, with Voegeli completing his work by December 1982.

The Empire Strikes Back was figuratively and literally a Valentine to fans, premiering on February 14, 1983. To prepare, NPR would begin an unprecedented public relations campaign while Brian Daley began another kind of rebel mission, this time to the planet Ord Mantell.

12

Some Herb Stew and a Side *Mission to Ord Mantell*

Although Yoda did not feature prominently in the original advertising wave for the film version of *Empire* as a strategy to keep the character's identity a secret, the opposite was true for the radio drama. Yoda was the fulcrum upon which National Public Radio (NPR) Director of National Promotions Linda Devillier and Senior Publicist Jan Hausrath pivoted. Devillier had been hired by Frank Mankiewicz with the goal of bringing more national awareness to NPR radio when he began his tenure as president. Of working on the promotions for both radio dramas, Devillier said, "Lucas gave NPR the radio broadcast rights to the series for a very modest fee. It was a grand adventure working with the Lucasfilm team."[1]

Because Yoda had been the break-out character from *Empire*, and because he was voiced in the radio drama by John Lithgow, recently nominated for an Academy Award for his memorable supporting role of Roberta Muldoon in the critically and commercially successful 1982 film *The World According to Garp*, it made sense to feature the Jedi Master as the advertising focus of the effective and expansive campaign.

Similar to the Griffith Observatory event for the *Star Wars* radio drama, Devillier and Hausrath arranged a premiere for *Empire* with the press, this time at New York's Hayden Planetarium at the American Museum of Natural History on February 14, 1983, from 6:00 until 8:00 P.M. Appropriately, the invitation journalists received with the press kit was Valentine's Day themed. Artwork of Yoda in a heart-shaped frame greeted the invitee on the cover. It may have been more appropriate to use Tauntauns as the mascot for the invitation since those who went to the premiere had to battle the remnants of what is now known as the Megalopolitan Blizzard of 1983, a historic blizzard that set records for snow along the Eastern Seaboard from February 10 until February 12, 1983.

Yoda also featured prominently when NPR contracted with the celebrated *New York Times* restaurant critic, Chef Craig Claiborne, to create a recipe for "Yoda's Herb Stew." Published in newspapers and magazines around the nation, the recipe promoted the upcoming premiere of *Empire*. Some local NPR stations got creative themselves, partnering with restaurants to sell Yoda's Stew with proceeds going to the radio affiliate. *The Pantagraph* journalist Betty Zimmerman reported on how fans could support WGLT-FM 89.1, the Bloomington, Illinois, NPR station, by getting a bowl of Yoda's stew from "Kup Tcheng, who with his brother, Khe Thi, a recent Vietnam emigrant, owns and operates Shanghai Express."[2] The brothers cooked up a batch for a taste-testing by Zimmerman, who pronounced it "delicious."[3] Much the same was occurring in Detroit, Michigan, where patrons of Woodbridge Tavern could get a bowl of Yoda's stew with proceeds benefiting WDET-FM 101.9.

When Richard Toscan and John Houseman had discussed the idea of creative scandals, one such scandal had occurred when some at NPR, both locally and nationally, thought *Star Wars* would not draw many younger fans to the radio because of their unfamiliarity with radio as anything except a music delivery device. The positive Arbitron ratings and reception to the first radio drama among younger listeners had proven that argument erroneous and that concern unsubstantiated. With the *Empire* radio drama, everything changed, and a much more vigorous effort to appeal to the junior market was an important part of the advertising plan. Many local stations had Yoda coloring contests for school-aged fans and Darth Vader meet-and-greets on a larger scale than had been done before. Winners of the coloring contest sponsored by WMFE-FM 90.7 in Orlando, Florida, received prizes as diverse as an appearance on WUCF-TV Channel 24's *Postscript* program and copies of *The Art of* The Empire Strikes Back book, a Yoda mug, a Yoda hat with ears, or John Williams's score.

Radio station WITF-FM 89.5 in Harrisburg, Pennsylvania, gave winners a Yoda t-shirt and received more than 1800 submissions. WKAR-FM 90.5 in East Lansing, Michigan, hosted a meet Darth Vader Day at the Impression 5 Museum on Saturday, February 19, 1983. For a $1.50 ticket, with discounts available at local Burger King restaurants, JCPenney stores, and in newspaper ads, fans could meet the Sith Lord in person. More than two thousand people attended, setting a record for the museum as the largest single-day crowd, prompting Mayor Terry McKane to declare it "Darth Vader Day." In Kailua-Kona, Hawaii, Ala Moana Centerstage was the location of a Darth Vader–themed event that helped KHPR-FM 88.1 on February 26 and 27, 1983. At these events, young fans could take pictures and get autographs, while the radio dramas were promoted and local NPR stations received the proceeds to help defer costs and plan future programming.

The *Empire* radio drama poster would showcase Yoda, surrounded by colorful creatures from Dagobah. The artwork was done by *Star Wars* artist Ralph McQuarrie, who had designed C-3PO, Darth Vader, the Stormtroopers, and many of the vehicles and locations of the original *Star Wars* and *The Empire Strikes Back* films. McQuarrie was born in Gary, Indiana, on June 13, 1929. Art was inspiration from his earliest memories, and during grammar school he started taking art classes. The face of his professional experiences always had one eye on the future and space technologies, working as a technical illustrator for the Boeing Aerospace Company and Litton Industries. His artwork defined real space travel for a generation, as the CBS News Network used his illustrations during their news programs covering the NASA *Apollo* missions.

Writer and director Hal Barwood, a friend of George Lucas and fellow University of Southern California alumnus, who would later produce *Corvette Summer*, Mark Hamill's first post–*Star Wars* movie, had met McQuarrie while he was a graduate student and talking with McQuarrie about an internship. Barwood later commissioned McQuarrie to create artwork for a science fiction film he was working on and recommended him to George Lucas who had begun preproduction on his own space film. "Ralph's contribution to the *Star Wars* world is incalculable," said George Lucas in the documentary *Ralph McQuarrie—Tribute to a Master*, "Him bringing the characters that I described as words to life as visuals, so I was able to see what they looked like, you know, was a very key component of being able to put the whole story together, because it's one thing to describe things and it's one thing to actually be able to hold a picture up."[4]

In addition to preproduction art and matte painting for the films, McQuarrie also contributed to many ancillary *Star Wars* projects and products. He had a long relationship with Judy-Lynn del Rey, and Del Rey and Ballantine Books, doing covers for everything from the original 1976 *Star Wars* movie novelization, to science fiction book covers, to the publishing of his own artwork. According to McQuarrie archivist and historian John Scoleri, when del Rey saw McQuarrie's artwork for *Star Wars*, she thought that it was akin to "seeing money."[5] When Del Rey commissioned McQuarrie to create a cover for a children's book in 1980, he chose to use Yoda. Authors Brandon Alinger, Wage Lageose, and David Mandel shared the details in their two-volume book *Star Wars Art: Ralph McQuarrie*, the most comprehensive collection of McQuarrie *Star Wars* work ever produced. They wrote, "The illustration was created as a cover for a children's book, but was deemed too scary upon completion and was not used. It was later used as cover art for *The Jedi Master's Quizbook* (published November 1983)."[6]

As with McQuarrie, Daley would play an important part in the *Quizbook*. As an expert, he had been asked to vet the questions and answers and provided Anita Gross at Lucasfilm and Judy-Lynn del Rey a long list of edits of both grammar and *Star Wars* trivia. Among his edits was that it is

Dak, not Dack, when referring to the Rebel Pilot who was Luke's gunner at the Battle of Hoth. In addition to the *Quizbook*, McQuarrie's Yoda painting would later be used as a sticker included in the *Official Star Wars Fan Club* membership kit.

Perhaps the most intriguing repurposing of the Yoda art was for the *Empire* radio drama poster. The poster, at 28" × 17⅜", features the words *The Empire Strikes Back* in alternating white, yellow, orange, and purple, matching the colorful pallet of McQuarrie's painting. The poster promised that the drama was "Coming Soon to a Radio Near You" and, once more with the Yoda theme, bids fans to "Listen as Luke Skywalker meets Yoda, the Jedi Master and learns the secret behind the Force." While McQuarrie passed away on March 3, 2012, his designs continue to influence *Star Wars* television shows and movies.

The wide net of Yoda-centric advertising caught its prize, as the ratings and critical response on *Empire* exceeded expectations. The program premiered on 90 percent of NPR's then 281 affiliates to reviews as impressive as those for the original radio drama. Steve Hill of *The Tampa Tribune* wrote, "The directors, the talented cast, including several of the film's performers, and the special effects wizards, have created a masterpiece in sound for this National Public Radio production.... Since the listener's mind can do with those aural images whatever it pleases, the production is really sort of 'personalized' for each listener by his own imagination.... John Madden and Tom Voegeli and writer Brian Daley have pulled together a stunner."[7]

David Hugh Smith of *The Christian Science Monitor* agreed, "This 10-part series gives evidence that radio drama is not obsolete—it's just waiting for fresh productions and compelling stories.... Because of the popularity of its film predecessor, *Empire* must both recall the images of the movie, for those who have seen it, and simultaneously spin the tale for the uninitiated. On both counts, judging from the first six episodes made available by press time, *Empire* succeeds with zest."[8]

Most local stations were pleased by the reception of both radio dramas and their ability to bring in diverse audiences, "We're especially pleased that kids who are used to seeing a film at the movies or on TV are calling to tell us how much they enjoy the radio dramas," said WVIK General Manager Don Wooten.[9]

Another symbol of the appeal of the *Empire* radio drama is that the only known vinyl record of any *Star Wars* radio drama was made for *Empire*. The U.S. Armed Forces Radio and Television Service created five records, with an *Empire* episode on each side, to distribute to its networks. There are only a few sets known to have survived because the records were considered property of the U.S. Department of Defense and never available for retail purchase.

Because of the success of *Empire*, it seemed a radio adaptation of *Return of the Jedi*, the third film scheduled to premiere May 25, 1983, was a likely prospect. About the possibility of an NPR *Jedi* drama occurring, Brian Daley shared, "I would be very disappointed if it didn't. Radio is very, very habit forming, especially for someone who writes novels most of the time."[10] NPR began preliminary discussions with Lucasfilm during the autumn of 1983. On October 19, 1983, Anita Gross provided John Bos at NPR a copy of the *Return of the Jedi* continuity script to begin the process. By October 20, 1983, Madden and Voegeli had agreed to return to their roles for *Jedi*. The third part of the radio drama creative trio, Daley, would have to be reached rather unusually to have the offer made to him.

James Luceno and Daley were trekking through Nepal at this time, on one of their famous and frequent world excursions. Daley had bought a plane ticket with a sixty-day open-ended return. His plan was to return to the United States either when he ran out of money or at the end of the sixty days. In October, Daley received a telegram from Lucia St. Clair Robson. It read, "ATTN: BRIAN. BOS DOING JEDI. HAS MADDEN AND VOEGELI. WANTS YOU, PRODUCTION MEET 1st OF DEC. IN NEW YORK. LOVE LUCIA."[11] Daley was thrilled by the news. Luceno described Daley's reaction, "Brian and I were in Nepal, trekking in Nepal. He got word that the funding had come through, and that he was going to write it. He searched all over Kathmandu for a bootleg VHS tape of *Return of the Jedi* because he wanted to show all the Sherpas that had been with us. They didn't know what to make of it, but it was a really fun evening."[12] Around that same time, Brian thought of the last line he wanted to use for *Jedi*. He had ended each of the two previous radio dramas with a line by Luke Skywalker. He now had the perfect line to have Luke close out the saga during the victory party on Endor, and he wrote the words on a scrap of paper to keep with his files until he began writing the script.

Bos designed a preliminary schedule that would have included:

December 1, 1983: A production meeting of Bos, Daley, Madden starts the process.
January 15, 1984: Daley completes the first script as Voegeli goes to Lucasfilm to obtain *Jedi* sound effects from Ben Burtt.
February 19 until February 29, 1984: Recording at A&R Recording Studio occurs.
March 1 until May 30, 1984: Voegeli edits during post-production.
October 3 until November 14, 1984 or December 19 until January 30, 1985: premiere of *Jedi* radio drama.[13]

The budget for the seven, eventually six, episodes of *Jedi* was $287,095. James Fifield, executive vice president of the General Mills

Toys Group, owners of Kenner Toys, had been interested in underwriting the project with the promotional synergy helping to promote the *Star Wars* toys and games.

But none of this would occur, at least not then, and not as planned. By the late spring and early summer of 1983, at the same time the last episodes of the *Empire* radio drama were premiering, serious problems with NPR on several fronts were becoming known which even a Jedi Knight couldn't fix. Mankiewicz had many successes during his tenure as president of NPR. His ideas, including his faith in the *Star Wars* radio dramas, tripled NPR's audience from 1977 to 1983. Under his leadership, NPR transformed the delivery of radio for the industry, one which had once been dominated by the distribution of programming via telephone lines and now did so by using satellites. It was NPR, not commercial radio, that was the first to implement a national satellite network. Mankiewicz had other big ideas, especially weaning NPR from its near-total dependency on federal government financing. He wanted to get more corporate sponsorships, using the slogan "NPR means business."[14]

Despite these gains, it was not enough to deal with a serious reduction in federal funding that occurred. Nor the rivalry for limited resources that eventually led to a civil war within NPR and the creation of a competitor network, American Public Radio (APR), composed of five of the most influential local NPR stations, most especially Minnesota Public Radio and KUSC, the station that had been granted the rights by George Lucas for the *Star Wars* radio drama. Adding to the list of headaches was a reduction of about $3 million in audience donations, the result of the recession of the 1980s that wreaked havoc with finances.[15] Forty of the 458 employees of NPR lost their jobs as a budget shortage of nearly $3 million—eventually much more—became obvious. Mankiewicz resigned on May 11, 1983.

Richard Toscan remembered this as the day he finally understood why Wally Smith had said he was right about NPR not doing *Empire*. Toscan shared, "Despite the success of *Empire* with listeners, its huge production costs following those of the original series ended up being one of several last financial straws on the camel's back at NPR. *Star Wars* saved NPR back in 1981 but along with other financial extravagances, Frank's resignation as NPR's President came only three months after the premiere of *Empire*. In all the smoke rising from NPR's budget woes, his contributions to NPR's programming, audience development, and the future of radio drama were lost. Frank deserved better for all he accomplished at NPR."[16]

Specific to *Jedi* was the decision of General Mills Toys Group not to sponsor the radio drama. Additionally, it turned out that while 20th Century–Fox and Lucasfilm had donated the music rights for a small sum, the contracts with the London Symphony Orchestra did not permit radio programs. A fee of $50,000 was required to get the music rights for the *Jedi* recordings. As a practical reality, then, after deducting that amount from the planned expense of $287,095, the *Jedi* budget would be greatly affected. All things considered, *Jedi* was shelved along with other NPR cultural projects to give Douglas J. Bennet, Jr., the new NPR president who had previously led the United States Agency for International Development, time to deal with these numerous crises.

Tom Voegeli tried to keep *Jedi* alive, however, even approaching NPR competitor APR with the idea of their producing and having the rights to premiere it, and then those broadcast rights reverting to NPR. APR agreed. NPR did not.

For Daley, the disappointment was heartfelt; however, he was not someone to let disappointment define him, as demonstrated by his willingness to adapt and learn when Del Rey rejected his first novel. Daley moved on to other projects, some of which were *Star Wars* related, some bringing him to write for other franchises, and others that were his own creations.

For fans of the radio drama, it is not too far afield to claim that Daley's script for the children's audio adventure *Rebel Mission to Ord Mantell: A Story from the Star Wars Saga* qualifies as episode zero to his *Empire* radio drama. Released in 1983 by Buena Vista Records, a subsidiary of the Walt Disney Company, with a running time of 29:43, almost the exact length of a *Star Wars* radio drama episode, *Rebel Mission to Ord Mantell* was produced by Jymn Magon and engineered by George Charouhas. Daley originally had the idea for *Rebel Mission* in 1980. Deborah Call of Lucasfilm publishing had asked Daley then if he would write an eight-week script for the *Star Wars* syndicated daily newspaper comic strip. Because of Lucasfilm's confidence in Daley, he would not be required to submit a synopsis. His idea was to answer the question of what happened when Han says "the bounty hunter we ran into on Ord Mantell changed my mind" in the *Empire* film.[17]

Although that project never materialized, the added scenes that Daley produced for the *Empire* radio dramatization that begins with Imperials doubting Darth Vader's hunch that the Rebels would escape to a snow planet when their Yavin 4 equipment and resources were designed for a warmer planet, inspired again the idea to explore Ord Mantell. Daley provided details of exactly how the Rebels were able to afford the purchase and acquisition of new snow-adapted equipment in *Rebel Mission*. The story of *Rebel Mission* begins with something unusual for Han, piloting an X-Wing. He and Luke are trying to leave obvious hints that the Rebels are reconnoitering jungle planets to make the Empire think the Rebellion was searching for environments similar to that of Yavin 4, when in reality, they are already on Hoth.

After their mission achieves its objective, Han, Leia, Luke, Chewbacca, and the droids begin a new mission to Ord Mantell. The plan is to abscond with funds invested in a company by Leia's royal family of Alderaan before her planet's destruction. Those credits would go to great measure in funding the Rebellion. Their contact is a bug-like alien named Phoedris who is eventually revealed to actually be Cypher, a famous bounty hunter. As Han and Leia deal with that complication, Luke and Threepio must try to escape on the cargo ship loaded with the money.

There are many similarities when comparing *Rebel Mission* to the NPR radio dramas. Daley limited the narration of *Rebel Mission* to the beginning and ending of the adventure, as with the radio drama. The lack of narration is one reason *Rebel Mission* is more sophisticated than traditional children's albums, which rely on the recitation of exposition. Daley trusted the listener to be able to appreciate the narrative through the dialogue, sound effects, and music, the same idea that Richard Toscan had inspired Daley to do with the radio dramas. Also, C-3PO is given good treatment in *Rebel Mission*, helping to rescue the day by using subterfuge as he did in the original *Star Wars* and by piloting the cargo ship. As with the radio dramas, Luke gets the last word of dialogue.

The most important difference is the voice actors. None of the actors from the radio dramas appear in *Rebel Mission*, although some would return for future Disney and Buena Vista Records *Star Wars* children's albums. For *Rebel Mission*, the narrator was Chuck Riley. Pat Parris was the voice of Leia, while Tony Pope performed the voices of C-3PO and the dual roles of Phoedris and Cypher. Pope would voice Threepio and an A-Wing pilot in the *Star Wars Trilogy Arcade* video game and reprised Threepio, among other characters, in the video game *Star Wars Rebellion*. He was also the voice of the Furby electronic toy. Pope passed away on February 11, 2004.

An excellent imitation of Mark Hamill's Luke Skywalker in *Rebel Mission* is provided by voice actor Corey Burton, whose contributions to *Star Wars* are many. Modern fans know Burton as the voice of bounty hunter Cad Bane in the television shows *The Clone Wars*, *The Bad Batch*, and *The Book of Boba Fett*, among others. He was the voice of Count Dooku in *Clone Wars* and *The Clone Wars* animated shows and has performed on many *Star Wars* video games. Burton dubbed the voice of Rebel Derek "Hobbie" Klivian in *The Empire Strikes Back* film.

But Burton's association with *Star Wars* began with his 1979 portrayal of Luke for a read-along children's recording of *Star Wars* and with *Rebel Mission* four years later. Speaking to Bonnie Burton for StarWars.com,

Corey Burton shared, "When I first saw *A New Hope* I identified with Luke Skywalker. I even did some looping for *The Empire Strikes Back* and met Mark Hamill. At the time, I had been cast as a sound-alike for Mark for the Disney Storyteller Read-Along records. Mark always impressed me with his absolute, real-guy, genuine openness. He has none of that pretension. He had me autograph the record (laughs)."[18]

Rebel Mission effortlessly works in concert with the *Empire* radio drama even considering the voice performance differences. If played before *Empire*, *Rebel Mission* sets the stage for the events that open Daley's expanded radio adaptation. Daley also had another idea for a second Buena Vista Records recording. The 1977 interviews that Carol Titelman conducted with George Lucas where he answered questions in character became a kind of divination for Daley's imagination and for many of his proposals during those years. Thinking of these interviews, Daley proposed an adventure revealing how Han was cashiered out of the Imperial service and his initial rescue of and meeting with Chewbacca. Daley wrote, "As per George's concept, I included slavers and a card game with a cheating angle—one I figured Bret Maverick would've gotten a yuck out of."[19]

Other franchises beckoned. In 1986, Daley, Lucia St. Clair Robson, and Luceno each wrote episodes of the pioneering American anime series *The Adventures of the Galaxy Rangers*, a space western about a group of Rangers that keeps peace while battling the Crown Empire led by the Queen of the Crown. Daley contributed five scripts, Robson two, and Luceno six. Of the experience, Luceno shared:

> That was another thing Brian dragged me into (laughs). I hadn't done anything like that. I hadn't done any science fiction or anything. He was working with a producer named Robert Mandell and Brian said to me, "Look, you know, this show needs scripts. Why don't you at least try it?" And so I did. We never wrote any scripts together for that show. We had a real interesting crew of writers on that show. I was sad that didn't continue. During that time, animated shows had been driven by marketing and toys and there just weren't any for that show. And so, we never saw a second season.[20]

Daley and Luceno would write novels together, appropriately since, as Luceno explained:

> I started traveling when I dropped out of college. I met so many interesting people, in my travels in Africa and South America that I just started keeping notes. And out of those notes, my first novel emerged. I hadn't really thought about writing as a career before that. My first novel was *Headhunters*. It was about the early cocaine trade in Peru during the early 70s. It was fiction, but it was based on people that I met. Events that occurred while I was on the road. A mingling of fact and fiction. It was through Brian that the book was published because

Brian's *Doomfarers of Coramonde* had found a home at Del Rey, and his editor was Owen Lock. Brian gave Owen a copy of *Headhunters*, which Owen passed on to the mass market division at Ballantine and they picked it up. It is one more thing that I owe to Brian. He is, in many ways, a mentor for me in science fiction, so I paid close attention to just about every line he wrote.[21]

Together, the friends wrote under the singular name Jack McKinney. Their chosen nom de plume was the result of a rather unusual inspiration. Luceno explained, "The name was on a toolbox that I inherited from my father. It was the name of the person who had owned the toolbox before my father. When my father left the Marines, he became a carpenter. I guess he must have worked with a Jack McKinney at one time and ended up with Jack McKinney's toolbox which came down to me."[22]

Starting in 1987, Daley and Luceno would start writing the first of twenty-one books in the *Robotech* series. A combination of adaptations of the animated *Robotech* series episodes and then eventually original stories set in the *Robotech* universe, the novels were published by Del Rey. "The reason why we were together on that, by the way is because we worked on *Galaxy Rangers*. So when *Robotech* came to Del Rey, someone there said, 'Why don't you two guys think about doing this project?' We spent a couple of weeks in California with the producer Carl Macek and watched all the episodes," Luceno detailed. "Then, I remember that we came back and spent a week or two plotting the 12 books. Brian said, 'All right, I will take number one, you take number two,' and we just went like that. At the same time he was working on number one, I was working on number two. Because we had the source material, we had all the animation, we had the scripts, and then we would just give each other our manuscripts and kind of work on our style trying to get the Jack McKinney style and make whatever corrections need to be made in each other's manuscripts."[23]

It was the rapidity of writing the *Robotech* novels that inspired Daley, albeit reluctantly, to finally make the move to computers instead of typewriters. "When he came to live here, I had one story on my home. I had a second story built on the house, which drove Brian crazy because there was carpentry going on and he was trying to focus," Robson shared.

Before I did that, there was an L shaped porch around the one side of the house. I had that enclosed with windows and we turned the porch into an office for him. The shelves were lined with books, most of them his. He had a tall desk with a tall stool because he was a long-legged guy. That's where he did his work. He never really used computers. When they had to do *Robotech*, they had to be turning out a chapter a week practically. It was really hardcore, typing. That is when Brian did get a computer, but it was so that he could keep up with Jimmy and so that he could send Jimmy his work..[24]

The collaboration was as strong as their friendship, and Daley and Luceno, as Jack McKinney, would continue to write books not only for

Robotech also but for their *Black Hole Travel Agency* series during the early 1990s.

Daley crafted a series of novels that were published in 1985 and 1986 chronicling the adventures of Hobart Floyt, a Terran bureaucrat who gets an inheritance from the ruler of an interstellar empire, and Alacrity Fitzhugh, a rogue sent by Earth's government to ensure that Floyt gets the money. The result was *Requiem for a Ruler of Worlds*, *Jinx on a Terran Inheritance*, and *Fall of the White Ship Avatar*. Continuing his association with Disney that had started with his novelization of *Tron* in 1982, Daley wrote the script of *The Story of* WarGames, a Buena Vista Records adaptation of the 1983 film, produced by Ted Kryczko and Jymn Magon.

There were two more *Star Wars* ventures that Daley worked on, but neither achieved fruition. Daley's first unproduced writing was the episode arc he proposed in 1984 for the *Star Wars: Droids* animated series. The program ran with other writers from 1985 to 1986 on the ABC television network, produced by Lucasfilm, 20th Century–Fox, and Nelvana, the company that made the frequently heralded *The Faithful Wookiee* animated short featured in the *Star Wars Holiday Special*. Daley wrote expanded outlines of the four episodes that composed his "Worldrush" tetralogy.

"Episode 1: Messengers from the Stars" starts with C-3PO and R2-D2 on the planet Thwacket working in a traveling acting troupe. In a scene reminiscent of the opening of *Han Solo's Revenge* when Han and Chewbacca play the wrong holodocumentary for the audience at Kamar, the performance goes awry when someone alters Threepio's script, causing him to inadvertently insult and anger the crowd. By "Episode 2: The Wreckers," the droids find themselves on the planet Sellatat, a world where farmers are oppressed by the Owner. The droids join protagonists Odal and Elj who dream of winning the Worldrush, a contest where participants stake claims to plots of land by building structures that meet specific requirements.

"Episode 3: A Stake in This World" features the appearance of many familiar beasts of burden from the Star Wars films, such as banthas, dewbacks, and even a "very warm Tauntaun" as Daley described it.[25] The concluding episode, "There's No Future in Yesterday" begins with what Daley likened to a twist on the "bunnies and birds making Cinderella's gown," as the droids fashion clothes for Odal and Elj. It is worth noting that Daley converted what could have been merely a comedic scene, Threepio having a tough time constructing an oil bath, and made it into a triumph for the droid. It is another demonstration of the affinity Daley had for the character. Had the episodes been produced, they would have been something of a reunion for Daley and Anthony Daniels, who voiced Threepio on the animated television program.

Unfortunately, Daley's script would not be produced. With *Droids* lasting a total of thirteen episodes, plus a special episode, "The Great Heep," which was written by Ben Burtt, there was never enough time on the schedule for what could have been yet another Daley-scripted *Star Wars* adventure.

By the late 1980s and early 1990, during a five-year stretch known in fandom as The Dark Times, *Star Wars* had drifted out of the public consciousness and there were not many products for sale. Without any idea of when the next film would be released, fandom had, it seemed, moved on. Except for the occasional item like role playing game materials, there were no comics, no books, and no action figures. Nearly nine years to the day of the premiere of the original *Star Wars* in theaters, Marvel Comics ceased producing *Star Wars* comics on May 27, 1986. That same year, Kenner slowed production on *Star Wars* toys, eventually abandoning them until almost a decade later. Store shelves once replete with Darth were now experiencing a dearth instead.

During this time, Del Rey and its parent company Ballantine were trying to maintain their *Star Wars* book license but having trouble convincing Lucasfilm that they were the best ushers for a new line of books. The plan at Del Rey was for Daley to be the writer of this new saga. Luceno remembered:

> When Ballantine was struggling to hold on to the license and was trying to pitch Lucasfilm on a new series of books, Brian was going to be doing what essentially Timothy Zahn ended up doing, taking the series forward. It was kind of Arthurian, in the sense that Luke was going to find other Force-sensitive beings and put together kind of a Round Table. And I was supposed to write a book about the Force. It was kind of a fiction-nonfiction book that was going to be about Jedi and aphorisms and all sorts of other things and the way of the Force. We submitted a lot of stuff to Lucasfilm, but a lot of it just got shot down. Then Ballantine lost the license and it then went to Bantam and then came Tim Zahn, and a new era.[26]

It would be Zahn's bestselling *Thrawn Trilogy* (which began in 1991 with *Heir to the Empire*) that ended the Dark Times and began a revitalization of *Star Wars*.

Even after Bantam's phenomenal success with their books, Del Rey continued to generate ideas for *Star Wars* books that might not be covered by the Bantam license. Daley would write various proposals, some on his own, some with Luceno, and some at the request of Owen Lock. One of the most fascinating was *Star Wars Voices* that Daley proposed on April 12, 1994. Daley called the idea the result of "Jim's stroke of genius" inspired again by George Lucas and Carol Titelman's 1977 interview sessions. *Star Wars Voices* was to be a compilation, presented as real-world "transcripts from various dialogues, colloquies, logs and personal journals, archival interviews, debriefings and so forth, for all the major *Star Wars* characters and many of the more popular supporting players."[27] Daley recommended that perhaps fans could send actual questions to their favorite characters to be answered in the book. Specifically, Daley proposed an interview with Chewbacca by the Galactic Ethnographic Society, a publication of the letters that Obi Wan Kenobi wrote to his brother Owen Lars,[28] a debriefing by the Tatooine Educational Cybernet of Owen and Beru Lars when they registered Luke for school, and the never-transmitted Luke Skywalker application to the academy.[29] Daley also proposed a *Jedi Advisory* text that would be a compendium of details about the galaxy gathered from Jedi adventures.

Star Wars was never far from Daley's thoughts even as he continued to write. A common theme of *Star* Wars is the importance of hope. Sometimes, if someone was lucky enough, or dedicated enough, hope can become something more. Hope can become possibilities. Many of the radio drama actors, John Madden, Voegeli, and Daley kept a flicker of hope that perhaps someday the trilogy of radio dramas would be completed. Thirteen years later, it would be. Thirteen—Daley's lucky number.

There would indeed be one last *Star Wars* radio adventure for Daley to write, even as his own future was limited by the news of pancreatic cancer. Thanks to the 1990s phenomenon of books on tape, Daley and his colleagues would make the *Jedi* return.

13

The Rise and *Return of the Jedi*

Technologies are always transformative. Designed originally for voice dictation, the compact cassette tape was developed in September 1963 by Philips. The cassette became a common medium for music during the 1970s and 1980s, as innovations like the Sony Walkman in 1979 provided both music portability and convenience. By 1989, cassette decks had become standard accessories in automobiles. As commuting and automobile congestion combined in the 1980s and 1990s to make daily travel for workers a protracted stress, audiobooks became a popular means to pass the time in traffic. By 1992, sales of audiobooks on cassette had reached $1 billion.

New chain stores such as Earful of Books in Dallas, Texas, were appearing whose sole function, similar to the then ubiquitous video stores, was to rent and sell audiobooks. Chief executive of Bestseller Audiobooks of Scottsdale, Arizona, Edvard Richards, said, "Time is becoming more compressed. The time for pleasure reading is something that's gone out the window, so people are looking for other alternatives to reading their favorite novels."[1] Agreeing with Richards was B. Daltons Bookstore manager, Jane Frank, "Many people just don't know the radio stations, and they get tired of turning the dial all the time. It's a different kind of person who buys the tape. It's usually a person more pressured for time."[2] When anti-skip technology made the compact disc (CD) a viable option for cars, that soon became a competitor to the cassette. Both technologies meant that people began listening to books more frequently than some were reading them.

The *Star Wars* and *Empire* radio dramas were perfectly suited to this emerging social trend. In fact, they were superior because they were full dramatic presentations, with music, voice acting, and sound effects, rather than individual narrators, the dominant way of presenting most early audiobooks. Sam Holt, senior vice president of programming at NPR, had the idea to sell the original *Star Wars* radio drama on cassette early on, but uncertainties about sales rights and logistics between NPR, KUSC, Lucasfilm, and 20th Century–Fox Music shelved the idea. By the 1990s, those issues had been resolved and two changes would result in the ability to retail the cassette and CD recordings of the *Star Wars* and *Empire* radio dramas at exactly the right time for on-demand listening by fans and commuters.

First, HighBridge Audio, which was founded in 1981, had become a major player in the audiobook game by the 1990s. Started by Minnesota Public Radio (MPR), which had a long association with the *Star Wars* radio dramas because of Tom Voegeli and his postproduction of the series at MPR facilities, HighBridge published and distributed both original productions of audiobooks and programming featured on public radio. *Star Wars* was a natural, and in 1993, it became one of the first audio projects to be released on CDs in addition to cassettes.

Second, there was a new director of publishing for Lucasfilm, Lucy Autrey Wilson, who has the distinction of being the first permanent employee ever at Lucasfilm, starting with the company in September 1974 as a bookkeeper and assistant to George Lucas. Wilson would work at Lucasfilm until 2003 and then directly for George Lucas until 2010. Wilson's contributions to *Star Wars* are legion, eventually ushering in a new era of *Star Wars* publishing that included more than 1,500 books. The thriving world of *Star Wars* publishing that Wilson supervised was a more hospitable environment for the idea of having HighBridge release the radio dramas.

In 1993, both *Star Wars* and *The Empire Strikes Back* went on sale in cassette and CD formats. They were instant bestsellers. The popularity of the radio dramas did not go unnoticed, and it cleared the way for other audio projects. In 1994, Time Warner AudioBooks made a deal with Lucasfilm to convert popular *Star Wars* comics and books into radio drama audio productions with full casts, sound effects, and music. Audiobook adaptations of expanded universe materials, including *Star Wars: Dark Empire* (June 1994), written by John Whitman from Tom Veitch's original Dark Horse Comics series on cassette, garnered impressive sales that earned the audiobook a ranking on *Publishers Weekly* bestseller list.

Talking with *The Baltimore Sun* in 1993, Brian Daley could see the first rays of hope that perhaps the *Return of the Jedi* audio drama could get produced, "I think that with the whole books-on-cassette development, people are used to hearing drama again."[3] Bolstered by the sales of radio dramas, Del Rey published Daley's original scripts which for the first time gave listeners the chance to read in conjunction with the radio dramas as they listened on cassette or CD, even glimpsing subtle changes of lines and scenes that were edited during recording or postproduction. Richard Toscan shared that the only time Lucasfilm's Carol Titelman said "No" to him was when he proposed publishing Brian's *Star Wars* radio scripts in 1981, but the passing of thirteen years—Daley's magic number again—made a difference. Daley wrote the introductions to both the 1994 Star Wars: *The National Public Radio Dramatization* script book and the 1995 Star Wars: The Empire Strikes Back: *The National Public Radio Dramatization* script book. Sensing that the tide was changing in favor of *Jedi*, Daley wrote in his *Star Wars* introduction, "I closed both radio serials with a line from Luke Skywalker, since the trilogy is, at its core, his story. And I've got one for the victory party in that Endor forest canopy—care to hear it? In that case, tune in if and when *Return of the Jedi* comes to radio."[4]

A perfect storm had arrived. HighBridge was experiencing healthy sales of the original *Star Wars* and *Empire* radio dramas, as was Hodder Headline Audiobooks, who published the radio dramas for British fans. Lucasfilm was deeply involved in readying the special editions of the original *Star Wars* trilogy for a new theatrical release in anticipation of the forthcoming prequel films. Lucasfilm publishing wanted new material to continue its expansion of *Star Wars*. Meanwhile, NPR had worked through many of its 1980s crises. In sum, the Dark Times were done. And if there was any doubt about the idea that maybe *Jedi* could recoup its costs by being sold as cassettes and CDs, sales of the first two radio dramas were selling out at the proverbial lightspeed from 1993 until 1995. HighBridge sold out of its collector's limited edition of the *Star Wars* and *Empire Strikes Back* radio dramas.

Improving upon previously available sets, the collector's edition went on sale May 31, 1993. It was limited to five thousand copies and featured twenty-three episodes on twelve discs, with thirty-three bonus recordings, including the original NPR promotional advertisements, alternative credit narrations, the new Voegeli-composed music, director's scenes restoring some of the 1983 rerun edits, and *The Making of* Star Wars *for Radio: A Fable for the Mind's Eye*, the audio documentary that played on NPR at the time of the original radio drama premiere.[5] Another bonus feature is a printed interview about the making of the films, with comments by George Lucas, Carrie Fisher, Harrison Ford, screenwriter Lawrence Kasdan, and model maker Jeff Mann.

After the success of the collector's limited edition, and with favorable conditions at NPR and Lucasfilm aligned, Sallie Neall, the HighBridge director of marketing, began to compile a proposal, with a $300,000 budget for the *Return of the Jedi*. With shades of the original partnership idea of NPR and the British Broadcasting Corporation (BBC) on the *Star Wars* radio series, Neall negotiated with a British audio company to finance some of the costs. Seventy thousand copies of the *Jedi* radio drama were planned to go on sale October 15, 1996, with NPR affiliates premiering the series in two segments on October 19 and October 20. Some stations chose the repeat date of October 26 and 27, while others customized the days and times with an episode per week or as a marathon. This arrangement preserved the charity aspect that was the *raison d'être* of the entire *Star Wars* radio drama project since its inception, with NPR using *Jedi* during funding campaigns.

Despite the good news, there was the fact that the budget, with inflation considered, was actually less money, not more, than the original productions. This meant that compromises needed to be made. The most important of these compromises was that *Jedi* would have fewer chapters when compared with its predecessors—only six episodes—which meant that the radio drama would be three hours and twelve minutes, providing Daley sixty-one minutes of additional time to add expanded scenes. Voegeli said, "It was about getting it done for audio publishing, as opposed to NPR radio, and there were only six episodes to save time and money. I think it was hurt by that."[6] Author Michael Kogge, as part of a series on the radio dramas for the *Star Wars Insider*, uncovered a hand-drawn chart by Daley that further demonstrated the dilemma faced by the *Jedi* production team. Daley wrote "Return of the Jedi" in the center of a triangle, and at the corners wrote, "Cast Size Limit," "Six Episode Limit," and "Star Wars Canon." As a reminder that Daley couldn't have everything he wanted this time around, he wrote, "Pick any two."[7]

While the quantity of episodes could be compromised, quality would not, and HighBridge reunited as much of the original team as possible despite the passage of thirteen years. Daley returned to write; John Madden to direct; Tom Voegeli to sound design, produce, and conduct post-production editing; and Mel Sahr to serve as production coordinator and casting director. Lucasfilm again donated the rights, including sound and music. Most of the original actors returned, including Anthony Daniels, Perry King, Ann Sachs, Brock Peters, Bernard Behrens, John Lithgow, Paul Hecht, and narrator Ken Hiller. However, Mark Hamill and Billy Dee Williams did not reprise their roles. During preproduction and recording of the *Jedi* radio drama, Hamill appeared as Colonel Christopher Blair in the *Wing Commander IV: The Price of Freedom* video game, as Dr. Sam Stein in the revival of *The Outer Limits*, and as a voice actor on nearly fifty episodes of television shows in addition to other acting work. Williams was busy with television movies and film roles, in addition to creating his fine art paintings.

In December 1995, Daley supplied Sahr with a preliminary cast list so she could begin the process of casting new roles and recasting Luke and

Lando. Daniels shared what it was like to get the call in the introduction he wrote to Star Wars: Return of the Jedi: *The National Public Radio Dramatization* script book, "It was good to hear Mel Sahr's voice again.... I remember the fun we had making them and the continuing unease I felt that we never completed this incarnation of the trilogy."[8] Sahr asked if Daniels would like to reprise his role. Daniels asked if Brian Daley was writing the scripts and the answer sealed the deal. "Yes, he was. Yes, I would."[9] With Daniels onboard, the *Jedi* radio drama was able to maintain that extra authenticity that his voice always brought to *Star Wars* productions.

Knowing that the team would be returning to Westlake Recording Studios during the first week of February 1996, the location where the original radio drama was produced, Sahr looked for Los Angeles actors to fill the needed roles. Considering the short window Sahr had, she sought the help of Susan Loewenberg, the founder and producing director of L.A. Theatre Works (LATW), a nonprofit media arts group formed in 1984. What makes LATW unique is that it records its live theater productions as radio dramas, experimenting with various formats to help bring the theater experience to more people. The LATW produced read along e-book versions of their plays and had a weekly radio show on local stations and streaming online. Actors such as Lithgow, Laurence Fishburne, Héctor Elizondo, Marsha Mason, Annette Bening, and Ed Asner have appeared in LATW productions. With its close similarity to radio dramas, LATW was a perfect source for actors who could make the transition to the *Jedi* production. Sahr found many of the actors who worked on *Jedi* through LATW, saving her needed time as the proverbial clock ticked to production. Ed Asner (Jabba the Hutt), Arye Gross (Lando Calrissian), Ed Begley, Jr. (Boba Fett), Nia Vardalos (various voices), and Tom Virtue (Major Bren Derlin), among others, were LATW alumni. As was the new Luke Skywalker, Joshua Fardon. On December 7, 1995, Daley and Loewenberg chatted by telephone about the radio drama and the characters to help with actor recommendations.

Joshua Fardon (Luke Skywalker)

Born October 23, 1965, in Kansas City, Missouri, and growing up in Knoxville, Tennessee, Joshua Fardon had been a *Star Wars* fan since the beginning. "I saw *Star Wars* when I was 11 years old at the Kingston 4 cinema," Fardon said.

> This was on Kingston Pike, out in the county, pretty much the middle of nowhere. There was a line to get in that wrapped around the cinema. I knew about the film early on because I would pretend to be a Hollywood mogul and

my uncle, as a joke, gave me a subscription to *Variety*. I had seen all these ads in *Variety* for this weird movie that was opening in the summer. But outside of that, there wasn't a huge amount of hype until it got released. And then there was this massive enthusiasm. I made my dad stand in line with me for three hours. When you're that young and you see something mythic in the way *Star Wars* is mythic, it speaks to you viscerally. I had a connection and infatuation with the film which was matched by everybody I knew. Later, I watched *The Empire Strikes Back* with a great amount of anticipation and was not at all disappointed. I actually think it's a better film. And then *Return of the Jedi*.[10]

I wasn't interested in being an actor at that time. Then, when I was 15, I'd do imitations at the dinner table. My family sent me to a summer stock theater called The Hampton Playhouse and I instantly fell in love. I knew this is what I wanted to do. I studied theatre at Northwestern as an undergraduate and at the Yale School of Drama as a graduate. I considered myself a Shakespearean actor, I'd done a bunch of regional theater. I got into this production of *Julius Caesar* that was produced by LA Theatre Works. The cast had celebrities like Richard Dreyfus, Kelsey Grammer and Stacy Keach. It was quite impressive. I had a tiny little part.[11]

As proof of the adage that there is no such thing as a small part, Fardon's performance at LATW was enough to make Sahr take notice.

I got a call asking if I would come in and read for something. I didn't know what the part was. When I got there and realized it was Luke Skywalker. I was like, "Oh, that's just ridiculous. Why am I even here? I'm never going to get this." Then they called me back. They call me back several times. I got increasingly nervous each time. They would have me there with John Madden and Tom Voegeli and I would be reading the scene where we are on the speeder bikes and really getting into it. I told John and Tom what a geek I was and I think they were pleasantly surprised by that. I was like, "I *love* these films."[12]

At the time of the audition, I had been going through a terrible breakup, sleeping on the floor of a friend of mine's house while looking for a new place. I landed a job at the Mark Taper Forum as an understudy for the play *Three Tall Women*, which is a play about three tall women. There are no men in the play, except for the final twenty minutes, when a guy walks in and holds hands with a dummy. He doesn't have any lines. And I was his understudy! That's my glamorous Hollywood Life (laughs)! While doing that, I was waiting to hear about the radio drama. And I waited and waited. Eventually, I assumed I didn't get the part because such a long time passed. Then Mel called. It felt really surreal. It didn't ever stop feeling surreal. And it's still surreal.[13]

Although Fardon has never met Hamill personally, there was always an admiration for Hamill and the character he originated. Fardon explained:

I'm a huge fan of Mark Hamill. I love Mark Hamill. I follow him on Twitter. The amount I see Luke in myself is probably not too far removed from the amount that I think anyone would see Luke in themselves. I think Luke

> Skywalker is probably a much better person than I am. He's certainly much braver. I'm a neurotic playwright who lives in Chicago. I don't completely identify with the character, but there are certain things about Luke I greatly admire. He goes on quite the journey through the three films. It's interesting to think about how much difference there is between the Luke who discovers his home ravaged on Tatooine in the first film and the Luke who fights against Jabba and the Sarlacc in the third film. Much more confidence, much surer of himself. He's grown up. There's something very Joseph Campbell about it.[14]

Arye Gross (Lando Calrissian)

At the time that Los Angeles–born Arye Gross was hired to play Lando Calrissian, he was about to finish his third season as Adam Green on the television sitcom *Ellen*. As with many of the new *Jedi* actors, Gross had performed at LATW. Gross, who had no easy task playing a character so popular and identified so strongly with the ever-cool Billy Dee Williams, would return to the role of Lando for the 2015 reboot of the Walt Disney Records Read-Along Storybook edition of *Star Wars: Episode V: The Empire Strikes Back*, a children's book featuring new art by Brian Rood.

Ed Begley, Jr. (Boba Fett)

Daley thought a great deal about the purpose and function of bounty hunters both for his radio drama scripts and for a piece that he wrote for *Star Wars Galaxy Magazine*. In his article, Daley wrote something that demonstrates exactly how much he understood the *Star Wars* galaxy, prefiguring *The Book of Boba Fett* by twenty-five years. "He has scored startling triumphs and survived devastating defeats," Daley wrote of Fett. "It seems certain that the Force has spared him to play out some defining role in the great pattern of the *Star Wars* epic."[15]

While Fett is silent in the film version of *Return of the Jedi* except for a yelp when Han activates the bounty hunter's jetpack, Daley expanded Fett's role in the radio drama with a dramatic scene in episode 2, "Fast Friends" where Fett visits Han Solo and Chewbacca in Jabba's prison. After their taunts and banter, Han yells something at Fett when the bounty hunter leaves. Now knowing what fans know about the death of Fett's father Jango, Han's threat must have stung Fett profoundly. From Daley's script:

> HAN: (SHOUTING AFTER HIM) You think a little thing like death's gonna slow us down? You'd better be looking over your shoulder, bounty hunter. 'Cause sooner or later we'll find you! I'm gonna rip your helmet off with your head inside![16]

Playing the more talkative Fett in the *Jedi* radio drama was Ed Begley, Jr. No stranger to science fiction, Begley was Greenbean, a recurring character in the 1978–1979 television show *Battlestar Galactica*. He was known to audiences for his role as Dr. Victor Ehrlich on the popular television show *St. Elsewhere*, earning Begley six Emmy Award nominations. He is a member of LATW, which is how his association with *Star Wars* occurred.

Ed Asner (Jabba the Hutt)

Before his passing in 2021, there were few television actors with the pedigree of Ed Asner. Born in Kansas City, Missouri, on November 15, 1929, Asner initially thought he would be a journalist, taking classes at the University of Chicago. He changed his major to drama and started doing plays. While serving in the U.S. Army, he continued to learn about acting while performing at Army bases. A successful theater career followed until he was selected to play Lou Grant on *The Mary Tyler Moore Show* in 1970, a role he performed for seven years, and again for five seasons on the drama *Lou Grant*. Asner helped pioneer the television mini-series format with his roles in *Rich Man, Poor Man* and *Roots*. The acting awards Asner has earned are more than impressive—they are historic. He had been honored more than any other male actor by the Academy of Television Arts & Sciences, winning seven Emmy Awards and five Golden Globe Awards.

Asner was an actor at LATW and voicing Jabba was a fun experience that Asner wanted to pursue. He could be part of the *Star Wars* saga, while continuing the LATW mission of helping to equalize access to the arts, since *Jedi* would play on NPR for free in addition to being available on cassette and CD. Fardon has fond memories of being a young actor and getting to learn from Lithgow and Asner. Asner could change from his real self to Jabba at the turn of a newspaper page.

> There was a parade of fantastic people who came through while we were recording. It was a very bizarre experience to be reading the scene with John Lithgow as Yoda. That is not something every actor does! That was pretty incredible. Ed Asner was just hilarious. He would be reading a copy of the *New York Times* while waiting for the scene to start, then he would turn to the mic, and say, "Ah ab godda ta neecho boke ooh neetah," which was phonetically written out for him. The production was very exacting about those things.[17]

Tom Virtue (Major Bren Derlin)

Playing the role of Derlin, originated by John Ratzenberger in *The Empire Strikes Back*, was character actor Tom Virtue. Born in Sherman,

Texas, Virtue was a member of The Second City and LATW. One of the most appealing things about playing a hero like Derlin on radio is that because the performance is audial rather than visual, Virtue could adapt to play almost any kind of character. With radio, Virtue detailed, "I can play a character that I can't usually play on stage or in film because I just look a certain way. I could play an old guy or get to play someone who's very young, who's different than I am. So that's the fun of it for me."[18]

Sahr learned of Virtue through LATW. "I started doing voice work really through Susan Loewenberg," Virtue remembers. "She funneled a lot of the talent into the *Jedi* radio drama. Susan is someone who really could have been a very successful film or television producer, but she loved radio. She loves audio. I'd done a bunch of roles for her. I always wanted to be a voiceover artist more than an on-camera actor. You get into a certain niche, and then that's your thing. Susan was one of the only people to recognize it about me. She's been one of the best benefactors for me."[19]

Yeardley Smith (EV-9D9)

Actor, writer, and comedian Yeardley Smith, a member of LATW, is best known as the voice of Lisa Simpson on *The Simpsons*, a role she has played continuously since 1987. In *Jedi*, she performs supervisor droid EV-9D9. Smith enjoyed the chance to play a character very different from Lisa Simpson, "It's a really gruesome, foul, drooly creature—that appealed to me ... they ran me through a fancy sonic meat-grinder. It was a little discombobulating."[20] As with many of those who worked on the *Star Wars* radio dramas, Smith thought of the experience as doing something of value. "I like radio," she said. "It's a lively art both in the literal and cultural sense of the phrase. It's so vital that we preserve it."[21]

During spring 1995, Daley would experience an abrupt life change. Months before any of the actors were contacted by Sahr, Daley was writing his novel series *GammaLAW* when he started to feel ill. "He got very sick and was in the hospital," Lucia St. Clair Robson remembered:

> He didn't complain so I didn't know exactly where he was hurting, but I knew he was in pain. I'll tell you what the doctor said. I was in the room at the hospital when he came in to give the prognosis. He said it was pancreatic cancer and "Unless you get hit by a bus, you'll be dead in six months." I just remember how horrible it was to get that news delivered in that manner. We were both stunned. I remember sitting on the bed holding his hand. What can you say? He had a death sentence. It was a matter of time and he wanted to finish his book before it happened.[22]

In July 1995, Daley endured a six-hour surgery known as the Whipple procedure and started chemotherapy and a regimen of other drugs. He wrote to a friend, "I live one day at a time. I don't know what will happen, but I'm enjoying life in the meantime. Each hour is very, very precious. I am still writing and so is Lucia."[23]

Daley focused as much as he could on making each day worthwhile. LaReine Johnston was inspired by how much her cousin Daley thought of others. With other writers, Johnston remembered that Daley:

> ... was very encouraging. You had to be careful with Brian. If you were to tell him that you were interested in writing something, he would be like, "Oh my God! What? Where is it? Let's see it! Great idea! Get to work on it!" You didn't feel that he was insecure or condescending. He was encouraging. For instance, a friend of mine was beginning to write and she had met Brian out here. One time she called [him] about her project she was writing and did not know how sick he was. This was near the end. She calls him and they talk. He says, "Send me your draft." She thought that was great. She sent it to him. He looks through the whole thing from beginning to end and takes notes and sends them back to her. And this was during the last few months before he passed. But that is how encouraging he was to people.[24]

Something good, though, was occurring despite the cancer. Daley wrote to his friend Anthony Daniels on September 5, 1995, "Dear Tony. Just an added note on the audio/radio side. I presume you've heard that Tom Voegeli feels funding for the serial adaptation of *Return of the Jedi* is a better than even bet?"[25]

On October 26, 1995, Daley received the official word and confirmation about *Jedi,* and he began plotting the outline of the six-episode script. He would be providing Sue Rostoni and Lucy Autrey Wilson at Lucasfilm copies for approval. As a realist and a humble person, Daley did not want to burden others with his diagnosis, nor with something that was inevitable. He went to Los Angeles for a preliminary meeting with Voegeli and Madden, although he would not be healthy enough to go to any of the future conferences. "When he came to LA, Brian was very sick. We were having wine, you know, typical LA. Sipping wine on the patio roof. Brian was a beer drinker, he was a *Heineken* fan," Voegeli said. "He came to say hi and everyone was a little shocked at how fast the cancer was progressing. We didn't know until that moment that he had cancer. He hadn't broadcast it."[26]

Madden recalled, "It is deeply imprinted in my mind. It was probably the first time I was aware of pancreatic cancer. It was the first time I got some kind of close ups on how absolute that journey was."[27]

Those closest to Daley—from Robson to best friend James Luceno, from his brother David and sister Myra—were seeing Daley affected by the cancer even as he continued to write. "That was just such a difficult time," Luceno shared.

> *Jedi* was like a shot in the arm that he would get to do this finally. That was just a wonderful thing to happen in the midst of all this terrible stuff that was going on. My memory is that that he found out after he'd been diagnosed. It was really bad because I kind of knew before he told me. You know, he'd been having these symptoms, and I was kind of watching him lose weight. I was very worried about him. He was seeing a physician who I thought had the wrong sense of what was going on. I've lost several friends to pancreatic cancer. My wife's father died of pancreatic cancer. I've seen this often. Too often. It is a roller coaster, you know, where you are despondent and then something comes along that you are more hopeful. After Brian had what was called the Whipple procedure, which is kind of a re-sectioning of your pancreas and your intestines, that made things better for a while. Then he was on chemotherapy, and then things would get worse, and then things would get a little better. But, you know, five months or so into that, even while he's continuing to work and be productive, he understood that he was not going to survive this. And we had some real heartfelt discussions about the future. So it was a really, really tragic period.[28]

During the week of October 30, 1995, Daley set aside the sixteen-hundred-page manuscript he had already crafted for *GammaLAW*, comfortable with a promise from Luceno to finish the series someday should Daley not be healthy enough. Daley concentrated his writing on the *Jedi* script, finally collecting the array of ideas and notes he had been keeping for the last thirteen years just in case. He would have this one last adventure to share with fellow *Star Wars* fans.

14

An Incomplete Family Reunion at Westlake

Mythologists Joseph Campbell and Vladimir Propp may have somewhat different approaches to studying folktales, but the scholars share a common denominator when exploring the hero's journey. Both Campbell and Propp write that the heroes of myths and fairytales always return to their places of origin before facing a final challenge. Where the heroes were once naïve, they return worldly. Where the heroes were once reluctant, they return with confidence. Where the heroes were once diffident about their abilities or gifts, they return transformed by their experiences, proficient in their abilities.

That is the journey that George Lucas created for Luke Skywalker. At first, Luke hesitates when Ben Kenobi asks for his help in *Star Wars*, uncertain about his abilities and unknowing of the reality of his circumstances. It is fine for Luke to dream about leaving Tatooine and his provincial world, but it is another thing entirely when he is given that chance. It takes the loss of his Aunt Beru and Uncle Owen for Luke to join Ben on his mission. During *The Empire Strikes Back*, Luke learns about the truth of the Force from Yoda, the world from Han Solo, and his own past from Darth Vader. In *Return of the Jedi*, Luke begins the film in the place he once told Ben Kenobi he doubted he would ever return to, Tatooine. However, Luke is no longer the farm boy he once was. He is nearly a Jedi Knight, and he is able to take on Jabba's army and rescue his friends because of everything he has gained during his previous adventures.

As Daley began writing the *Jedi* script during the autumn of 1995, he would rely on this narrative archetype of the hero's return. In his September 5, 1995, letter to Anthony Daniels, he asks Daniels about the scene in the *Jedi* film where C-3PO narrates the previous adventures of his comrades to the Ewoks. "I was thinking about Campbell and *The Power of Myth*," he told Daniels. "It seems likely the Ewoks would ask, at some point, 'Where are *we* in this word magic? Tell about us!'"[1] Campbell was very much on Daley's mind.

In his original ideas for episode 1, which he named "Cry Solo," later, "Tatooine Haunts," Daley wrote opening scenes that would eventually be removed from the final version of the script. One version had Luke returning to Cloud City, the place where he first learned that his father was Darth Vader, and then to Tatooine. The narrator would have said, "Luke Skywalker, after long training and many adventures in his efforts to become a Jedi Knight and learn the ways of the Force, has returned to the wreckage of Cloud City, floating high over the gas giant planet Bespin. His only companions are the droids C-3PO and R2-D2. There he has kept a solitary vigil for a day and a night, preparing himself for a final test of his powers before facing the great trial he foresees in the days ahead."[2] Cloud City is abandoned and listing, causing great concern for C-3PO. Luke is there to prepare himself for the rescue of Han Solo and presumably to find needed parts to build a new lightsaber.

In a second version of the first episode, Daley has Luke return to Tatooine as he begins to implement the subterfuge against Jabba the Hutt. A few hours before C-3PO and R2-D2 make their journey to Jabba's palace, where the film version introduces them, the radio drama would find them with Luke Skywalker on a rope footbridge above the Clamor Chasm gorge on Tatooine.

Threepio asks how the footbridge facilitates the rescue of Han Solo. Luke says it doesn't. He is there for another purpose. While in Anchorhead, Luke learned that two of his former friends would be using the bridge to transport a war droid they built, with the plan of giving the dangerous Gunmetal droid to Jabba as proof they could be valuable to his organization. Luke knows this is a mistake, as Jabba has a reputation of being fickle with the fates of those he employs. As the friends approach, Luke hides his face using his cowl and adopts an artifice that Daley describes as a variation of the Clever Peasant persona Yoda used when Luke first arrived at Dagobah. Luke blocks the footbridge, and the audience learns that the friends are Fixer and Camie from the original *Star Wars* radio dramas. Although Fixer never realizes the identity of the man who stops his plan, Camie certainly knows according to Daley's script:

> **Camie:** I assume nobody calls you "Wormie" these days, Luke.
> **Luke:** (in his normal voice.) No. Other things but not that.
> **Camie:** I'm not even gonna ask how you did this, or why. But thanks. Fixer'll appreciate it too, eventually—although I won't bother his head with details.[3]

The idea that when heroes return home, they go unrecognized by their community is another thread in the tapestry of mythological archetypes according to Campbell. The transmutation from what they were to what they are becoming is so complete that others, as with Fixer, cannot process the change. Daley experienced this in reality; his sister Myra Daley DiBlasio described how Daley was physically and psychologically transformed by his time serving in the military.[4] On a personal level, Daley understood how war changes a person. The scene that Daley wrote exemplifies the idea of Campbell and Propp that the hero returns to their origin place near the end of their adventure, though now fully ready to face challenges and transformed with maturity and abilities unknown when the hero was younger. It is Luke now, not Fixer, who is the leader. The roles have reversed since their scenes together in the *Star Wars* radio drama. This scene would not be included in the final version of the script, in favor of a more efficient beginning.

Daley submitted his script to Lucasfilm in December 1995. He planned to once again be at the recording sessions, writing Anthony Daniels on December 6, 1995, "If not before, I'll see you in L.A. in February."[5] By then, unfortunately, the effects of chemotherapy meant that travel and active writing were becoming too difficult. Disappointed, Daley would not be able to make revisions nor be present at story conferences or the recording. With a scheduled recording date at Westlake Recording Studios for the week of February 5, 1996, it would mean that any script changes would need to be made soon. To facilitate rewrites, Lucy Autrey Wilson brought in author John Whitman. Perhaps best known to *Star Wars* fans for his 12 *Galaxy of Fear* young adult reader books that were published in 1997 and 1998, Whitman had a good deal of audio drama experience already at the time of the *Jedi* radio drama. He had adapted the Dark Horse Comics series *Dark Empire* and its sequel *Dark Empire II* for the Time Warner fully dramatized audio books in 1994 and 1995. He also adapted *Empire's End* and co-wrote, with Ryder Windham, the twenty-two-minute children's audio adventure, *Star Wars: The Mixed-Up Droid.*

One edit that was requested was to excise the Cloud City and Fixer scenes in favor of an opening that included a scene deleted from the *Return of the Jedi* film, that of Luke actually constructing his new lightsaber. As filmed by director Richard Marquand and included in the *Jedi* novelization by James Kahn, the scene was brief, but interesting. The cloaked Luke Skywalker provides the first clue that he is now much more than when audiences first met him in *Star Wars* when he did not even know what a lightsaber was, let alone how to complete the challenging task of assembling one. The *Jedi* radio drama would expand that scene a great deal, once again showing that it is important for Luke to learn to trust his instincts. Each time he tries to follow the instructions in the books he found in Ben Kenobi's hut, he failed to construct his lightsaber. It is only when Luke trusts himself that the saber ignites.

Daley, Madden, Voegeli, and indeed the entire troupe of actors had always depended upon the recommendations of Anthony Daniels, especially as it pertained to the characterization of C-3PO and to *Star Wars* lore more broadly because he had one of the longest associations with the franchise, except for George Lucas and early Lucasfilm employees. Daniels's previous radio drama acting experience, combined with the authenticity and understanding he brought to his character, had always been valuable to the radio drama team. Daniels would participate in story conferences to share his ideas, one of which would eventually result in a beloved expanded universe character, previously featured in books and comics, to make an appearance in the *Jedi* radio drama.

Daniels was once again impressed by Daley's script and what he added to the character. In the *Jedi* radio drama, C-3PO serves many functions, from translator to deity, from Ewok storyteller to a character who has grown enough to stand against the taunts of Han Solo. "One of the problems I had with *The Empire Strikes Back* was that Threepio was used purely, as far as I remember, for comedy and he didn't have a purpose," Daniels said.

> After that, I did have a talk with George and said he needs a role, a proper role and it'd be great if he was kind of a leader that, for instance in those old cartoons, where you have somebody running at the back, hiding behind everybody and then suddenly everyone turns around and he's at the front and he's leading the way. That kind of reversal. But I like to think, and I'm probably totally wrong, that eventually Threepio becoming the king of the Ewoks was that kind of seed. That by some quirk of fate, Han Solo becomes the kid on the block. Threepio does need a purpose and I do speak in the present tense. And it's kind of complicated because you wonder how much does he really know? He's quite savvy. He's not meant to lie in robotic terms, but of course, he does. He can fudge the truth. You know, the scene from *Star Wars*, "I got to take my counterpart down to maintenance...." So he lies to the Stormtroopers. One of my favorite moments is where—because basically Threepio has been bullied in each of these films—he suddenly turns on Han Solo [in the film version of *Return of the Jedi* when Han continually gives orders to Threepio] and in no uncertain terms gives the look of death. That's one of my proudest moments, because it took me thinking about Harrison's timing, interrupting, and giving him the totally evil eye. Makes me laugh every time. And then of course, we did that, we achieved that in radio terms because of Brian.[6]

In the film, of course, the scene ends with Threepio giving Han that famous double-take. That would not work on radio, so Daley gave Threepio a classic line as the denouement.

Han: And hurry up, will ya? I haven't got all day.
Threepio: Why, sir? Are there other droids you need to drive to distraction before retiring?[7]

"One of the things I suggested they change in *Return of the Jedi*," Daniels recalled, "Was that Brian had Threepio talking to Boba Fett in Jabba's Palace. Well, Threepio knew that Boba Fett was kind of a baddy and it didn't seem right to me. Also, Boba Fett doesn't really speak in the movie. So to have him go from quiet to suddenly voluble was pushing it a bit."[8] As originally scripted by Daley, Fett and Threepio's interactions included:

Boba Fett: (voice processed by battle armor helmet com.) You. Translator droid.
3PO: Yes sir, Captain Fett?
Fett: You know who I am?
3PO: You are Boba Fett, sir. The bounty hunter who brought Captain Solo here to Jabba the Hutt.
Fett: And you were Skywalker's droid. Does he really mean to come here?
3PO: I have never known Master Luke to lie, sir.[9]

Daniels continued, "John Madden listened to me and they found another character that could have been there. Arica. The female voice changed the dynamics and it turned out nicely."[10] Arica, it would turn out, is actually the alias used by Timothy Zahn's expanded universe character Mara Jade while she was at Jabba's Palace gathering information about Luke Skywalker and hoping to get close enough to him to achieve the orders of her master, the Emperor. Jade, as Arica, is cozying up to Threepio with the hopes that Skywalker will arrive soon to rescue the droid. Arica's inclusion by Whitman connected the fan favorite *Thrawn Trilogy* and other expanded universe adventures, such as the 1995 short story "Sleight of Hand: The Tale of Mara Jade," to the radio drama.

Of his contributions that improved the radio dramas, Daniels is reluctant to take too much credit. "I can edit. I can say, 'That's really good. But what about this? Or this a better turn of phrase.' Threepio developed a slightly arcane, archaic turn of phrase that makes him sound old fashioned and stuck up, which he is. So, people know now that anything I do, I am going to edit. Not making him more. But making it more him. Because the writers have come maybe to this as a new project. I've been with Threepio for all these years. So, respectfully on both sides, we come together."[11]

Daniels and Daley would have had a chance to continue their collaboration with a Dark Horse Comics project. "Wow, I didn't know what it takes to write a comic book," Daniels laughed. "Never again!"[12] Before *Jedi* was approved for radio, editor and author Ryder Windham asked Daley and Daniels to write a *Droids* comic book. Originally named *Unfriendly Persuasion*, Daley started plotting the comic with Daniels's contributions.

With the need for alacrity once Daley signed to write the *Jedi* radio script, he delayed work on the comic. Due to his illness, Daley was never able to get back to the project. Windham assumed Daley's writing responsibilities with Daniels, and the result was the 1997 *The Protocol Offensive* with Daley credited as plotter. Both C-3PO and R2-D2 are representing the Tion Hegemony, a reference to *Han Solo and the Lost Legacy,* during negotiations with the planet Tahlboor as the droids become embroiled in a civil war.

With Daley's radio drama script approved thanks to Whitman's revisions, recording began at Westlake. While Voegeli and Madden's friendship meant they saw each frequently, in many instances, the actors returning for *Jedi* had not seen each other for years. Ann Sachs thought of the recording session as a great reunion. "After so many years, it was wonderful to see everybody again," Sachs reminisced.[13]

For Joshua Fardon, his first day at Westlake was a mixture of every kind of emotion. The seasoned actors and Madden helped Fardon navigate the challenges of voice acting:

> I was under the giant shadow of Mark Hamill, who, in my mind, as I was doing it and to this day, even when I listen to myself doing it, *is* Luke Skywalker. Mark Hamill as Luke is fused in my brain. But I had to be Luke Skywalker. And once you decide to just play, once you really embrace it, it's like being a kid. I mean, everyone wants to be Luke Skywalker! And I started to really get into it. I'd be reading lines with Threepio and then I look over at Anthony Daniels and think, "Wow, holy smokes." It was just really surreal.
>
> My first day was terrifying. I entered the studio and there was Anthony Daniels and Perry King from *Riptide.* The very first thing John had me perform was the scene of Luke assembling his lightsaber. I didn't know what I was doing. Radio drama was a rare medium. John asked me to do the scene several different ways. I believe that it went very badly, that first take. I think they thought that there needed to be some adjustment to the writing, but I was nervous, thinking, "I am not doing well, I don't know what I'm doing and it shows." The next scene they recorded was the unfreezing of Han from carbonite. I sat in the booth in the studio and watched Perry King. He got in front of the mic, and physicalized everything, which was the opposite of what I thought you would have to do. Watching Perry was a very fast education. I realized, "This is a bit like doing Shakespeare. It's visceral, it's physical and there's the mythic element. And Brian's writing is really wonderful." Once I realized that I got much more comfortable.
>
> On the first day, I also had scenes with R2-D2 who wasn't really there. I had to respond to Artoo as if he were speaking to me. To react appropriately, I had to figure out what Artoo was actually saying and allow it to trigger a truthful response. That's hard, having to generate the other character's dialogue in the imagination. It's akin to reading a book. Because unlike being in a play or film on set, you're not really in costume. You're in a sound stage. There's a desk with

papers, there's a microphone, there are all these technical things you have to worry about.

You have to trust that you're going to dive into the scene. You're going to become Luke Skywalker, talking to Yoda as Yoda is dying. Because if you're not able to do that, if you're not able to go into that kind of mode in your head, then the audience won't either. So, you have to get there. And that was part of the reason also for physicalizing scenes. Physicalizing also brings out a vocal quality. By the end of the first day, I realized I was surrounded by a bunch of people who were extremely professional and very actively involved in the scenes, and that I just had to respond as truthfully as I could, under the circumstances.[14]

Madden was as much mentor as director to Fardon on how to voice act.

John helped me tremendously. He took a huge risk putting me in this. He was super patient. And I felt like there was a great sense of trust. He was also very, very smart. If I were saying something like, 'Leia is my sister,' with too much enthusiasm he would say, 'No, say it softer. You will be more intense if it's softer.' He would give you a direction that provided you with a new way of thinking about the line—and it always worked gorgeously. During the scene when I'm fighting against Palpatine, John stood over me playacting that he was zapping me with lighting out of his hands. He was very involved.[15]

While Fardon, a bit like Luke at the start of his own journey, may have been hesitant about his voice acting abilities at first, his colleagues thought otherwise. Sachs believed, "Josh did a great job of coming on and he was the only one in that position. He had the stuff it takes to do something like that."[16]

Another actor joining the group was Tom Virtue, playing Major Bren Derlin, who in the *Jedi* radio drama is the aide-de-camp of General Han Solo. Around the time of the radio drama, Virtue had a reunion of sorts with radio drama co-star John Lithgow. As production of the movie *Shrek* began, the voice actors were recorded to help inform the animation process. Lithgow played Lord Farquaad. However, when an animated film has script changes, it is usually too expensive to ask the original actors to return during revisions. Instead, they will record again at the end of the process once the animation is completed. Virtue was the voice of the temporary Farquaad during that process, sandwiched between performances by Lithgow.

They would record John Lithgow at the beginning. And then the animators and director work on the film for four years. A lot of times, they will do a scene and then they would scrap it. When they tried a new scene, I would come in and do his lines. I would do it trying to imitate his kind of voice manners and then they would use that as a scratch track. Then the studio and producer

> Jeffrey Katzenberg would either approve it or not, and that's how they would build the movie. Someone did it for Eddie Murphy. Someone did it for Mike Myers. They only get those guys at the beginning and at the end when they've got it all set. They have them re-record it.[17]

On the radio drama, Virtue enjoyed working with a diverse group of actors. Some, like Ann Sachs, were most associated with stage acting, while others, like Perry King, were most associated with film and television. Radio acting was freeing for Virtue:

> It is always a problem having to use memory when acting. When you have the words right in front of you as with radio, you are a lot freer to do the performance as long as you don't get caught up sounding like you are reading. But if you can kind of get the line ahead of time, it helps that you don't have to memorize for that. It isn't as restrictive as when you have to have your memory, particularly if you haven't done the performance for six months or something when you may still have to think, "What's my next line?" We can create suspense, just getting closer to the mic and creating something, a close-up or a long shot, or a lot of different illusions, just by proximity, with acting to a microphone.[18]

Radio frees not only the actor, Virtue believes, but the audience, also. "There's almost a governor on your imagination when it comes to film, but not in radio. There's something even with *Star Wars*, as visually creative as it was, that there may be things you could do with it on radio that can create even more in your imagination that could go beyond what you could create visually."[19]

An example of Virtue's idea is the moment when Darth Vader, now restored as Anakin Skywalker, asks his son to remove his mask. Madden thought that the scene was one of the most effective of the radio dramas and revelatory of the special magic of radio. The convention that was used was to have Brock Peters as Vader perform the role until the helmet is removed and another actor take on the role after that. The emotional effect of the scene surprised even Madden. By its nature, film shows the audience everything it needs. However, because as Madden believes, what we are most interested in during that scene is the internal emotional life of the character, the radio drama creates a focus on that which is most important. Fardon thought that working with Brock Peters on scenes such as this was one of the best experiences, too. "Brock was just spectacular. I mean, *To Kill a Mockingbird*. His Darth Vader was great. It was even great in the room before Tom Voegeli added any sound effects. Brock has that voice. It was easy to be freaked out by the presence of Darth Vader!"[20]

Something that had not changed since June 1980, when the actors first recorded the original radio drama, was the fun and camaraderie balancing out the challenges of performing such a complex drama using solely the voice. Fardon has memories of those fun moments, "There was a discussion about whether it was pronounced 'Daygo-bah' system or 'Dag-obah' system. They actually called Lucasfilm to ask! The whole week was like Christmas. It was such a great group of people. So much fun. They were so welcoming, helping me with this impossible task of replacing an icon and being patient. Anthony Daniels and I would go to lunch. He was just awesome, just the nicest, kindest person."[21]

Lucasfilm even got in on the fun. Howard Roffman, who has served various roles at Lucasfilm from legal counsel, to chief operating officer, to president of Lucas Licensing, has a cameo as a rebel.

In his autobiography, *I Am C-3PO: The Inside Story*, Daniels wrote about that special kind of affection radio wrought, "At the mere hint from the stage directions Perry apparently swept a sighing Princess Leia into his arms and lavished her with kisses. The truth is more prosaic. Perry at mike three. Ann at mike four, some feet away. Perry held his script in his left hand while leaning closer to the mike. Ann holding her script and breathing heavily. Perry's right hand came up to his lips, his breathing heavier. He passionately kisses the back of his hand. Ann went, 'Mmmmmm.' In the control room it sounds like total passion. In the studio everyone rolls around in helpless mirth."[22]

But everyone was keenly aware, despite the antics, that one of their own was missing. Brian Daley had been at every recording session of *Star Wars* and *Empire*, yet his illness had progressed, and he could not be there for *Jedi*. Madden and Voegeli would call Daley every day to let him know about the status of the recordings. Everyone wanted to let Daley know how much they missed him. Voegeli had the idea of recording messages from the actors to which he would add sound effects. The plan was that each of the actors would start their message in character and then break character at the end to share their thoughts with Daley. "I recall all of us becoming aware of Brian's illness," Fardon remembered.

> We did that recording of everyone to wish him well. There was a very tragic aspect to the whole thing. Spiritually, Brian was very much in the room while the recording was happening. His presence was everywhere. It wasn't until the second or third day I was told he was sick. I didn't know him personally, so when we sent him messages, I didn't write mine—John and Tom wrote it for me. It was much better than anything I would have come up with. I was really honored to participate and to be surrounded by a group of people who loved and respected Brian so deeply.[23]

Daniels wrote about the messages to Daley in his introduction to the *Jedi* script book, "We had kept Brian up to date with phone calls, but at the end of recording on the last Saturday, various cast members scribbled on the back of their scripts and came up with their own lines, which we then taped. Far from trying to show Brian that anyone can write if they have a pencil, rather, our jottings were a tribute to his imagination, his skills, his personality, which we had all appreciated with fond admiration."[24]

The messages begin with a crowd, including Voegeli and Madden, cheering Daley's name. Perry King and Ann Sachs collaborated on a scene where Leia is communicating via hologram with Daley, and Han gets jealous, saying, "Fine. I understand. When he comes back, I won't get in your way." To which Leia shares that Han has nothing to worry about because, "Han. He's the writer," riffing a moment from the actual radio drama. It ends with King and Sachs making certain Daley knew they missed and loved him.

Fardon's script begins with the joke of Artoo wondering if something is wrong since he does not recognize Luke, to which he is told, "No, it's fine. I just took over for another actor." Ed Asner uses his Jabba speak to wish Daley the best before he has Jabba take a nap. Artoo and Luke plot a course for the Baltimore system to go visit their old friend, Daley. Brock Peters has Vader kneeling before Daley, awaiting his orders, and then, breaking character, wishing that Daley, "Get well… Rejoin us, soon… Love." Paul Hecht as the Emperor reveals that he is pleased with the words that Daley wrote and commands him to get better.

Daniels wrote his message with appropriate banter between C-3PO and R2-D2. "Master Brian," Threepio goes on to say, "Artoo and I want to say that it has been a distinct honor and joy to work with you. With our thanks, we send you our very best wishes." Then, the droid duo shuffles on, with Threepio arguing how Hollywood has affected Artoo's circuits, until a fade-out.

With the recording of the radio drama and the message to Daley completed late on Saturday, February 10, Voegeli called to share the news with Daley, "I got Lucia and she said, 'Oh, Tom, he's about to die.' It was always such an important project to him that I've always wondered whether he was holding on to hear that the recording was done."[25]

Jedi co-producer Julie Hartley of HighBridge had previously arranged a wrap party at a restaurant on Melrose Avenue. The event was blend of joy and relief that *Jedi* had finally been completed and sadness that Daley was not there with them. Daniels recalled what it was like to lose Brian:

> It was the worst. Brian's timing was brilliant, actually, in a negative way. Because we knew he was ill right from the beginning of the last episode.… We kept him in touch with what we were doing. And always talked about him and always laughed at huge jokes in his absence. John and Tom would get in touch with him. He really was virtually present in the studio. His spirit was totally there because we were reading his voice, his take on George's original

creations. I remember so vividly the dinner party we all had at the end as a celebration, because it had been very intense that period of work. We had literally raised our glasses to Brian, to absent friends, and early the next morning, John Madden rang me and said Brian died. And it was like—I am getting goose bumps remembering. It was a bit of a punch in the face. We had recorded spoof little episodes for him, as though all the characters were looking for him. I read the bit where the last ones in the studio are Artoo and Threepio and we are talking about him. Then, they just walk away into the distance. It may have been the intensity of his work, which we had been doing even though he wasn't there. But suddenly, at the end of this block of energy, and him, there was this complete cessation. An ending. And nothing more. Nothing more except that we are talking about him now, which is a good thing.[26]

15

Losing Brian

"I miss him all the time," said Lucia St. Clair Robson, thinking about the early morning hours of February 11, 1996, when Daley died. In the few days before he lost his battle with pancreatic cancer, Daley had been progressively getting worse. "He was here at home, not in good shape. He didn't want to go to the hospital. Brian had worked as long as he could, but after a while he was mostly in bed. It was hard for him because I live up two flights of stairs from the garage. It wasn't easy getting him down the stairs. It wasn't a good place for him, but Brian wanted to spend his remaining days here."[1]

Daley's sister Myra Daley DiBlasio was by this time a registered nurse managing a Joint Commission on Accreditation of Healthcare Organizations (JCAHO) survey at a hospital in New Jersey and was unable to visit Brian in Maryland. She had been talking regularly with her brother during his illness, using a technology he would normally eschew, but which provided him the ability to communicate without worrying Robson. "America Online or AOL had just come out," DiBlasio recalled.

> Most people really didn't even know what the internet was then. The only reason why I knew was because Brian called me and told me that I need to get this thing called AOL. I was like, "What are you talking about?" I got an account. He had learned he had pancreatic cancer. He was starting to get sick. He didn't really want to talk about it with Lucia to spare her the pain of it. He would wait till she was out and then he would call me. Or he would use AOL to email me. He told me, "Don't ever tell Mom I'm sick. Don't tell her anything." He wanted to protect her. The stress of not telling Mom gave me an ulcer. I didn't tell Mom until the end. She was shocked when it happened.[2]

James Luceno remembered Daley's concern about Robson:

> Brian had always been a joyous guy. This one took that out of him. It took that away from him. He was, unfortunately, pretty despondent at the end. Brian didn't always have the healthiest habits, you know, like having a great diet. And he was kind of wondering, you know, whether he could attribute it to eating too many hotdogs, drinking too many beers, whatever. Brian didn't like to

go deep into his personal life or his personal feelings. So some of the conversations we had, towards the end, were very, very hard for him, because it was clear where everything was headed, but he just didn't want to really process it. Trying to keep it at arm's length. We went to a movie, I don't know which, but we went to see it and we had a talk afterwards. And it was at this point, it was all about what was going to happen to Lucia and would I be there for her and that sort of thing. He was resigned at that point.[3]

Despite Daley's attempts to protect Robson, she knew what he was doing. "He was downplaying it so I wouldn't be upset. He was always very protective." That instinct of Daley to worry about how his situation would affect Robson was on display from the very first day they had learned the news of the cancer months before. "That day, things were pretty muted. He came home and I remember we were lying in bed. I said, 'If I could take this, I would.' He said, 'The only reason I would agree to that is because it's the one who is left behind that has the harder job.' He was right."[4]

The same day that Madden, Voegeli, and the actors had finished recording *Jedi*, Myra, with the required JCAHO survey finished at the hospital, got in her car and drove to Maryland.

I knew from our frequent conversations that Brian was losing his fight. My father died at home of lung cancer and when I saw Brian, I understood why he choose to spare my mother the sordid details of his illness. I think once Brian knew that the radio show was finished, and that I was there with Lucia and she would be okay, that was it. He felt it was okay and that it was time. I was trying to make him relax. We gave him some medication after talking with hospice. I was never a science fiction expert like Brian, but I said to him, "Just close your eyes and relax. Go to one of those stars." I couldn't think of the name of the stars or planets from science fiction. He opened his eyes and said, "Well, which one you want me to go to?" I was thinking, "And he still wants me to be specific. How do I know which star or planet?" That was the last thing he and I said to each other.[5]

Surrounded by Lucia and his sister Myra, Brian passed away. Robson remembered, "It was so emotional. My hand was on his heart when it stopped beating."[6]

Anthony Daniels called, speaking with Robson for an hour about their memories of Daley and how she was doing. It is something which still provides comfort to Robson. When the time arrived to collect Daley's ashes, Robson had to drive past the funeral home twice before gathering the nerve to go in. There were two remembrance ceremonies for Daley, one in Baltimore, one in New Jersey.

The one in Baltimore was arranged by Robson and Luceno, with Daley's mother, siblings, other family, and friends there to celebrate his life. Daley enjoyed going to the water near the Severn River to watch the sunset. It seemed like a good place to have the ceremony. "We had his memorial service under a bridge because it was pouring rain. A lot of people turned out. People drove from New Jersey. The guys from his karate group showed up. At their gym, his karate partners took Brian's photo and enlarged it, placing it on the wall, along with his obituary. They thought very highly of him."[7]

At the New Jersey memorial, the first song they played was "Away in a Manger," the song the nurses had sung to Daley the day he was born during that snowstorm that had stranded the family at the hospital. "That was Brian and my Mom's song for the rest of their lives," Myra recalled. Even though Tom Voegeli knew that Daley would never be able to hear the messages everyone had recorded at Westlake, he still wanted to complete the recording. He shared it with Robson, and it was played at the New Jersey ceremony. Myra said, "There wasn't a dry eye in the place. The recorded messages were a perfect gift" to the family.[8]

Loss and grief encourage remembrance of times gone by. They also inspire creativity in finding ways to keep those remembrances alive. For Daley's friends and family, they would find ways to keep him near. Myra said:

> A short time after Brian passed away, I was surprised that Mom called me and told me about a science fiction book dinner club she wanted to go to that was planning a series of events to talk about Brian. Mom was not a science fiction expert. She was, by this time, very arthritic. She asked me to drive her to these meetings. I asked what we were going to do there. She said, "We're going to talk." I said, "What are we going to talk about? We are not Brian and I don't think we should talk about science fiction." She said, "I'm talking." It was a big event and my mother spoke about Brian. And it worked. They just wanted to hear anything about Brian. I was so proud of my brother and my mother and I found out that when you love someone, it is easy to talk about them.[9]

Myra knew that even though her mother was not a *Star Wars* expert, she was proud of her son. "A kid wrote to Brian. That was something else about Brian, he answered every fan letter he ever got. The letter said the kid had a learning disability and that his parents kind of gave up on him because he had trouble reading. Until Brian's books. Because of them, he learned to read. My mother was very proud of that letter to Brian because her son was able to influence someone like that."[10]

For Luceno, his own writings became the stratagem for honoring his friend, appropriate since they were collaborators and Daley had been a kind of writing mentor. Luceno kept his promise to Daley and completed the *GammaLAW* series. Doing so became a method for Luceno to get closer to his friend, despite him no longer being here. "That was really a chance for me to really look deeply into Brian as a writer, because I had all of his notes and I saw all of his directions, all of his different drafts, all of his research material. It was really eye opening, as well as I knew him, to take on this project, and wrap up this big saga of his."[11]

Poetically, considering that Luceno and Daley had first seen *Star Wars* together during summer 1977, Luceno was asked to write the *Agents of Chaos* duality, for Del Rey, which had recently recaptured the *Star Wars* book license. The books, *The New Jedi Order: Agents of Chaos I: Hero's Trial* and *The New Jedi Order: Agents of Chaos II: Jedi Eclipse*, dealt with the death of Chewbacca and Han's grief. Luceno added as many nods to Daley as possible in the books. Han teams again with Roa, a character that appeared in *Han Solo's Revenge* by Daley as the first smuggler to take Han on the famed Kessel Run. How Roa deals with the loss of his wife Lwyll, also a character from Daley's book, is a catalyst for Han's decisions in *Agents of Chaos*, making Daley's inspirations more than mere cameos. However, there are some amusing Daley character cameos, as when Han thinks a labor droid is his old friend Bollux from all of the original Daley Solo books. Luceno reflected on what writing the books meant to him and how they happened:

> Those books are totally, totally for Brian. I wasn't even going to write for *Star Wars*. I ended up writing by accident because Lucasfilm was planning this large series of 22 novels, and they wanted someone who had an experience with a saga of that dimension. And because of *Robotech*, they thought that I would be someone who could come in as kind of a consultant to how you handle a big series. Then, only like a month or two into it, someone said, "Would you want to write one of the books?" And I said, "Sure," because we had already plotted where the series was going to go, and then to get the one where Han is grieving was like an extraordinary irony, in a way. But of course, I jumped right at the chance, because it was my way to kind of bring in Brian as much as I could.[12]

Almost symbolic of Brian's adventures with Luceno, Daley's ashes have been scattered around the world. Robson wrote:

> A bit of Brian has wafted from the peak of Huayna Picchu in Peru. He swims in the river that runs through the Mayan ruins at Palenque. He keeps company with other soldiers at the chapel dedicated to Vietnam War veterans in Angel Fire, NM. Some of his ashes share his mother's coffin next to his father in a cemetery in Paramus, NJ. He resides in Canyon de Chelly, AZ, in the Chesapeake Bay, a river in New Hampshire, a back yard in New Jersey, a front yard in Maryland, in an old U.S. Army building in Berlin, Germany, and in a film canister in the pocket of one of his fatigue shirts displayed in the living room of an Army buddy. A friend requested some of his cremains to scatter in an unusual place. In 2003, a memorial to the Indian combatants was added at the site of the Little Bighorn Battlefield National Monument. Its designers included a

stone opening as a Spirit Gate to welcome the dead, both Indian and Anglo. Members of some tribes feel that the existence of such a doorway poses a danger to this world. They asked my friend to put dust from a grave in the portal to seal it shut and protect our earthly plain. The friend, who has read Brian's books, thinks Brian would accept the "challenge and the duty of protecting our world from an inter-dimensional rift." He could be right.[13]

For Robson, though, it is remembrances of Daley that keep him most present. "My fondest memory is dancing to music here in the living room, barefoot on the floor," he said. "I often wonder how he would have aged; how would he look now. Would he lose his hair? It wouldn't matter because that's not what I was in love with. I was in love with that personality and that brilliance, his intellect."[14]

On July 26, 1995, about a month after learning about his cancer, Daley wrote a letter to be given to fans and friends upon his death. It said:

Greetings ... and farewell.

I hope and believe that I'll be forgiven by all of you whom I didn't contact personally since the diagnosis of my cancer. The hardships of treatment combined with the pressures of preparation for my operation left little time to collect thoughts and calm, and I simply couldn't make all the calls and write all the letters it would have taken to contact everyone for whom I care and who, I know, cares for me. You were in my thoughts, and now I'm in yours; that will have to suffice us in this imperfect world.

Your good thoughts and prayers would be welcome now no less than when I was alive. I hold it as an article of faith that there are many paths to the Light, and one day we'll get to do the catching up we missed this time around.

My love and best wishes to all. My life, even these last days, has been one of exceptional good fortune, luminous joys and gifts, and the people who came to be important to me were foremost among these.

Until we meet again...

BRIAN.[15]

16

Audio Drama That Was, Audio Drama to Be

What began in the administrative offices of Frank Mankiewicz at National Public Radio (NPR) and Richard Toscan at the University of Southern California more than forty years ago has shaped the future not only for NPR but for modern *Star Wars* storytelling; for the formation of podcasting; and for those inspired by the words Brian Daley wrote and the actors John Madden and Tom Voegeli brought to life.

The extraordinary ratings, publicity, and boost in donations that resulted from the 1981 *Star Wars* radio drama could not have arrived at a better time, providing irrefutable data on the relevancy of NPR and permitting the avoidance of a devastating congressional funding reduction. Mankiewicz hoped that *Star Wars* could bring a new audience to NPR, and Toscan hoped that it could bring a new audience to the art form of radio drama. *Star Wars* achieved both goals, in droves. The reverb of the creative scandal that was the *Star Wars* radio dramas continued in its immediate wake and to this day. Toscan reflected, "When that first series started airing, we were all caught up in the euphoria of what was really unimaginable success, thinking we were ushering in a new age of radio drama in America. What none of us realized then was that for it to become a mass entertainment medium again, radio drama had to be freed from the radio."[1]

The eventual sale of the radio dramas on cassette, and their pioneering availability on CD, shaped the early days of audiobooks, introducing those who were fans of the saga to the then new medium of books on tape and CDs as merely one example of *Star Wars*' continued influence. Sales of new editions continued long after the initial release and are one more example of the radio dramas' enduring relevance. Shortly after the premiere of *Jedi*, HighBridge created *The Complete Star Wars Trilogy: Original Radio Dramas: Collector's Limited Edition*. With only 7,500 individually numbered copies available, this fifteen-disc set featured the entire trilogy with bonuses, including comments from Anthony

Daniels, Joshua Fardon, Perry King, and John Madden recorded by co-producer Julie Hartley during the February 1996 Westlake sessions. Voegeli included the raw recording of the speeder bike chase scene as it was recorded in the studio and the completed scene for comparison. Most specially, the get-better messages to Daley played at his memorial ceremony rounds out the new bonus features. This set does not, however, have all the bonus features of the previous 1993 limited edition twelve-disc set of *Star Wars* and *Empire*.

Although these collector sets were labeled as complete, there was some dialogue included in the 1981 radio broadcast that had been edited from the 1983 radio re-broadcast for time considerations, and this dialogue could not be located when Voegeli remastered the dramas for the CDs. Perhaps the most important piece was a conversation between Luke and Camie about dreams where Luke mentions that he thinks he dreams about his parents sometimes; this scene is included in Daley's script and was part of the original broadcast in 1981.[2]

Additionally, when the *Star Wars* radio drama originally played, the opening narration began with "*NPR Playhouse*. The sounds of theater from National Public Radio. *Star Wars*. An adaptation for radio in 13 parts. Based on characters and situations created by George Lucas." When the radio dramas were converted for cassette and CD, the *NPR Playhouse* reference was removed, as was the idea that it was adaptation for radio. During 2007, yet another version of *The Complete Star Wars Trilogy: The Original Radio Dramas* was retailed, only this time with no bonus features. That same edition was released as a portable MP3 through the Playaway Digital Audio company in 2008.

HighBridge Audio and Topps Company, Inc., the licensee of *Star Wars* trading cards, collaborated to produce a 2013 collector's edition of Star Wars: A New Hope: *The Original Radio Drama*. Limited to 7,500, there were two covers available to the MP3 CD sets. The Light Side edition featured art by Matt Busch, and the Dark Side edition had art by Randy Martinez. The covers gave fans their first look at original radio drama characters like Lord Tion and Heater, who Busch modeled after original Jabba the Hutt actor Declan Mulholland, who played the character in the scenes deleted from the 1977 theatrical release. Each set included an exclusive trading card that matched the cover art, bonus behind-the-scenes audio content, and a booklet with images of the recording sessions.

That same year, Topps created a *Star Wars Illustrated* card set that for the first time visualized the original radio drama and its expanded scenes. Composed of one hundred cards, plus bonus and premium cards, the set permitted fans to follow along, listening to the radio drama as they leafed through the deck. The year 2015 would see the *Star Wars Illustrated:* The

Empire Strikes Back sequel card set, focusing the hundred cards on scenes from the *Empire* radio drama.

Humble Bundle gave charity-minded fans a chance to buy downloadable versions of the *Star Wars* audio dramas using their pay-what-you-want model during 2015. Those donating $15 could get all the radio dramas, plus *Star Wars* audio books. Proceeds supported First Book and UNICEF.

Although Daley shied from media appearances, one sure strategy for getting his participation in an event was if it helped new writers. In 1990, for example, he returned to lecture about writing at his alma mater, Jersey City State College. It is not taxing, then, to imagine that Daley would have been pleased to know that his Han Solo books and audio drama scripts continue to influence a new generation of storytellers. Alexandra Bracken, author of *Star Wars: A New Hope: The Princess, the Scoundrel, and the Farm Boy*, wrote in her preface to her imaginative novelization, "One final note: for this adaptation, I pulled directly from three sources: my imagination, George Lucas' film script, and Brian Daley's masterful 1981 radio drama script."[3]

Jason Fry shared in his piece "The First *Star Wars* Book I Loved," published on the official *Star Wars* website: "Sadly, I'll never get to meet Brian Daley—he was taken from his friends long ago, and far too young. But re-reading *Stars' End*, I realize he was one of my teachers—and man, did he ever teach me a lot."[4]

Star Wars, with its focus on the Skywalkers, in its original film form and as a radio adaptation, is about a family. Perhaps one reason for its meteoric success and cultural relevance is that *Star Wars* appeals to families who enjoy and share the saga. With its roots in the Golden Age of Radio, the *Star Wars* radio dramas even more effectively bring different generations together. That generational quality of the influence of the radio dramas is something that those involved in their production have experienced.

Myra Daley DiBlasio gives an example of how her brother's inspiration has never abated:

> A few years ago, I was at the bookstore in my town. I was getting a preorder and I noticed there was a line outside the bookstore and around the corner. There were about five or six Stormtroopers. It was a *Star Wars* author signing books. All the fans had cameras. I was trying to make my way through the crowd because I only needed to get my book and I had ice cream and groceries waiting. When I got to the front, the owner of the bookstore helped me. I said, "Oh, you know, years ago, my brother wrote a *Star Wars* book." The owner asked my brother's name and I said, "Brian Daley." The author stopped signing and came running to us. He loved Brian. Now it was chaos. Everyone was asking to take my picture. I was like, "You don't understand. I didn't have

> anything to do with it." It didn't matter. They wanted pictures with Brian's sister, I guess. They asked me questions. It was very nice. I couldn't believe this many years later fans would have that reaction.[5]

Samuel Sachs Morgan has a unique perspective, as both a fan and the son of Princess Leia voice actor Ann Sachs. During the interview for this book, he spoke to his mother.

> It's interesting to me the longevity of *Star Wars*. Every now and again somebody will reach out to me and say, "Was your mom, Princess Leia?" Every now and again somebody will reach out to us through social media. Through the years I think social media has certainly changed that in terms of accessibility or being able to get in touch with somebody. *Star Wars* endures. It has had a great impact on so many people. The fact that it endures and keeps going and sort of reinventing itself is just such an amazing thing."[6] Sachs then turned to his mother, "It makes me proud that you were a part of it.[7]

Joshua Fardon, as a parent, has a similar, yet reversed, experience from Samuel Sachs Morgan.

> My stepdaughter is into anime and cosplay. There's a very large interest in voice actors among the younger generation. As a theatre artist that gives me great hope, because theater is primarily an oral medium. It's somewhat visual, but not nearly as visual as film. It's much more dependent on words. Out of necessity radio drama is also word dependent. Radio requires you to be a participant. You can't just be a passive listener. You have to imagine this world. You have to create these things in your head, which is really, really healthy.[8]

Brian Daley is never far from the thoughts of his family and friends. Lucia St. Clair Robson wonders about what Daley would be like today, knowing that "Brian would have written a ton more if he would have been allowed to live."[9] James Luceno wonders the same. "Lucia and I talk about that. What he might have been doing? He was not a tech person, even when computers were becoming important. He was writing on some piece of junk, using some word processing system that no one was using anymore. He was more comfortable writing using a typewriter actually. I think he would have been certainly involved in *Star Wars* again, because when the license went back to Ballantine and Del Rey, he would have certainly been their first choice."[10] Anthony Daniels reflected on Daley, "You know, he loved *Star Wars* and respected it, and could do it. It would have been interesting if he had been part of the newer teams, if he stayed around to do other stuff. But he didn't...."[11]

For Voegeli, it would be something to revisit that galaxy far away on radio. "The whole thing was an amazingly wonderful working experience for me. I wish I could go back to it. I mean, I wish Lucasfilm had wanted to go on to new radio dramas based on all the films that have followed. I would have been happy to do them as radio dramas."[12]

The original *Star Wars* radio drama premiered to a world in 1981 where entertainment and technology were neither digital nor democratized, and rarely on-demand. It was not until May 1982, that *Star Wars* was available for rental on VHS and Betamax tapes. On September 1, 1982, fans could purchase it. The price was $79.99, more than $300 in 2024 dollars. Before the video revolution, fans could revisit *Star Wars* through Super-8, but only selected scenes or the abridged *Story of Star Wars* cassette tape and record narrated by Roscoe Lee Browne. In terms of audio or visual, those were the options, short of going to a film re-release at theaters—that is, until the radio drama, which gave fans the entire narrative and then some.

In many ways, the radio dramas were the precursor to today's podcasting revolution. There is a through-line of both purpose and imagination that connects the radio dramas of the Golden Age to *Earplay* to the *Star Wars* radio dramas to audiobooks to podcasts. Today, popular podcasts and audio adventures have, as the original radio dramas had with Anthony Daniels, Billy Dee Williams, and Mark Hamill, *Star Wars* film actors turning their energies to voice acting. Oscar Isaac (Poe Dameron in the sequel trilogy of the *Star Wars* films) stars in *Homecoming*, and Kelly Marie Tran (Rose Tico in the films) leads the cast in *Passenger List*. Toscan noted another more subtle influence. "In the midst of the ending credits for the radio episodes, Ben Burtt is credited as 'sound designer for Lucasfilm.' The term 'sound designer' was just coming into use in recognition of that essential role in the coordination of music, sound effects, and dialogue, and its use in the first series contributed to the increasing stature of sound professionals. While most listeners may not have noticed, those laboring in those behind-the-scenes sound roles in audio drama did."[13]

Star Wars fans have also turned to podcasts as a creative outlet. More than two hundred podcasts relate to *Star Wars*, made by fans for fans. *Blast Points Podcast*, *Coffee with Kenobi*, *Fantha Tracks Radio*, *Rebel Force Radio*, *The Resistance Podcast*, *SW Action News*, and *Tarkin's Top Shelf* are some of the popular podcasts and have been given stage time at official Star Wars Celebrations. Through audio, podcasters give opinions, review products, provide a forum for discussion, and otherwise share their affinity, and sometimes ire, with aspects of the *Star Wars* universe. Some continue that familial quality that defines *Star Wars*, as with *Father and Son: A Star Wars Podcast*.

Filmmaker and director Kyle Newman was so inspired by the radio dramas and Brian Daley that he created two live audio dramas that were performed at Celebration VI at Orlando in 2012 and Celebration Anaheim in 2015. *Smuggler's Gambit* and its sequel *Smuggler's Bounty* focus on the characters of Han Solo and Chewbacca, much like Daley's novels. The audio adventures were a chance for fans to experience what it was like during the Golden Age of Radio as *Star Wars* actors from various animated series and films such as Dee Bradley Baker, Ashley Eckstein, Tom Kane, Matt Lanter, Daniel Logan, Catherine Tabor, James Arnold Taylor, and Matt Wood, with Lucasfilm sound designer, voice director, and sound effects editor David W. Collins as Han Solo, performed the script live. Newman wrote about his motivation, "Brian's lovingly crafted audio iterations of *A New Hope* and *The Empire Strikes Back* were no mere retellings of the films that I knew so well; they breathed a life of their own and stood proud on their own artistic and technical merits. But most importantly, they explored corners of the galaxy that I had never experienced before and even brought to life scenes that, until then, were things of folklore... And it proved to me that *Star Wars* would never die."[14]

Star Wars is sometimes thought of merely as popular culture, but it is much more than that. Unlike most popular culture which is, by its nature, ephemeral, *Star Wars* transcends generations, has transformed the cinema, and has given the world a new mythology. The *Star Wars* radio dramas endure for many reasons, but they do endure. Unlike many iterations of popular culture, the *Star Wars* radio dramas were not commercial. They were a charitable gift created from the heart. George Lucas and Lucasfilm donated the rights for $1 to help the University of Southern California and to give everyone free access to *Star Wars*. The actors did it because they supported that mission and because it gave them the chance to act in an unusual medium. Richard Toscan wanted to help not only NPR but to introduce a new generation to a classic art form. The idea Toscan, Joel Rosenzweig, and John Houseman conjured was a boon to NPR, saving the network at a time when it needed it the most. John Madden, who by the time of *Jedi* had already become an established film director, returned to direct the radio play for those very same artistic and community-minded reasons. Tom Voegeli put months of work into the postproduction because he understood the purpose and creative challenge required when taking *Star Wars* from the theater to radio.

Brian Daley did it for all those reasons, too, and because, most of all, he loved *Star Wars* and what it represented. The last lines of dialogue Daley wrote to be spoken by Luke Skywalker at the Ewok Celebration are as much an epitaph of sorts for Daley as they are a conclusion of the radio dramas: "Their fire is back in the universe. Let it burn high and bright, to be seen by friend and foe. The Jedi have returned."

Perhaps Anthony Daniels sums it up best, "One of the things that I'm proud of is the radio series.... The radio series was valuable. They were good things to do.... Yes, those days have gone now. But they exist forever. On the medium of sound."[15]

Appendix A

Related *Star Wars* Audio Projects

As with Brian Daley's *Rebel Mission to Ord Mantell* adventure, there are many related *Star Wars* audio projects featuring those who had originally contributed to the radio dramas. This is a brief history of the making of those adventures.

***The Story of* Star Wars.** Buena Vista Records. 20th Century–Fox Records Corporation. 1977.
The Story of* Star Wars: The Empire Strikes Back: *The Adventures of Luke Skywalker. RSO Records, 1980. Buena Vista Records. 1983.
***The Story of* Star Wars: Return of the Jedi.** Buena Vista Records. 1983.

Each of the original *Star Wars* films was adapted as an abridged audio adventure featuring original dialogue, music, and sound effects. Both the *Star Wars* and *Empire* recordings were adapted by E. Jack Kaplan and Cheryl Gard-Wornson. The narrator on *Star Wars* was Roscoe Lee Browne, who science fiction fans may know as the voice of Box in the 1976 film *Logan's Run*. Browne was a noted Shakespearean actor and Emmy Award winner, and had made his stage directorial debut in 1966 with the play *A Hand Is on the Gate* which starred James Earl Jones. His narration of *Star Wars* helped it become a Gold Record Seller, with more than 500,000 copies sold. A picture disc of C-3PO, R2-D2, and Darth Vader; LP record; eight-track; and cassette tape version were available. A sixteen-page book with photographs was included in most releases.

Empire had two releases, one in 1980 featuring impressive cover art by Jeff Wack and art direction by Glenn Ross and Tim Owens. Darth Vader and Luke Skywalker battle on the cover, framed by moments from the film. A 1983 release by Buena Vista Records followed, with a different cover, this time of the Battle of Hoth. The later version included a sixteen-page book. The narrator for *Empire* was Malachi Throne, a reliable character actor who had memorable appearances in the original *Star Trek*. These recordings were available on LP record and cassette.

Jedi featured Chuck Riley as narrator, heard on many of the Buena Vista Records Star Wars Read-Along records and tapes during the 1980s, including *Rebel Mission to Ord Mantell*. As was tradition, a sixteen-page book was included featuring images from the film, and *Jedi* was sold as a picture disc featuring Luke Skywalker and Wicket W. Warrick, LP record, and cassette. On each of the *Star Wars* story of adventures, the original film dialogue recordings of Mark Hamill and Anthony Daniels were included, giving fans a precursor to the radio dramas that were to follow.

1-800-521-1980. Writer: Craig Miller. Lucasfilm, Ltd. 1980.

A most important contributor to early *Star Wars* fandom, Craig Miller served as director of fan relations for Lucasfilm from 1977 until 1980. Among his many contributions was producing the January 1980 segment of *Sesame Street* featuring Anthony Daniels as C-3PO and R2-D2 and shepherding the *Official Star Wars Fan Club*. While thinking of strategies to get fans engaged during the pre-premiere publicity for *The Empire Strikes Back*, Miller had an inspired idea: create a toll-free phone number where fans could call once each month and hear a different message from the characters, voiced by original film actors.

George Lucas approved of the idea, and Miller wrote the scripts. Mark Hamill, Anthony Daniels, Carrie Fisher, and James Earl Jones recorded their lines in December 1979 during breaks while looping their dialogue from the film. Harrison Ford was recorded at his home because his looping had already been completed. Each character would give hints as to their adventures in *Empire*, with Anthony Daniels as C-3PO ending the message with an invitation to see *Empire* when it premiered on May 21, 1980, hence the phone number's clever numbering system. There would be a new character message each month for the five months prior to the film's release.

Of all the messages, C-3PO's was the one that gave the most hints, and while it was doubtful anyone who had not seen the film would catch it, Threepio literally reveals his fate in the movie. "And when we got to the Cloud City, I just went all to pieces. Oh dear. I can't go on. Talking about it is too upsetting."[1] All to pieces, indeed.

And all to pieces is exactly what occurred. So popular was the number that it caused the entire 800 phone line system of Illinois to grind to a halt for several hours. Miller explained in his book *Star Wars Memories*, "AT&T couldn't handle it. There were so many calls coming in, their system couldn't generate busy signals to all of them. Or any other sort of signal. No 'fast busy.' No 'out of service.' No nothing. The 800 system for Illinois crashed and shut down for several hours."[2] The press took notice, including the *Des Moines Tribune*, which reported, "Phone the Empire. How about a little chat with Han Solo, *Star Wars* fans? Han will tell you all his troubles if you call him, toll-free, at 1–800–521–1980. In between dodging Imperial ships, Solo is promoting the new *Star Wars* movie *The Empire Strikes Back*. Warning: The phone lines are quite busy."[3] Busy, indeed. Promptly, more lines were added and fans could get through. Hamill's and Daniels's recordings for the 800 number took place six months before they would reunite for the original radio drama recordings at Westlake Recording Studio.

Star Wars: The Empire Strikes Back: *A Radio Interview Special.* Backstage Productions, Inc. 1980.

The *Star Wars: The Empire Strikes Back* was a vinyl record produced and distributed by Backstage Productions, Inc. It was not a retail item. Rather, it was sent free to local radio stations as a promotional item for the *Empire* film. Mark Hamill, Billy Dee Williams, and Anthony Daniels, who each reprised their roles for the radio dramas, along with Harrison Ford, Carrie Fisher, David Prowse (Darth Vader), director Irvin Kershner, and producer Gary Kurtz are interviewed on the record. Each station was permitted to edit and use the cue scripts and timings that were provided to customize a radio program according to their formats and schedules. Occasionally, the record is sold at auction, although few are known to exist.

Christmas in the Stars. RSO Records. November 1980.

Recorded in 1980, *Christmas in the Stars* (CITS) may be the most unique audio adventure in the *Star Wars* pantheon. The holiday album was produced by Meco Monardo, whose 1977 disco version of the "*Star Wars* Theme/Cantina Band" was certified Platinum, the number-one song on the *Billboard* charts for two weeks in October 1977. Meco's *Star Wars and Other Galactic Funk* LP album scored Platinum with sales of more than 1 million. The setting of CITS is a droid factory owned by an S. Claus. Featuring songs by Yale music professor Maury Yeston, sound effects by Ben Burtt, and narration and singing by Anthony Daniels as C-3PO, the recording was available as both an LP record and cassette. There is much that makes CITS a fun collection of holiday songs, with titles like "What Can You Get a Wookiee for Christmas (When He Already Owns a Comb?)." It is also an important artifact of 1980s popular culture. The album was the first professional recording by Jon Bon Jovi who, as his birth name John Bongiovi, sings "R2-D2 We Wish You a Merry Christmas." Lead vocal credits are Daniels, Bongiovi, Yeston, and Rod McBrien. Writing credits include, among others, Meco, Yeston, McBrien, Sammy Cahn, Lawrence

Grossman, and Denny Randell who wrote the Four Seasons song, "Working My Way Back to You." The CITS cover is an image of Claus sitting in front of a fireplace in his workshop, with Threepio and Artoo, painted by *Star Wars* visualist Ralph McQuarrie. The album is one of the first of its kind recorded on a Sony 1600 PCM Digital Recorder, which had been introduced in 1978.

CITS was produced with the textbook definition of alacrity. The concept approval, writing of the songs and dialogue, and recording all had to occur within a few months to be ready for Christmas 1980. Meco told the story of how the album came together in a 2005 interview with fan website Rebelscum and The Force.net staffer Shane Turgeon:

> I wrote a letter, nine pages long. It starts: "Dear George, you don't know me personally, but you know who I am." And I reiterated all the things I had done with *Star Wars* ... eventually saying, "I think we should do a Christmas album together?" And then I had the one and only telephone conversation I ever had with George Lucas.[4]

The recording sessions were primarily at the famous Power Station, owned by CITS co-mixer Tony Bongiovi, cousin of John, who credits the financial success of *Star Wars and Other Galactic Funk* with making it possible to build his studio in the first place.[5] Additional recording occurred at Celebration Studio. Daniels told journalist Andrea Warner in 2016, "I was actually rehearsing for a play in London, rehearsing every day of the week, and then [RSO Records] needed—as a lot of things are in show business—it now.... We go to the studio and it was just me; sadly there was no orchestra there. It was all just click tracks and all that kind of thing and very little rehearsal time, very little preparation...."[6]

Originally, Daniels was not the only film actor who was supposed to be featured on the record. Frank Oz was supposed to play Yoda; however, due to a schedule conflict that occurred while he was working on *The Muppet Movie* in London, he had to focus on that obligation rather than the album. The song he was to appear on, "Meaning of Christmas," had to be revised anyway because of Lucasfilm concerns about it being too religious.

Daniels told Warner that despite some people thinking of the album as odd, it is also "sort of charming ... you get away with it at Christmas, you know."[7] Many fans must have agreed, as *Christmas in the Stars* charted on *Billboard* for six weeks in December 1980. The dialogue interstitials and the unified narrative of *Christmas in the Stars* qualifies it as an audio adventure in addition to a Christmas album. Riffing on the lyrics to "The Odds Against Christmas," it could be argued that the odds against Christmas being Christmas without *Christmas in the Stars* really are 365 to 1.

Star Wars Adventures in ABC. Buena Vista Records. 1984.
Star Wars Adventures in Colors and Shapes. Buena Vista Records. 1984.

Perhaps as a result of the experiences and challenges that George Lucas had faced in grammar and high school as a student, Lucasfilm has always had a commitment to finding ways to use entertainment as a portal to education. Those students with hip teachers in 1978 may have been lucky enough to have them use the *Star Wars Teaching Kit* from George Lucas, Contemporary Motivators, Pendulum Press, Inc., and Eye Gate Media. Filmstrips, a comic book, a classroom poster, comic books, and *Star Wars*–themed activities helped make learning fun. Accompanying the reading was a cassette tape with a full audio adventure that did not feature any of the film actors. *The Young Indiana Jones Chronicles* 1992 television series, for example, was meant to teach as much as it amused. Today, the tradition continues with *Star Wars* used to teach coding, science, technology, engineering, and math.

In 1984, when technology was less digital and more analog, the medium of educating while entertaining was achieved with vinyl records and tapes. Disney's Buena Vista Records made two such *Star Wars* adventures, one for learning the alphabet, the other for learning about colors and shapes. Both feature Daniels as C-3PO and were produced by Ted Kryczko, one of the Walt Disney Company's most prolific and honored producers. Kryczko began his career working on the Read-Along version of Steven Spielberg's *E.T.: The Extra-Terrestrial.* He would eventually move from director of product development to vice president of the A&R Catalog at Walt Disney Records. Kryczko was nominated for fourteen Grammy Awards, winning two, and his records have sold more than 70 million copies. Fans will note his name on many of the Buena Vista Records and Walt Disney Records *Star Wars* recordings.

Adventures in ABC uses rhyming schemata as listeners learn the alphabet by describing *Star Wars* characters or technology that begins with each letter. A is for AT-AT, T is for Tauntaun. Daniels takes turns with the other narrator William Woodson with fun fare, such as "B is for Bantha / A Bantha does not have a name…. If I had a Bantha, / I'd name it 'Samantha.'" Reference materials for the art must have included the Kenner action figures, as Greedo is drawn wearing a costume that is the same as the figure, not the actual film costume. Additionally, the *ABC* book makes the same error as Kenner toys by substituting 4-LOM for the letter Z character Zuckuss.

Adventures in Colors and Shapes is more of a traditional tale, with C-3PO and R2-D2 on a mission to help Han Solo and Chewbacca locate a Fulstar plate needed to repair the *Millennium Falcon*. The problem is that Han's typically dismissive dealings with Threepio had the droids running around in proverbial circles to find the needed plate in the needed color and shape. As C-3PO shares with Luke, "The plate cannot be a circle, Master Luke. It must have straight sides, but not three sides like a *triangle* and not five sides like a *pentagon*. It must have exactly four straight sides. Just what are we to do?" Daniels's performance is a welcome addition to the project, helping, as the back cover of the accompanying Read-Along books promise, to make the experience "A *Star Wars* Adventure in Learning Fun."

Star Wars: Heir to the Empire. Bantam Audio Publishing. 1 June 1991.
Star Wars: Dark Force Rising. Random House Audio. 1 May 1992.
Star Wars: The Last Command. Random House Audio. 1 April 1993.

During the early days of audiobooks, *Star Wars* was an important contributor to the new medium. Anthony Daniels narrates the abridged audiobook versions of the last two *Thrawn Trilogy* books. *Heir to the Empire*, the first book of the series, was narrated by Wedge Antilles actor Denis Lawson. With versatility, Daniels not only provides the exposition, but also he plays all the roles, giving fans the treat of hearing his interpretations of favorite characters.

Star Wars: A New Hope *Read-Along.* Walt Disney Records. 1997.
Star Wars: The Empire Strikes Back *Read-Along.* Walt Disney Records. 1997.
Star Wars: Return of the Jedi *Read-Along.* Walt Disney Records. 1997.

In order to align the *Star Wars Read-Along* recordings with the 20th Anniversary Special Editions of the film released in 1997, modern adaptations were produced for record and cassette that same year, featuring images from the film in the twenty-four-page companion book. Adapted and produced by Randy Thornton, the additional and modified scenes from the new versions of the films were included. Kryczko returned as executive producer. (These versions of the *Star Wars* films would get a 2015 re-release, this time on CD, featuring art by Brian Rood.) The narrator was once again Chuck Riley.

What is most special about these *Read-Along* recordings is that they constitute a reunion of sorts for the actors who worked on the radio dramas. Although the actors did not record their parts together as they did for the NPR radio dramas, the credit roster of the 1997/2015 *Read-Along* recordings is familiar to any fan of the National Public Radio (NPR) series. Daniels reprises his role as C-3PO, Perry King is Han Solo, Brock Peters is Darth Vader, Arye Gross is Lando Calrissian, and Joshua Fardon is Luke Skywalker. Other roles were played by *Rebel Mission to Ord Mantell* alumni Pat Parris, who was Leia Organa, and Corey Burton, this time as Yoda. The *Read-Along* adventures did not merely use lines from the radio dramas. They featured new dialogue with new recording sessions conducted during 1996, a separate project than the *Return of the Jedi* radio drama but recorded near the same time. Listen for cameos by *Read-Along* producer Thornton as Jabba the Hutt and recording engineer Jeff Sheridan as an Imperial Commander.

Fardon enjoyed returning as Luke, but the experience of recording was very different when compared with the radio drama, "That was produced by Disney. They had me do all three movies at the same time, but the dialogue was select. It would be a line from *Star Wars*. Then, some lines from *The Empire Strikes Back*. Then select lines from *Return of the Jedi*. It wasn't a drama so much as a narrated story with a few lines here and there."[8]

The Incredibly Improved New Wonder Column in Space Written and Performed by Anthony Daniels. Lucasfilm Ltd. and A Mad Dan Production. 1999.

Before the Internet, there was Dan Madsen. Fan experiences would not be the same if not for Madsen, not only for those who love *Star Wars* but *Star Trek*, too. For twenty-five years, Madsen was president of the *Official Star Trek Fan Club* providing fans with information about actors, writers, artists, and crew. For more than 150 issues, Madsen published *The Star Trek Communicator*, which in its various versions was the source for the latest *Star Trek* news. More than that, the *Communicator* was social media before it ever existed, as fans communicated with each other and with celebrities through the pages of Madsen's creation.

Madsen was a typical Colorado kid during the 1960s and 1970s, except that he was a little person. What he wasn't was a science fiction fan. After a rather harsh day at school due to bullying, he grabbed a snack and sat on the couch to ruminate. *Star Trek* was on, as his brother was a fan. The episode was "Plato's Stepchildren," which featured actor Michael Dunn as Alexander, whose short stature made him the person of constant ridicule for the Platonian characters in the episode. Captain Kirk tells Alexander that where he comes from, size, shape, or color make no difference and nobody has more power than anyone else. By the time Alexander beams away to join Captain Kirk, Madsen was along for the ride. Thus started his lifelong love of science fiction.

Although Madsen's career goal was to be an actor, he was inspired by *Star Trek: The Motion Picture* to start a newsletter to help promote the show. Instead of pay, Madsen took a job with a local printer to learn the business and to print his *Star Trek* newsletter. The newsletter was enjoyed by *Star Trek* creator Gene Roddenberry, who would read each issue. In 1982, Madsen would receive a phone call that would change his life. The call was from Paramount Pictures. They wanted Madsen to know that he could not write the newsletter, as *Star Trek* was copyrighted. Madsen told them that he wasn't making money; rather, it was costing him money! He was merely trying to help the show and movies. Actually, Paramount knew this, and then because of what they called his proper mix of "fanaticism and professionalism," Madsen learned the real reason for the phone call. At Roddenberry's request, Madsen was being asked to run the Official *Star Trek* Fan Club. During the next decades, Madsen would have nearly 105,000 subscribers to the *Communicator*, create exclusive products, and employ more than a hundred people with the idea of providing fans with the best access to news about the franchise.

Despite his love for *Star Trek*, Madsen discovered in 1977 that there was, as Yoda might say, another. Said Madsen:

> The first time I ever heard of *Star Wars* was at a *Star Trek* convention. It was Star Con in Denver. Guests were James Doohan and Grace Lee Whitney. At that point, you know, *Star Trek* was king. There was nothing really else out there. The convention was all focused on *Star Trek*. On the back page of the convention program booklet was an ad for this thing called *Star Wars*. I remember it said the film was going to be showing in 70 millimeter at the Cooper Theater, one of the biggest, nicest theaters we had in Denver. Big surround sound, big screen that went all the way around. I still have that program booklet. It is really kind of special to me, because it literally is the first time I was ever introduced to *Star Wars*.
>
> I was 13 at the time. I had to go in for surgery on my both my legs as a result of my dwarfism. This was right after the convention. I think it was the week or two weeks after *Star Wars* had premiered. My cousin, who is much older than I and loves science fiction like me, said, "Oh my God, Danny you've got to see this new movie *Star Wars*. It blows *Star Trek* away." And I'm like, "Come on." I couldn't walk at this point. And my cousin says, "I'll carry you into the theater, and we'll go see the movie." My mom and dad said fine and my cousin pulled the car up in front of the theater and talked to the manager. He carried me to the front row of the balcony which had this bar in front of it so I could sit in the seat and my feet would rest on the bar.
>
> I was absolutely blown away when that opening scene with that Star Destroyer occurred. It didn't take long before I had taken down everything I had of *Star Trek* and my entire room was full of *Star Wars* posters. I went to a hobby shop and that was just heaven. I could actually build an X-Wing fighter and hang it on my ceiling. It was a love affair that began instantaneously. That same cousin took me to a magic store that sold the rubber masks and I was able to buy the Don Post C-3PO mask. I thought that was the greatest thing. I remember getting that and putting that on my shelf. I went to the local comic

> book store when I learned the first issue of the *Star Wars* by Marvel Comics was out. These are always such favorite, special memories to me, because you know, it was so innocent. And there wasn't this whole mass marketing and merchandising and everything. Every new thing that came out was like this treasure.[9]

In 1987, Madsen was asked by George Lucas to a meeting, where they discussed the idea that perhaps Lucasfilm would like to start a new fan club, but unlike the previous one, it would be run by an outside company. Would Madsen be interested? It was a dream for Madsen, making him the fan club president and publisher for his two favorite franchises. Madsen has many favorite memories of Lucas. One was a conversation, where Madsen was asking Lucas about the early days of *Star Wars*. "George said to me his initial idea was to make Luke and Leia little people. The problem was that he couldn't find any actors that were good enough to play that."[10] Out of that original idea, however, would eventually emerge *Willow*, a film that Madsen auditioned for as the main character:

> When *Willow* came out, I was also trying to pursue a career as an actor. I had an L.A. agent. He called me one day and says, "I got an audition for you out here. It's for a new film George Lucas and Ron Howard are doing." I'm like, "Wow, you're kidding me. What character am I auditioning for?" He says, "Willow." I had to be out the next day. I go to Los Angeles, took a cab to the casting director's office, waited my turn, and read for the part of Willow. They called me and said they liked what I was doing in the audition, and that it was between me and two other actors. They asked if I could come back and read again. I stayed an extra day, went back to the casting director's office, read different pages of the script. They said, "Okay, that's good. We will let you know what happens." Obviously, nothing happened, as we now know today. But here's the irony of it all. It was just months later that I got this call from Lucasfilm about doing their fan club. The first project was *Willow*. They send me to the set. I'm spending a week on the set, interviewing everybody, Ron Howard, and here I am interviewing Warwick Davis, who beat me out for the role. I told him that story. He just got the biggest kick out of it.[11]

Another favorite memory was Madsen's *The Phantom Menace* cameo as Dams Denna, the kaadu wrangler who helps Jar Jar during the celebration on Naboo. That occurred at the request of George Lucas.

For the first issue of the *Official Lucasfilm Fan Club* newsletter, later renamed *Star Wars Insider*, Madsen would begin a sincere friendship with Anthony Daniels, who would be the first actor interviewed for the magazine. Actually, Madsen had met Daniels years before as a fan during 1983:

> When I was a kid, they had a special screening of *Return of the Jedi* at the biggest, nicest theater here in Denver. It was before the movie actually had its real premiere. They had characters from the film there, the real thing. Lucasfilm

> brought them out. And Anthony Daniels was there. I got to go. As I remember, I said, "Mr. Daniels, could I get a picture with you?" And he was like, "Sure." I got a picture of me and Anthony, and Darth Vader, standing outside the theater. But that was long before I ever got the Fan Club license. Long before he and I met professionally. It was me being a fan, Dan, and asking for a picture with Anthony with Darth Vader in costume. Years later, I interviewed Anthony for the very first issue of the *Lucasfilm Fan Club Magazine* and we really became good friends. He was in London and we enjoyed the interview so much.[12]

It was Madsen who shepherded the very first Star Wars Celebration, beginning a tradition of conventions that endures twenty-five years later. Madsen was not given much time to arrange the event, and he turned to Daniels for advice and to ask him to be the emcee. Madsen had arranged for the event to be at the Wings Over the Rockies Air and Space Museum from April 30 until May 2, 1999. The event would be focused on *The Phantom Menace*, featuring the first convention appearances for many of the film's actors, behind the scenes panels, a three-quarters scale X-Wing fighter, and the world premiere of the "Duel of the Fates" music video. Twenty thousand fans were going to gather those days to celebrate. Yet neither Madsen nor Daniels could imagine the challenges that awaited them.

On April 20, 1999, the devastating attacks at Columbine High School stunned the world and sent the communities closest to the suburb, including Denver, into mourning and shock. Lucasfilm thought it appropriate to cancel the event, and an emergency meeting was convened via telephone. Madsen had been part of that community his entire life, and he was concerned about what canceling the event would do to those fans who needed to have something positive, something affirming, during the days after the tragedy. There was also the practical concerns about the many fans from other nations and out of town who were traveling to the convention. Would they be able to get their airplane tickets refunded? Some of those fans had already arrived in Denver. Madsen called the mayor of Denver to ask his opinion and the mayor felt the community needed something positive to happen. The mayor sent a letter to Lucasfilm and the event was on. However, there would be some changes. Fans were asked not to bring any prop weapons out of respect for those suffering. The convention became a charity event, to help raise funds for the families affected.

Then, the bad weather came, some of the worst rains the area had seen. Because much of the event was outdoors, with tents for shelter, this was another problem for Madsen and Daniels. The water was everywhere, as were concomitant problems, such as making certain the celebrities would not get shocked by the microphone wires now near puddles. Despite this, and perhaps because of it, the first Celebration became a kind of Woodstock for the *Star Wars* generation. Good spirits, comradery, respect for each other, joy, and friendship were more on display at the event than anything else. Soon the weather cleared, and it truly was a celebration.

Madsen recalled, "Tony and I became really close, obviously, especially with the first Celebration he and I did. Then, as Celebration came around, he flew out two weeks prior to the show and we went out to dinner each night. He came over to my house several times and we worked on the preparations. Doing this. Doing that. Not once ever thinking. 'Okay, what do we do if it pours rain?'"[13]

At the same time Madsen and Daniels were planning Celebration, they were collaborating on a special audio adventure. From 1995 until 1999, Daniels had written a regular piece for the *Star Wars Insider* alternatingly named "The Wonder Column" or the "The New Wonder Column." Daniels said:

> I'd always written "The Wonder Column" to kind of amuse myself. To keep my brain going. Back in the day, I got the impression quite a few times that people thought I must be a real numb-nut to play a robot in a fiberglass gold suit. You know, that people thought that I clearly didn't have a brain. And I found that quite difficult, really. Some people were quite condescending. Maybe I became a bit of a smartass in return.... I did get fed up with being put down and ignored.... And one of the ways I kept my brain alive, because I was no good at cryptic crosswords, don't play Chess, don't play Bridge, was that I could write these stories. And they were all true. I recognized very quickly, though, that to make the story interesting, you do have to give it a shape. Think of seeing a man walking down the road and he steps on banana skin. That is a fact. But you need to shape it, mold it, give it a modeling and give it a presentation, really or the story isn't funny or interesting.[14]

"The Wonder Column" ran from issue 26 until 42. Daniels continued:

> I began to really enjoy wordsmithing, if you will, in a very minor, minor way. And I would love it and I would send it to Dan, and he would just be excited. He's a very good audience. I love working with him, totally love work with him. He worked so hard to make the Fan Club work. All things were against him, sadly. Then, I realized that I had run out of humorous, funny things to say about *Star Wars*, and all that was left were some rather negative memories. I decided it was better to stop because *Star Wars* is so beloved by millions of people. When I published my book, around that time I was becoming aware of how books work. The newspapers have that so-and-so's biography is out and there are shock headlines. I don't know, all sorts of things they don't really need to say and I don't want to know. Just to sell the book. That hurts the main product. George's film is a very fine piece of art. Why would I want to smear it? ... I was honest about a lot of things in the book. But there are many things that I wanted to say and then decided actually, maybe, that is private.[15]

But the last "Wonder Column" was not the last expression for Daniels's writings. *Star Wars Insider* Editor-in-Chief Jon Bradley Snyder had an idea. Madsen described Snyder's proposal:

> Jon is an audio aficionado and album collector. He told me, "You know, Anthony's column is so popular." And they were popular. We got people who were always talking about how much they loved Anthony's columns. They were written with wit, a tongue in cheek sarcasm that he would use to describe different things that he felt and thought in his columns. Snyder said, "We could do a whole CD of this and have Anthony read these." I said, "That's a great idea." I called Anthony and he was on board.[16]

The Incredibly Improved New Wonder Column in Space was available in two editions, one autographed by Daniels though the fan club. It featured the music of John Williams and authentic sound effects from the films. Additional music and sound were added by Peter Hutchings. Daniels edited the columns to be a more audio-friendly experience, and more, he created a wrap-around story by which C-3PO and R2-D2 are making delivery runs to Endor. Threepio is happy to see the Ewoks again since they revere him as a deity. What appears to be an asteroid storm suddenly appears, and the droids endeavor to save the ship. However, it turns out not to be a storm at all. Rather, the ship is being bombarded by pieces of Daniels's "Wonder Column." The droids then listen to the stories and fragments of the column, with Threepio making the postmodern comment that he is very aware of who Daniels is and that he considers him "the most wonderfully gifted and modest human being." The audio then alternates between Daniels sharing real anecdotes of making the films and the continuing adventure of C-3PO and R2-D2.

Madsen recalled, "Everything had to be vetted by Lucasfilm licensing. They had to approve the whole idea of the CD. They provided the sound effects."[17] The result is a CD that makes for a good companion to the radio dramas and shares details about the making of the films that only those like Daniels who were there know. In 2021, Daniels would write a special anniversary "Wonder Column" for the two-hundredth issue of the *Star Wars Insider*, which sported a variable cover, one of which was a nod to the first issue created by Dan Madsen more than thirty years before.

I Am C-3PO: The Inside Story. Daniels, Anthony. Dorling Kindersley Ltd. 2019.

The audiobook version of his 2019 autobiography *I Am C-3PO: The Inside Story* features Daniels performing an unabridged reading of his book. The nine-disc set includes music from John Williams scores for *Star Wars*, *The Empire Strikes Back*, *Return of the Jedi*, *The Phantom Menace*, and *The Force Awakens*. The nine hours, twenty-seven minutes were recorded in just a five-day period. Writer and director J.J. Abrams recorded the foreword. Daniels explained how it all happened. "Wonderful JJ. He said one day, 'You should write a book.' Then he said, 'Are you?' because he is very sharp. I said, 'Yes. Would you write the foreword?' He said, 'That would be an honor!' And then of course, very cheekily, when we decided to make an audio version, I went back to him in post-production and asked if he would record his foreword, and he said, 'Of course.'"[18] Included in the audiobook are Daniels's thoughts and feelings about the *Star Wars* radio dramas and an emotional tribute to Brian Daley.

For fans of the *Star Wars* radio dramas hungry for more, these related projects above are a bonus, with more audio adventures to share with Anthony Daniels, Mark Hamill, Joshua Fardon, Perry King, Brock Peters, and Arye Gross. Reflecting on everything, Daniels shared, "So many memories encapsulated in those films and in the audio dramas. Suddenly it occurs to me, it wouldn't have been the same without Brian ... because he was the right choice."[19]

Appendix B

NPR Affiliates

The following is a sampling of the National Public Radio (NPR) stations that aired the *Star Wars* radio drama during its premiere. While local stations customized the days and times of each broadcast, the official NPR schedule for the *Star Wars* radio drama was:

March 7, 1981: "A Wind to Shake the Stars"
March 14, 1981: "Points of Origin"
March 21, 1981: "Black Knight, White Princess and Pawns"
March 28, 1981: "While Giants Mark Time"
April 4, 1981: "Jedi That Was, Jedi to Be"
April 11, 1981: "The *Millennium Falcon* Deal"
April 18, 1981: "The Han Solo Solution"
April 25, 1981: "Death Star's Transit"
May 2, 1981: "Rogues, Rebels and Robots"
May 9, 1981: "The Luke Skywalker Initiative"
May 16, 1981: "The Jedi Nexus"
May 23, 1981: "The Case for Rebellion"
May 30, 1981: "Force and Counterforce"

Star Wars

The following is a sample of local affiliate days and times for *Star Wars*. The location refers to the city of license. Unless otherwise noted, the affiliate aired *Star Wars* starting in March 1981.

KALW San Francisco, California (delayed premiere until April 1, 1981)
Wednesdays, 8:30 P.M.
KBBF Calistoga, California
Saturdays, 7:00 P.M.
KBKY Lexington, Kentucky

KBYU Provo, Utah
Fridays, 6:30 P.M.
KCCK Cedar Rapids, Iowa
Saturdays, 1:00 P.M.
KCRW Santa Monica, California
Tuesdays, 3:30 P.M.

KCSN Northridge, California
Mondays, 7:30 P.M.
KCUR Kansas City, Missouri
Mondays, 9:30 P.M.
KENW Clovis, New Mexico
Mondays, 5:30 P.M.
KESD Brookings, South Dakota
Mondays, 10:00 P.M.
KETR Greenville, Texas
Thursdays, 8:00 P.M. Repeats Sundays, 1:00 P.M.
KEYA Rolla, North Dakota
Wednesdays, 5:30 P.M.
KHPR Honolulu, Hawaii (delayed premiere until November 21, 1982)
Sundays, 6:30 P.M.
KLCC Eugene, Oregon
Sundays, 11:30 A.M.
KLON Long Beach, California
Mondays, 6:30 P.M.
KLSE Rochester, Minnesota
Saturdays. 8:30 A.M.
KMCR Montgomery City, Missouri
Sundays, 12:00 P.M.
KMUW Wichita, Kansas
Mondays, 6:30 P.M. Repeats Thursdays, 10:00 P.M. and Sundays, 11:00 P.M.
KOAC Corvallis, Oregon
Saturdays, 10:00 A.M.
KOPB Portland, Oregon
Saturdays, 10:00 A.M.
KPCS Pasadena, California
Unknown day and time
KQED San Francisco, California
Mondays, 6:30 P.M.
KRVS Lafayette, Louisiana
Wednesdays, 10:00 P.M.
KSBR Mission Viejo, California
Thursdays, 11:30 P.M. Repeats Saturdays, 8:30 A.M.
KSJN Minneapolis, Minnesota
Saturdays, 8:30 A.M.
KSJR Saint Cloud, Minnesota
Saturdas, 8:30 A.M.
KSMU Springfield, Missouri
Mondays, 9:35 P.M. Repeats Wednesdays, 6:30 P.M. and Saturdays, 9:35 P.M.
KSOZ Branson, Missouri
Mondays, 6:30 P.M. Repeats Saturdays, 8:00 A.M.
KSUI Cedar Rapids, Iowa
Fridays, 4:30 P.M. Repeats Sundays, 11:30 A.M.
KUAT Tucson, Arizona
Saturdays, 6:00 P.M.
KUER Salt Lake City, Utah
Saturdays, 10:30 A.M.
KUFM Missoula, Missouri
Saturdays, 9:30 A.M.
KUNI Cedar Falls, Iowa
Wednesdays, 6:30 P.M.
KUSC Los Angeles, California
Sundays, 6:00 P.M. Repeats Thursdays, 4:30 P.M.
KUT Austin, Texas
Tuesdays, 6:30 P.M.
KUWR Laramie, Wyoming
Tuesdays, 8:00 P.M. Repeats Saturdays, 8:00 P.M.
KVCR San Bernardino, California
Thursdays, 6:30 P.M.
KVLU Orange, Texas
Mondays, 6:30 P.M.
KVPR San Joaquin Valley, California
Saturdays, 6:00 P.M.

KWAX Eugene, Oregon
Saturdays, 7:30 P.M.
KWGS Tulsa, Oklahoma
Mondays, 9:30 P.M.
KWSU Spokane, Washington
Mondays, 7:30 P.M.
KXPR Sacramento, California
Saturdays, 8:00 P.M.
WABE Atlanta, Georgia
Mondays, 7:30 P.M.
WAMU Washington, D.C.
Mondays, 11:00 P.M. Repeats
Sundays, 12:00 P.M.
WBAA West Lafayette, Indiana
Mondays, 10:00 P.M. Repeats
Wednesdays, 4:00 P.M.
WBEZ Chicago, Illinois
Wednesdays, 7:00 P.M.
WBFO Buffalo, New York
Sundays, 4:30 P.M. Repeats
Mondays, 11:30 P.M.
WBHM Birmingham, Alabama
Sundays, 6:30 P.M.
WBJC Baltimore, Maryland
Sundays, 6:30 P.M.
WBKY Lexington, Kentucky
Mondays, 11:30 P.M. Repeats
Saturdays, 1:30 P.M.
WBST Muncie, Indiana
Saturdays, 1:00 P.M.
WCSU Dayton, Ohio
Mondays, 7:30 P.M.
WEBR Niagara Falls, New York
Saturdays, 7:00 P.M.
WEKU Lexington, Kentucky
Saturdays, 12:00 A.M.
WEPR Greenville,
South Carolina
Mondays, 7:30 P.M.
WERN Madison, Wisconsin
Mondays, 10:00 P.M.
WETA Washington, D.C.
Saturdays, 10:30 P.M. Repeats
Wednesdays, 6:30 P.M.
WETS Johnson City, Tennessee
Wednesdays, 6:30 P.M.
WFPL Louisville, Kentucky
Mondays, 3:00 P.M.
WGBH Boston, Massachusetts
Mondays, 10:30 P.M.
WGBO New York, New York
Sundays, 8:00 P.M.
WGUC Cincinnati, Ohio
Sundays, 12:30 P.M.
WITF Harrisburg, Pennsylvania
Sundays, 7:00 P.M. Repeats
Tuesdays, 12:30 P.M. and
Sundays 1:30 P.M.
WKAR East Lansing, Michigan
Saturdays, 8:00 P.M.
WKMS Paducah, Kentucky
Fridays, 10:30 P.M.
WKNO Memphis, Tennessee
Mondays, 6:30 P.M.
WKSU Kent, Ohio
Sundays, 6:00 P.M.
WKYU Bowling Green, Kentucky
Mondays, 6:30 P.M.
WLRN Miami, Florida
Mondays, 4:30 P.M.
WLTR Columbia, South Carolina
Tuesdays, 7:00 P.M. Repeats
Saturdays, 8:30 A.M. and
Sundays, 2:00 P.M.
WMFE Orlando, Florida
Mondays, 7:30 P.M.
WMUB Dayton, Ohio
Mondays, 7:30 P.M.
WNIU Rockford, Illinois
Saturdays, 7:00 P.M.
WNYC-AM New York, New York
Mondays, 7:30 P.M.

WNYC-FM New York, New York
Mondays, 10:00 P.M.
WPLN Austin, Texas
Sundays, 8:30 A.M.
WQED Pittsburgh, Pennsylvania
Saturdays, 10:30 A.M.
WRVO Oswego, New York
Wednesdays, 4:00 P.M. Repeats Wednesdays 11:00 P.M.
WSIU Carbondale, Illinois
Saturdays, 12:00 P.M. Repeats Saturdays 10:00 P.M.
WSKG Binghamton, New York
Tuesdays, 10:00 P.M. Repeats Sundays 7:00 P.M.
WSUI Iowa City, Iowa
Saturdays, 6:00 P.M.
WTSU Montgomery, Alabama
Sundays, 12:30 P.M.
WUNC Chapel Hill, North Carolina
Sundays, 6:30 P.M. Repeats Thursdays, 11:00 P.M.
WUOL Columbus, Ohio (delayed premiere until May 1981)
Saturdays, 9:00 A.M.
WUOT Knoxville, Tennessee
Sundays, 7:00 P.M.
WUSF Tampa, Florida (delayed premiere until November 11, 1982)
Thursdays, 7:00 P.M. Repeats Wednesdays, 11:30 P.M.
WUWF Pensacola, Florida
Sundays, 5:30 P.M.
WVIA Wilkes-Barre, Pennsylvania
Saturdays, 6:30 P.M.
WVIK Rock Island, Illinois
Saturdays, 10:30 A.M.
WVPR Burlington, Vermont
Mondays, 7:30 P.M.
WVPS Windsor, Vermont
Mondays, 7:30 P.M.
WVUB Vincennes, Indiana
Mondays, 6:30 P.M.
WXXI Rochester, New York
Saturdays, 11:00 A.M. Repeats Tuesdays, 10:05 P.M.
WYSO Dayton, Ohio
Thursdays, 8:00 P.M.

Partners:

Australian Broadcasting Corporation (premiered 1982)
BBC World Service (premiered April 1981)
BBC 1 (premiered July 2, 1981)
Canadian Broadcasting Corporation (premiered July 4, 1981)
Saturdays, 10:30 A.M.

Star Wars: The Empire Strikes Back

The following is a sample of local affiliate days and times for *Star Wars: The Empire Strikes Back*. The location refers to the city of license. Unless otherwise noted, the affiliate aired *Empire* starting in February 1983.

KCBX San Luis Obispo, California
Wednesdays, 9:00 P.M.
KCRW Santa Monica, California
Mondays, 3:00 P.M.

KCPB Thousand Oaks, California
Sundays, 6:00 P.M.
KCSM San Mateo, California
Mondays, 7:30 P.M. Repeats
Saturdays, 8:00 A.M. and
Sundays, 8:30 P.M.
KHPR Kailua-Kona, Hawaii
Sundays, 6:30 P.M.
KLSE La Crosse, Wisconsin
Saturdays, 8:30
KPBS San Diego, California
Mondays, 7:00 P.M. Repeats
Saturdays, 8:00 A.M.
KQED San Francisco, California
Sundays, 9:30 A.M.
KRVS Lafayette, Louisiana
Mondays, 10:00 P.M.
KSBR Viejo, California
Saturdays, 9:00 A.M. Repeats
Sundays, 7:00 P.M.
KSJN Minneapolis, Minnesota
Saturdays, 8:30 A.M.
KSOR Ashland, Oregon
Mondays, 9:30 P.M. Repeats
Wednesdays, 4:30 P.M.
KUAT Tucson, Arizona
Sundays, 6:30 P.M.
KUER Salt Lake City, Utah
Thursdays, 9:00 P.M.
KUFM Butte, Montana
Tuesdays, 9:30 P.M.
KUNI Cedar Falls, Iowa
Wednesdays, 6:30 P.M.
KUNM Albuquerque, New Mexico
Sundays, 7:00 P.M. Repeats
Tuesdays, 10:00 P.M.
KUSC Los Angeles, California
Sundays, 6:00 P.M.
KUSF San Francisco, California
Thursdays, 7:30 P.M. Repeats
Fridays, 10:00 P.M.
KVLU Beaumont, Texas
Mondays, 6:30 P.M.
KVPR Fresno, California
Sundays, 5:00 P.M.
KWIT Sioux City, Iowa
Mondays, 6:30 P.M.
KWMU St. Louis, Missouri
Saturdays, 2:00 P.M.
WABE Atlanta, Georgia
Thursdays, 8:00 P.M.
WAMC Albany, New York
Mondays, 8:00 P.M.
WAMU Washington, D.C.
(delayed premiere until March 6, 1983)
Sundays, 7:30 P.M.
WBHM Birmingham, Alabama
Saturdays, 8:00 P.M. Repeats
Sundays, 6:30 P.M.
WBKY Lexington, Kentucky
Saturdays, 9:30 A.M.
WBST Muncie, Indiana
Mondays, 8:00 P.M. Repeats
Saturdays, 10:00 A.M.
WBUR Boston, Massachusetts
Mondays, 6:30 P.M.
WCAL California, Pennsylvania
Mondays, 9:00 P.M.
WDET Detroit, Michigan
Fridays, 8:00 P.M.
WDUQ Pittsburgh, Pennsylvania
Wednesdays, 7:00 P.M.
WEKU Richmond, Kentucky
Sundays, 9:00 P.M.
WERN Madison, Wisconsin
Mondays, 10:00 P.M.
WETA Washington, D.C.
Saturdays, 12:30 P.M.
WFSU Tallahassee, Florida
Sundays, 7:00 P.M.
WGBH Boston, Massachusetts
Fridays, 4:30 P.M.

WGLT Bloomington, Illinois
Fridays, 5:30 P.M.
WHLA La Crosse, Wisconsin
Saturdays, 8:30 P.M. Repeats
Mondays, 10:30 P.M.
WHRO Norfolk, Virginia
Thursdays, 11:00 A.M.
WHRS Boynton Beach, Florida
Sundays, 6:00 P.M.
WHWC Menomonie, Wisconsin
Mondays, 10:00 P.M. Repeats
Saturdays, 7:00 P.M.
WHYY Philadelphia, Pennsylvania
Mondays, 7:00 P.M.
WITF Harrisburg, Pennsylvania
Unknown day and time
WKAR Lansing, Michigan
Saturdays, 8:00 P.M.
WLSU La Crosse, Wisconsin
Saturdays, 10:30 A.M.
WMFE Orlando, Florida
Sundays, 6:00 P.M.
WMKY Morehead, Kentucky
Mondays, 7:00 P.M. Repeats
Tuesdays, 4:00 P.M.
WMOT Murfreesboro, Tennessee
Mondays, 7:00 P.M.
WMRA Harrisonburg, Virginia
Mondays, 9:30 P.M. Repeats
Saturdays, 12:00 P.M.
WNYC-AM New York, New York
Mondays, 9:30 A.M.
WNYC-FM New York, New York
Mondays, 10:30 P.M.
WPLN Nashville, Tennessee
Thursdays, 7:00 P.M. Repeats
Sundays, 8:30 A.M.
WPNE Green Bay, Wisconsin
Mondays, 7:00 P.M. Repeats
Saturdays, 7:00 P.M.
WQCS Fort Pierce, Florida
Sundays, 10:00 P.M.
WQED Pittsburgh, Pennsylvania
Saturdays, 12:00 P.M.
WRFK Richmond, Virginia
Tuesdays, 6:33 P.M.
WSIU Carbondale, Illinois
Wednesdays, 10:30 P.M.
WSLU Canton, New York
Mondays, 7:00 P.M. Repeats
Thursdays, 1:30 P.M.
WUAL Tuscaloosa, Alabama
Mondays, 10:00 P.M.
WUNC Chapel Hill, North Carolina
Tuesdays, 11:00 P.M. Repeats
Fridays, 6:30 P.M.
WUOT Knoxville, Tennessee
Sundays, 6:00 P.M.
WUSF Tampa, Florida
Thursdays, 7:30 P.M. Repeats
Fridays, 10:00 P.M.
WVIA Pittston, Pennsylvania
Wednesdays, 8:30 P.M. Repeats
Sundays, 7:30 P.M.
WVIK Rock Island, Illinois
Saturdays, 9:15 A.M.
WXXI Rochester, New York
Saturdays, 10:30 A.M. Repeats
Tuesdays, 10:05 P.M.

Partners:

ABC Sydney, Australia (premiered April 25, 1983)
Sundays, 11:00 A.M.
United States Armed Forces Radio and Television Service

Star Wars: Return of the Jedi

The following is a sample of local affiliate days and times for *Star Wars: Return of the Jedi*. The location refers to the city of license. Unless otherwise noted, the affiliate aired *Jedi* starting in October 1996. NPR premiered *Jedi* as two 90-minute episodes during fundraising campaigns occurring on October 19, 1996, and October 20, 1996. Some affiliates delayed until October 26, 1996, and October 27, 1996, or customized the days and times and presented the program weekly.

KJZZ Phoenix, Arizona
Premiered as two 90-minute episodes October 19, 1996, and October 20, 1996, at 1 P.M.

MPR St. Paul, Minnesota (delayed premiere until November 10, 1996)
Sundays, 8:00 P.M.

WAMC Albany, New York
Thursdays, 8:30 A.M.

WAMQ Albany, New York
Thursdays, 8:30 A.M.

WBEZ Chicago, Illinois
Saturdays, Unknown time

WDUQ Pittsburgh, Pennsylvania
Sundays, 7:00 A.M. Repeats Sundays, 12:00 A.M.

WFPL Louisville, Kentucky
Saturdays, 9:00 P.M.

WNPR Hartford, Connecticut
Premiered as two 90-minute episodes October 26, 1996, and October 27, 1996

Chapter Notes

Preface

1. Daley, Brian. Star Wars: *The National Public Radio Dramatization*. New York: Del Rey, 1994, 307.

Chapter 1

1. Rogers, Julie. "A Timeline of NPR's First 50 Years." *NPR*. April 28, 2021. https://www.npr.org/2021/04/28/987733236/a-timeline-of-nprs-first-50-years.
2. "National Public Radio." *Influence-Watch.org*. https://www.influencewatch.org/nonprofit/national-public-radio-npr/.
3. Toller, Susan. "Radio Drama Is Coming of Age." *The Capital Times*. May 13, 1976, 25.
4. Toller.
5. Voegeli, Thomas. Personal interview. October 27, 2021.
6. Voegeli.
7. Voegeli.
8. Voegeli.
9. Madden, John. Personal interview. November 19, 2021.
10. Prosser, Willets, Jr. "National Public Radio—Let Us Shorthand that to NPR—is a Sort of Poor Stepsister of Public Television." *Cincinnati Enquirer*, [October?] 1977, 8. (Clipping in Brian Daley's library collection and/or personal files.)
11. Prosser.
12. Kerr, Jennifer C. "Aide Announced Kennedy's Death." *The Atlanta Constitution*. October 25, 2014.
13. Wolf, Ron. "Anatomy of NPR: Politic-plagued and Shortchanged." *Tallahassee Democrat*. August 28, 1983, 1G–5G.
14. Palmer, Chris. "NPR Chief Making Gentle (Air) Waves." *Bangor Daily News*. February 3, 1980, ME3.
15. King, Perry. Personal interview. September 21, 2021.

Chapter 2

1. Woodall, Bernie. "George Lucas Goes Back to the Film School He Shaped." *Reuters*. March 30, 2009.
2. Toscan, Richard. Personal interview. January 25, 2022.
3. Toscan.
4. Toscan.
5. Toscan.
6. Toscan.
7. Toscan.
8. Toscan.
9. Toscan.
10. Toscan.
11. Toscan.
12. Toscan.
13. Toscan.
14. Toscan.
15. Toscan.
16. Toscan.
17. Toscan.
18. Toscan.
19. Toscan.
20. Toscan.
21. Richmond, Ray. "National Public Radio Strikes Back with *Star Wars* Series." *Daily News*. February 1, 1981.
22. Rosenzweig, Marc. Personal interview. February 1, 2022.
23. Rosenzweig.
24. Rosenzweig.
25. Toscan.
26. Toscan.
27. Toscan.
28. Rosenzweig.
29. Rosenzweig.

Chapter 3

1. Lewis, Dennis John. "*Star Wars* to Try New Galaxy Via Radio Series." *The Washington Star.* January 3, 1981.
2. Lindsey, Robert. "Will *Star Wars* Lure Younger Listeners to Radio?" *The New York Times.* March 8, 1981.
3. Toscan, Richard. Personal interview. January 25, 2022.
4. Toscan.
5. Toscan.
6. Toscan.
7. Toscan.
8. Carter, Jimmy. "George Lucas Talks with Jimmy Carter About Radio, Film Editing and Movie Going." *YouTube. https://www.youtube.com/watch?v=HycL6kNX2hI.*
9. *Toscan.*
10. Brown, James. "*Star Wars* Series to Take to the Airwaves." *The Los Angeles Times.* April 28, 1979, 37.
11. Brender, Alan. "*Star Wars*' Latest Incarnation: It's a Radio Play." *Starlog* 47. June 1981, 23–24.
12. King, Perry. Personal interview. September 21, 2021.
13. Toscan.
14. Toscan.
15. Richmond, Ray. "National Public Radio Strikes Back with '*Star Wars*' Series." *Daily News.* February 1, 1981.
16. Kleiner, Dick. "May the AM and FM Be with You." *St. Joseph News Press Gazette.* June 30, 1979.
17. Toscan.
18. Toscan.
19. Toscan.
20. Voegeli, Thomas. Personal interview. October 27, 2021.
21. Toscan.
22. Toscan.
23. Toscan.

Chapter 4

1. Daley, Brian. *Han Solo at Stars' End.* New York: Del Rey Books, 1979, 73.
2. Woods, Bob. "An Interview with Brian Daley." *Star Wars Galaxy Magazine* 2. Winter 1995, 24–30.
3. DiBlasio, Myra Daley. Personal interview. March 16, 2022.
4. DiBlasio.
5. Luceno, James. Personal interview. November 5, 2021.
6. Luceno.
7. DiBlasio.
8. DiBlasio.
9. DiBlasio.
10. DiBlasio.
11. Robson, Lucia St. Clair. Personal interview. January 28, 2022.
12. DiBlasio.
13. Robson.
14. Daley, Myra. Personal letter to Brian Daley. July 1, 1967. Correspondences. Brian C. Daley Papers Collection. University of Maryland, Baltimore County Albin O. Kuhn Library & Gallery. Special Collections 26. Baltimore, MD.
15. Daley, Myra.
16. DiBlasio.
17. DiBlasio.
18. DiBlasio.
19. Robson.
20. Luceno.
21. DiBlasio.
22. del Rey, Judy-Lynn. Letter to Al Zuckerman. February 27, 1975. Correspondences. Brian C. Daley Papers Collection. University of Maryland, Baltimore County Albin O. Kuhn Library & Gallery. Special Collections 26. Baltimore, MD.
23. Daley, Brian. Lecture at Jersey City State College. 1990.
24. del Rey, Judy-Lynn. Letter to Brian Daley. July 7, 1976. Correspondences. *Brian C. Daley Papers Collection. University of Maryland, Baltimore County Albin O. Kuhn Library & Gallery.* Special Collections 26. Baltimore, MD.
25. Luceno.
26. del Rey, Lester. Letter to Brian Daley. April 30, 1977. Brian C. Daley Papers Collection. University of Maryland, Baltimore County Albin O. Kuhn Library & Gallery. Special Collections 26. Baltimore, MD.
27. Brooks, Terry. Letter to Brian Daley. March 25, 1977. *Brian C. Daley Papers Collection. University of Maryland, Baltimore County Albin O. Kuhn Library & Gallery.* Special Collections 26. Baltimore, MD.
28. Anderson, Kevin J. Letter to Brian Daley. August 15, 1980. Brian C. Daley Papers Collection. University of Maryland, Baltimore County Albin O. Kuhn Library & Gallery. Special Collections 26. Baltimore, MD.

29. Luceno.
30. Woods.
31. Luceno.
32. Madden, John. Personal interview. November 19, 2021.
33. Robson.
34. "Check Out Over 40 Years of *Star Wars: A New Hope* Novelization Covers." Starwars.com. March 9, 2018. https://www.starwars.com/news/check-out-over-40-years-of-star-wars-a-new-hope-novelization-covers.
35. Newborn, Alex. "A Fan Interviews Brian Daley." *The Star Wars Collector* 13–14 (October 1995). Additional questions by John Hansen, Peter Iorillo, Mike Jasman, Marlene Karkoska, Hans Kummer, and Dan Wallace.
36. Harrington, Richard. "Radio Notes." *The Washington Post*. April 25, 1981.
37. Luceno.
38. Robson.
39. Robson.
40. Robson.
41. Daley, Brian. *Han Solo at Stars' End*, 47.
42. Daley, Brian. *Han Solo at Stars' End*, 5.
43. Daley, Brian. *Han Solo at Stars' End*, 81.
44. Daley, Brian. *Han Solo and the Lost Legacy*. New York: Del Rey Books, 1980, 95.
45. T-bone. "Interview with Ann C. Crispin." *T-bone's Star Wars Universe*. September 20, 1998. https://starwarz.com/tbone/interview-with-ann-c-crispin-original-posting-september-20-1998/.
46. Fry, Jason. "The First *Star Wars* Book I Loved." StarWars.com. October 4, 2012. https://www.starwars.com/news/the-first-star-wars-book-i-loved.
47. Lacey, Kellie. "*Star Wars* Writer Explains the Appeal of Non-Jedi Stories Like Mandalorian, Boba Fett." *CBR.com*. February 6, 2022. https://www.cbr.com/star-wars-mandalorian-book-of-boba-fett-non-jedi-appeal/.
48. Toscan, Richard. Personal interview. January 25, 2022.

Chapter 5

1. Richmond, Ray. "National Public Radio Strikes Back with *Star Wars* Series." *Daily News*. February 1, 1981.
2. Madden, John. Personal interview. November 19, 2021.
3. King, Perry. Personal interview. September 21, 2021.
4. *The Derek McGinty Show. WAMU.* July 12, 1993.
5. Robson, Lucia St. Clair. Personal interview. January 28, 2022.
6. Johnston, LaReine. Personal interview. April 22, 2022.
7. Johnston.
8. Johnston.
9. Lucas, George, and Carol Titelman. Interview. August 5, 1977. Brian C. Daley Papers Collection. University of Maryland, Baltimore County Albin O. Kuhn Library & Gallery. Special Collections 26. Baltimore, MD.
10. Lucas, George, and Carol Titelman. Interview. August 11, 1977. Brian C. Daley Papers Collection. University of Maryland, Baltimore County Albin O. Kuhn Library & Gallery. Special Collections 26. Baltimore, MD. George Lucas' interview comments are also featured in the *Making of Star Wars* by J.W. Rinzler (New York: Del Rey Books, 2007).
11. Lucas, George, and Carol Titelman. Interview. July 23, 1977. Brian C. Daley Papers Collection. University of Maryland, Baltimore County Albin O. Kuhn Library & Gallery. Special Collections 26. Baltimore, MD.
12. Lucas and Titelman.
13. Lewis, Dennis John. "*Star Wars* to Try New Galaxy Via Radio Series." *The Washington Star*. January 3, 1981.
14. Woods, Bob. "An Interview with Brian Daley." *Star Wars Galaxy Magazine* 2. Winter 1995, 24–30.
15. Toscan, Richard. Personal interview. January 25, 2022.
16. Toscan.
17. Johnston.
18. Johnston.
19. Robson.
20. Toscan.
21. Daley, Brian. Star Wars: *The National Public Radio Dramatization*. New York: Del Rey Books, 1994, 7.
22. Toscan.
23. Daley, Brian. Star Wars: *The National Public Radio Dramatization*, 3.
24. *The Derek McGinty Show.*
25. *The Derek McGinty Show.*
26. Toscan.

27. Madden.
28. Madden.
29. Madden.
30. Madden.
31. King.
32. Daley, Brian. Star Wars: *The National Public Radio Dramatization*, 9.
33. Voegeli, Thomas. Personal interview. October 27, 2021.
34. Madden.
35. "*Star Wars* Radio Broadcast Slated." *The Villager (Austin, TX)*. February 13, 1981.
36. Silver, Robert. "The Force Returns, but Now It Emanates from a Radio." *Gazette*. March 11, 1981.
37. Daley, Brian. Star Wars: The Empire Strikes Back: *The National Public Radio Dramatization*. New York: Del Rey Books, 1995, n8.

Chapter 6

1. Madden, John. Personal interview. November 19, 2021.
2. Madden.
3. Arnold, Alan. *Once Upon a Galaxy: A Journal of the Making of* Star Wars: The Empire Strikes Back. New York: Del Rey Books, 1980.
4. Klinger, Judson. *Playboy*. March 1981.
5. Lindsey, Robert. "Will *Star Wars* Lure Younger Listeners to Radio?" *The New York Times*. March 8, 1981.
6. Klinger.
7. "*Star Wars* Radio Broadcast Slated." *The Villager (Austin, TX)*. February 13, 1981.
8. Lindsey.
9. Madden.
10. Voegeli, Thomas. Personal interview. October 27, 2021.
11. Sachs, Ann. Personal interview. November 12, 2021.
12. Klinger.
13. Daniels, Anthony. Personal interview. December 20, 2021.
14. Daniels, Anthony. *I Am C-3PO: The Inside Story*. London: Dorling Kindersley Limited, 2020.
15. Daniels. *I Am C-3PO: The Inside Story*.
16. Daniels. Personal interview.
17. Daniels. Personal interview.
18. Daley, Brian. Star Wars: *The National Public Radio Dramatization*. New York: Del Rey Books, 1994, 6.
19. Newborn, Alex. "A Fan Interviews Brian Daley." *The Star Wars Collector* 13–14 (October 1995). Additional questions by John Hansen, Peter Iorillo, Mike Jasman, Marlene Karkoska, Hans Kummer, and Dan Wallace.
20. Daniels. Personal interview.
21. Robson, Lucia St. Clair. Personal interview. January 28, 2022.
22. Madden.
23. L'Officier, Rany, and Jean-Marc. "The Man Inside: An Interview with Anthony Daniels." *Fantasy Empire*. March 1984, 54–58.
24. Daniels. Personal interview.
25. King, Perry. Personal interview. September 21, 2021.
26. King.
27. King.
28. King.
29. King.
30. Sachs.
31. King.
32. Sachs.
33. Collins, William B. "New 'Dracula' Without Fangs Is Delightful, Nutty." *The Philadelphia Inquirer*. October 22, 1977, 6.
34. Sachs.
35. Daley, Brian. Star Wars: *The National Public Radio Dramatiza*tion, 10.
36. Daley, Brian. Star Wars: *The National Public Radio Dramatization*, 10.
37. Sachs.
38. King.
39. Brender, Alan. "*Star Wars*' Latest Incarnation: It's a Radio Play." *Starlog* 47. June 1981, 23–24.
40. Daley, Brian. Star Wars: *The National Public Radio Dramatization*.
41. Browne, Kale. Personal interview. October 29, 2021.
42. Browne.
43. Browne.
44. Browne.
45. Browne.
46. Browne.
47. Toscan, Richard. Personal interview. January 25, 2022.
48. Newborn.
49. Voegeli.
50. Toscan.
51. Toscan.
52. Rosales, Lori. "Interview: David

Alan Grier." *Sidewalks*. 2018. https://vimeo.com/228580091.

53. Toscan.
54. Toscan.
55. Toscan.

Chapter 7

1. Tepper, Ron. "'Cal Tech' Analog Meets Digital Meets Video Meets..." *Billboard*. June 30, 1979.
2. Tepper.
3. Tepper.
4. Voegeli, Thomas. Personal interview. October 27, 2021.
5. Bowman, Pierre. "Kenobi, Vader & Co. on the Radio." *Star-Bulletin*. November 10, 1982.
6. Voegeli.
7. *Entertainment Tonight*. 1982 (date unknown).
8. Sachs, Ann. Personal interview. November 12, 2021.
9. Sachs.
10. Bittan, Dave. "WHYY-FM Strikes Back with *Empire* Series." *Philadelphia Daily News*. February 8, 1983.
11. Madden, John. Personal interview. November 19, 2021.
12. King, Perry. Personal interview. September 21, 2021.
13. King.
14. White, Timothy. "Slaves to the Empire: The *Star Wars* Kids Talk Back." *Rolling Stone*. June 12, 1980.
15. Daley, Brian. Star Wars*: The National Public Radio Dramatization*. New York: Del Rey Books, 1994, 10.
16. Daley, Brian. Star Wars*: The National Public Radio Dramatization*, 201.
17. Madden.
18. Sachs.
19. Sachs, Ann, and Samuel Sachs Morgan. Personal interview. November 12, 2021.
20. Daniels, Anthony. Personal interview. December 20, 2021.
21. Daniels.
22. Daniels.
23. Daley, Brian. Star Wars*: The National Public Radio Dramatization*, 6.
24. Toscan, Richard. Personal interview. January 25, 2022.
25. Sachs, Ann.
26. Daley, Brian. Star Wars*: The National Public Radio Dramatization*, 7.
27. Daley, Brian. Star Wars: The Empire Strikes Back*: The National Public Radio Dramatization*. New York: Del Rey Books, 1995, 9.
28. Sahr, Mel. Letter to Brian Daley. May 14, 1980. Correspondences. Brian C. Daley Papers Collection. University of Maryland, Baltimore County Albin O. Kuhn Library & Gallery. Special Collections 26. Baltimore, MD.
29. Madden.
30. Luceno, James. Personal interview. November 5, 2021.
31. Daniels.
32. Daniels.
33. Daniels.
34. Daniels.
35. Sachs.
36. Toscan.
37. Toscan.
38. Toscan.
39. Brender, Alan. "*Star Wars*' Latest Incarnation: It's a Radio Play." *Starlog* 47. June 1981, 23–24.
40. Daley, Brian. Star Wars*: The National Public Radio Dramatization*, 9.
41. King.
42. Browne, Kale. Personal interview. October 29, 2021.
43. Toscan.

Chapter 8

1. Strickler, Jeff. "Audio Wizard Strikes Back, Readies *Empire* for Airwaves." *The Star and Tribune*. November 5, 1982.
2. Voegeli, Thomas. Personal interview. October 27, 2021.
3. Voegeli.
4. *The Making of* Star Wars *for Radio: A Fable for the Mind's Eye*. Minnesota Public Radio. 1981.
5. Lycan, Gary. "*The Empire Strikes Back*." *Register*. February 11, 1983.
6. Voegeli.
7. Voegeli.
8. Voegeli.
9. Strickler, Jeff. "Audio Wizard Strikes Back, Readies *Empire* for Airwaves." *The Star and Tribune*. November 5, 1982.
10. Strickler.
11. *The Making of* Star Wars *for Radio: A Fable for the Mind's Eye*.
12. Sachs, Ann. Personal interview. November 12, 2021.

13. Voegeli.
14. Toscan, Richard. Personal interview. January 25, 2022.

Chapter 9

1. Toscan, Richard. Personal interview. January 25, 2022.
2. Toscan.
3. Toscan.
4. Toscan.
5. Toscan.
6. Toscan.
7. Toscan.
8. Tozian, Greg. "WUSF Chooses Not to Air *Star Wars* Series." *The Tampa Tribune*. March 2, 1981, 43.
9. *Woman's Day*. April 7, 1981.
10. Brown, James. "*Star Wars* Debut." *Los Angeles Times*. March 8, 1981.
11. Staten, Vince. "*Star Wars* Is Ready for Invasion of Radio." *Evening Dispatch*. March 5, 1981.
12. Jordan, Gerald B. "*Star Wars* to Blast Off as a Radio Series." *Kansas City Star*. March 2, 1981.
13. Malaspina, Rick. "Prepare for a Vivid View of *Star Wars*—in Mind's Eye." *Tribune*. March 2, 1981.
14. Toscan.
15. "NPR Strikes with *Empire* in 83." *Starlog* 61. August 1982, 14.
16. Schwartz, Tony. "Financial Troubles Threaten *National Public Radio*." *Minneapolis Tribune*. April 26, 1981.
17. Toscan.
18. Madden, John. Personal interview. November 19, 2021.
19. Hanauer, Joan. "People There." *UPI. News Tribune*. January 24, 1983.
20. Ford, Shelley. "*The Empire Strikes Back* Is Back." *Airwaves*. February 1983, 44–45.
21. Lucas, George. Letter to Brian Daley. April 31, 1981. Correspondences. Brian C. Daley Papers Collection. University of Maryland, Baltimore County Albin O. Kuhn Library & Gallery. Special Collections 26. Baltimore, MD.
22. Robson, Lucia St. Clair. Personal interview. January 28, 2022.
23. Bowman, Pierre. "Kenobi, Vader & Co. on the Radio." *Star-Bulletin*. November 10, 1982.

Chapter 10

1. "NPR Strikes with *Empire* in 83." *Starlog* 61. August 1982, 14.
2. "NPR Strikes with *Empire* in 83." *Starlog*.
3. Toscan, Richard. Personal interview. January 25, 2022.
4. Toscan.
5. Daley, Brian. Star Wars: The Empire Strikes Back*: The National Public Radio Dramatization*. New York: Del Rey Books, 1995, 4.
6. "Luke Skywalker Returns." *Missourian*. January 30, 1983.
7. Daley, Brian. Star Wars: The Empire Strikes Back*: The National Public Radio Dramatization*, 5.
8. 40 Years of *Star Wars*." *Star Wars Celebration Orlando 2017*. StarWars.com. April 13, 2017. https://www.youtube.com/watch?v=YI5QodTtlME.
9. "40 Years of *Star Wars*." *Star Wars Celebration Orlando 2017*.
10. "Luke Skywalker Returns." *Missourian*.
11. Sachs, Ann. Personal interview. November 12, 2021.
12. "Heading for the Stars: The Empire is Back." *Dimensions in Sound: The Monthly Program Guide for Supporters of WHRO-FM Program Fund*.
13. *The Graham Norton Show*. *BBC One*. November 24, 2017. https://www.youtube.com/watch?v=xtIiMgMDROg.
14. Daley, Brian. Star Wars: The Empire Strikes Back*: The National Public Radio Dramatization*, 8.
15. Voegeli, Thomas. Personal interview. October 27, 2021.
16. "Heading for the Stars: The Empire Is Back." *Dimensions in Sound: The Monthly Program Guide for Supporters of WHRO-FM Program Fund*.
17. King, Perry. Personal interview. September 21, 2021.
18. Daniels, Anthony. Personal interview. December 20, 2021.
19. Daley, Brian. "Beyond Light Speed." *KUAT Radio Program Guide*. February 1983.
20. *The Salt Lake Tribune*. February 11, 1983.
21. *The Salt Lake Tribune*.
22. Daley, Brian. "Script Treatment." *Star Wars: The Empire Strikes Back*. Brian

C. Daley Papers Collection. University of Maryland, Baltimore County Albin O. Kuhn Library & Gallery. Baltimore, MD.

23. Voegeli.

24. *Empire of Dreams: The Story of the* Star Wars *Trilogy*. Dir. Kevin Burns. Prometheus Entertainment in association with Lucasfilm, Ltd. October 2014.

25. Daniels.

26. Adamo, Susan. "'The Empire' Sounds Off." *Starlog* 69. April 1983, 26–27.

27. Daley, Brian. Star Wars: The Empire Strikes Back: *The National Public Radio Dramatization*, 86.

28. Daley, Brian. Star Wars: The Empire Strikes Back: *The National Public Radio Dramatization*, 96.

29. Lucas, George, and Carol Titelman. Interview. July 23, 1977. Brian C. Daley Papers Collection. University of Maryland, Baltimore County Albin O. Kuhn Library & Gallery. Special Collections 26. Baltimore, MD.

30. Daley, Brian. Star Wars: The Empire Strikes Back: *The National Public Radio Dramatization*, 235.

31. Harrington, Richard. "Radio Epics." *The Washington Post*. February 22, 1983.

Chapter 11

1. Edwards, Bob. "*Morning Edition* Interview with Mark Hamill." *National Public Radio*. June 23–24, 1982. Quoted from Cowan, Lisa, and Lee Vibber, editors. *On the Mark: The Newsletter for Mark Hamill Fans* 1, no. 4 (Fall 1982): 5.

2. "Heading for the Stars: The Empire Is Back." *Dimensions in Sound: The Monthly Program Guide for Supporters of WHRO-FM Program Fund*.

3. Daley, Brian. Star Wars: The Empire Strikes Back: *The National Public Radio Dramatization*. New York: Del Rey Books, 1995, 8.

4. Collins, Glenn. "Metropolitan Diary." *The New York Times*. June 16, 1982, C2.

5. Collins.

6. King, Perry. Personal interview. September 21, 2021.

7. Adamo, Susan. "'The Empire' Sounds Off." *Starlog* 69. April 1983, 26–27.

8. Newborn, Alex. "A Fan Interviews Brian Daley." *The Star Wars Collector* 13–14 (October 1995). Additional questions by John Hansen, Peter Iorillo, Mike Jasman, Marlene Karkoska, Hans Kummer, and Dan Wallace.

9. Daley, Brian. Star Wars: The Empire Strikes Back: *The National Public Radio Dramatization*, 7.

10. Harrington, Richard. "Radio Epics." *The Washington Post*. February 22, 1983.

11. Voegeli, Thomas. Personal interview. October 27, 2021.

Chapter 12

1. Kachmann-Geltz, Kim. "Testing the Limits: Ron and Linda Devillier." *Monthly Voice of the Lowcountry*. March 30, 2016. https://www.hiltonheadmonthly.com/people/profiles/3244-testing-the-limits-ron-and-linda-devillier.

2. Zimmerman, Betty. "Central Illinois Debut for Yoda's Herb Stew." *The Pantagraph*. March 9, 1983, 21.

3. Zimmerman.

4. "*Ralph McQuarrie—Tribute to a Master*." *Star Wars UK*. March 5, 2014. https://www.youtube.com/watch?v=tf6oSA28S_U.

5. Scoleri, John. "The Ballantine/Del Rey Paperback Covers of Ralph McQuarrie: A Checklist (1976–1987)." *Bare-Bones E-zine*. November 22, 2010. https://barebonesez.blogspot.com/2010/11/ballantinedel-rey-paperback-covers-of.html.

6. Alinger, Brandon, Wade Lageose, and David Mandel. Produced in cooperation with the Ralph McQuarrie Archives. Star Wars *Art: Ralph McQuarrie, Vol. 2*. New York: Abrams Books, 2016, 145.

7. Hill, Steve. "'Empire' Conquers the Airwaves." *The Tampa Tribune*. February 17, 1983.

8. Smith, David Hugh. "NPR Brings the Wrath—and Grandeur—of 'Empire' to Radio." *The Christian Science Monitor*. February 17, 1983.

9. Arpy, Jim. "RI Radio Station Puts Movies on the Air." *Quad City Times*. February 1, 1983.

10. Ford, Shelley. "*The Empire Strikes Back Is* Back." *Airwaves*. February 1983, 44–45.

11. Robson, Lucia St. Clair. Telegram to Brian Daley. October 1983. Correspondences. Brian C. Daley Papers Collection.

University of Maryland, Baltimore County Albin O. Kuhn Library & Gallery. Special Collections 26. Baltimore, MD.

12. Luceno, James. Personal interview. November 5, 2021.

13. Bos, John. Return of the Jedi *Radio Adaptation*. October 20, 1983. Correspondences. Brian C. Daley Papers Collection. University of Maryland, Baltimore County Albin O. Kuhn Library & Gallery. Special Collections 26. Baltimore, MD.

14. Wolf, Ron. "Anatomy of NPR: Politic-plagued and Shortchanged." *Tallahassee Democrat*. August 28, 1983, 1G–5G.

15. Wolf.

16. Toscan, Richard. Personal interview. January 25, 2022.

17. *Star Wars: The Empire Strikes Back*. Dir. Irvin Kershner. Writer Lawrence Kasdan and Leigh Brackett, from a story by George Lucas. Lucasfilm Ltd., 1980.

18. Burton, Bonnie. "Corey Burton: Voicing Villains." StarWars.com. March 20, 2009. https://www.starwars.com/theclonewars/news20090320.html.

19. Daley, Brian. Letter to Lucy Autrey Wilson. December 6, 1993. Correspondences. Brian C. Daley Papers Collection. University of Maryland, Baltimore County Albin O. Kuhn Library & Gallery. Special Collections 26. Baltimore, MD.

20. Luceno.

21. Luceno.

22. Luceno.

23. Luceno.

24. Robson, Lucia St. Clair. Personal interview. January 28, 2022.

25. *Star Wars: The Empire Strikes Back*. Dir. Irvin Kershner. Writer Lawrence Kasdan and Leigh Brackett, from a story by George Lucas. *Lucasfilm Ltd.*, 1980.

26. Luceno.

27. Daley, Brian. Letter to Owen Lock. April 12, 1994. Correspondences. Brian C. Daley Papers Collection. University of Maryland, Baltimore County Albin O. Kuhn Library & Gallery. Special Collections 26. Baltimore, MD.

28. According to the 1983 novelization of *Return of the Jedi* by James Kahn, Owen Lars was really the brother of Obi-Wan Kenobi, not the stepbrother of Anakin Skywalker as eventually revealed in *Star Wars: Attack of the Clones*.

29. Daley, Brian. Letter to Owen Lock. April 12, 1994. Correspondences. Brian C. Daley Papers Collection. University of Maryland, Baltimore County Albin O. Kuhn Library & Gallery. Special Collections 26. Baltimore, MD.

Chapter 13

1. Associated Press. "Audiobooks Chain Making Noise in Dallas." *Fort Worth Star-Telegram*, July 2, 1993, 51.

2. Shah, Allie. "Why Read When You Can Listen?" *St. Cloud Times*. July 23, 1993, 5A–11A.

3. McKerrow, Steve. "Even on Radio, 'Star Wars' has the Force." *The Baltimore Sun*. July 9, 1993.

4. Daley, Brian. Star Wars*: The National Public Radio Dramatization*. New York: Del Rey Books, 1994.

5. Excerpts from the documentary are included on the bonus discs from *The* Star Wars *Vault: Thirty Years of Treasures from the Lucasfilm Archives*, a 2007 reference book by Stephen J. Sansweet and Pete Vilmur.

6. Voegeli, Thomas. Personal interview. October 27, 2021.

7. Kogge, Michael. "30 Years of Star Wars Radio Drama Part II: How the Empire Almost Won and the Jedi Returned Late!" *Star Wars Insider* 127 (August 2011).

8. Daniel, Anthony. Introduction. Daley, Brian. Star Wars: Return of the Jedi: *The National Public Radio Dramatization*. New York: Del Rey Books, 1996.

9. Daniels.

10. Fardon, Joshua. Personal interview. October 8, 2021.

11. Fardon.

12. Fardon.

13. Fardon.

14. Fardon.

15. Daley, Brian. "Predators." *Star Wars Galaxy Magazine* 6. Winter 1996, 32–37.

16. Daley, Brian. Star Wars: Return of the Jedi: *The National Public Radio Dramatization*, 1996.

17. Fardon.

18. Virtue, Tom. Personal interview. September 27, 2021.

19. Virtue.

20. Covert, Colin. "Stars in Your Ears." *Star Tribune*. October 15, 1996, 39.

21. Covert.

22. Robson, Lucia St. Clair. Personal interview. January 28, 2022.

23. Daley, Brian. Letter to Masakazu Kawamoto. October 11, 1995. Correspondences. Brian C. Daley Papers Collection. University of Maryland, Baltimore County Albin O. Kuhn Library & Gallery. Special Collections 26. Baltimore, MD.

24. Johnston, LaReine. Personal interview. April 22, 2022.

25. Daley, Brian. Letter to Anthony Daniels. September 5, 1995. Correspondences. Brian C. Daley Papers Collection. University of Maryland, Baltimore County Albin O. Kuhn Library & Gallery. Special Collections 26. Baltimore, MD.

26. Voegeli.

27. Madden, John. Personal interview. November 19, 2021.

28. Luceno.

Chapter 14

1. Daley, Brian. Letter to Anthony Daniels. September 5, 1995. Correspondences. Brian C. Daley Papers Collection. University of Maryland, Baltimore County Albin O. Kuhn Library & Gallery. Special Collections 26. Baltimore, MD.

2. Daley, Brian. "Episode One: Cry Solo." *Star Wars Part VI: Return of the Jedi.* Unused script excerpt. Brian C. Daley Papers Collection. University of Maryland, Baltimore County Albin O. Kuhn Library & Gallery. Special Collections 26. Baltimore, MD.

3. Daley, Brian. "Tatooine Haunts." *Star Wars: Return of the Jedi.* Brian C. Daley Papers Collection. University of Maryland, Baltimore County Albin O. Kuhn Library & Gallery. Special Collections 26. Baltimore, MD.

4. DiBlasio, Myra Daley. Personal interview. March 16, 2022.

5. Daley, Brian. Letter to Anthony Daniels. December 6, 1995. Correspondences. Brian C. Daley Papers Collection. University of Maryland, Baltimore County Albin O. Kuhn Library & Gallery. Special Collections 26. Baltimore, MD.

6. Daniels, Anthony. Personal interview. December 20, 2021.

7. Daley, Brian. Star Wars: Return of the Jedi: *The National Public Radio Dramatization.* New York: Del Rey Books, 1996.

8. Daniels.

9. Daley, Brian. *Star Wars: Return of the Jedi.* Unused script excerpt. Brian C. Daley Papers Collection. University of Maryland, Baltimore County Albin O. Kuhn Library & Gallery. Special Collections 26. Baltimore, MD.

10. Daniels.

11. Daniels.

12. Daniels.

13. Sachs, Ann. Personal interview. November 12, 2021.

14. Fardon, Joshua. Personal interview. October 8, 2021.

15. Fardon.

16. Sachs.

17. Virtue, Tom. Personal interview. September 27, 2021.

18. Virtue.

19. Virtue.

20. Fardon.

21. Fardon.

22. Daniels, Anthony. *I Am C-3PO: The Inside Story.* London: Dorling Kindersley Limited, 2020.

23. Fardon.

24. Daniels, Anthony. Introduction. Daley, Brian. Star Wars: Return of the Jedi: *The National Public Radio Dramatization.*

25. Voegeli, Thomas. Personal interview. October 27, 2021.

26. Daniels. Personal interview.

Chapter 15

1. Robson, Lucia St. Clair. Personal interview. January 28, 2022.

2. DiBlasio, Myra Daley. Personal interview. March 16, 2022.

3. Luceno, James. Personal interview. November 5, 2021.

4. Robson.

5. DiBlasio.

6. Robson.

7. Robson.

8. DiBlasio.

9. DiBlasio.

10. DiBlasio.

11. Luceno.

12. Luceno.

13. Robson, Lucia St. Clair. "The Etiquette of Ashes." *LuciaStClairRobson.com.* https://www.luciastclairrobson.com/the-etiquette-of-ashes/.

14. Robson, Lucia St. Clair. Personal interview.

15. Daley, Brian. Personal letter. 26 July 1995. Courtesy Lucia St. Clair Robson.

Chapter 16

1. Toscan, Richard. Personal interview. January 25, 2022.
2. "Interview with David C. Fein." *SW Action News*. March 2009. http://swactionnews.com/.
3. Bracken, Alexandra. *Star Wars: A New Hope: The Princess, the Scoundrel, and the Farm Boy*. Glendale, CA: Lucasfilm Press, 2015.
4. Fry, Jason. "The First *Star Wars* Book I Loved." StarWars.com. October 4, 2012. https://www.starwars.com/news/the-first-star-wars-book-i-loved.
5. DiBlasio, Myra Daley. Personal interview. March 16, 2022.
6. Sachs, Samuel Morgan. Personal interview. November 12, 2021.
7. Sachs.
8. Fardon, Joshua. Personal interview. October 8, 2021.
9. Robson, Lucia St. Clair. Personal interview. January 28, 2022.
10. Luceno, James. Personal interview. November 5, 2021.
11. Daniels, Anthony. Personal interview. December 20, 2021.
12. Voegeli, Thomas. Personal interview. October 27, 2021.
13. Toscan.
14. Newman, Kyle. "SWCVI: Smuggler's Gambit—A Live Audio Adventure." StarWars.com. August 22, 2012. https://www.starwars.com/news/swcvi-smugglers-gambit-a-live-audio-adventure.
15. Daniels.

Appendix A

1. Miller, Craig. 1-800-521-1980. Lucasfilm, Ltd. 1980.
2. Miller, Craig. *Star Wars Memories*. Fulgens Press, 2019. *Facebook*. February 1, 2021.
3. "The Hot Line." *Des Moines Tribune*. May 2, 1980, 32.
4. Turgeon, Shane. Interview with Meco. May 2005. https://www.theforce.net/jedicouncil/interview/meco2005.asp.
5. Warner, Andrea. "The First-ever Oral History of *Christmas in the Stars: Star Wars* Christmas Album." *CBC*. December 16, 2016. https://www.cbc.ca/music/read/the-first-ever-oral-history-of-christmas-in-the-stars-star-wars-christmas-album-1.5051210.
6. Warner.
7. Warner.
8. Fardon, Joshua. Personal interview. October 8, 2021.
9. Madsen, Dan. Personal interview. October 15, 2021.
10. Madsen.
11. Madsen.
12. Madsen.
13. Madsen.
14. Daniels, Anthony. Personal interview. December 20, 2021.
15. Daniels.
16. Madsen.
17. Madsen.
18. Daniels.
19. Daniels.

References

Thank you to the authors, journalists, and researchers whose writings are an archive of great historical value.

All *Star Wars* books, characters, comic books, music, television shows, movies, and video games referenced in this book are owned by Lucasfilm, Ltd., and The Walt Disney Company. The *Star Wars* and *Star Wars: The Empire Strikes Back* radio dramas were produced by National Public Radio. The *Star Wars: Return of the Jedi* audio drama was produced by HighBridge Audio.

Adamo, Susan. "'The Empire' Sounds Off." *Starlog* 69 (April 1983): 26–27.

Alinger, Brandon, Wade Lageose, and David Mandel. Produced in cooperation with the Ralph McQuarrie Archives. *Star Wars Art: Ralph McQuarrie*, Vol. 2. New York: Abrams Books, 2016.

Anderson, Kevin J. Letter to Brian Daley. August 15, 1980. Correspondences. Brian C. Daley Papers Collection. University of Maryland, Baltimore County Albin O. Kuhn Library & Gallery. Special Collections. Baltimore, MD.

Arnold, Alan. *Once Upon a Galaxy: A Journal of the Making of* Star Wars: The Empire Strikes Back. New York: Del Rey Books, 1980.

Arpy, Jim. "RI Radio Station Puts Movies on the Air." *Quad City Times*. February 1, 1983.

Associated Press. "Audiobooks Chain Making Noise in Dallas." *Fort Worth Star-Telegram*. July 2, 1993, 51.

Bittan, Dave. "WHYY-FM Strikes Back with *Empire* Series." *Philadelphia Daily News*. February 8, 1983.

Bos, John. Return of the Jedi *Radio Adaptation*. October 20, 1983. Correspondences. Brian C. Daley Papers Collection. University of Maryland, Baltimore County Albin O. Kuhn Library & Gallery. Special Collections. Baltimore, MD.

Bowman, Pierre. "Kenobi, Vader & Co. on the Radio." *Star-Bulletin*. November 10, 1982.

Bracken, Alexandra. *Star Wars: A New Hope: The Princess, the Scoundrel, and the Farm Boy*. Glendale, CA: Lucasfilm Press, 2015.

Brender, Alan. "*Star Wars*' Latest Incarnation: It's a Radio Play." *Starlog* 47. June 1981, 23–24.

Brooks, Terry. Letter to Brian Daley. March 25, 1977. Correspondences. Brian C. Daley Papers Collection. University of Maryland, Baltimore County Albin O. Kuhn Library & Gallery. Special Collections. Baltimore, MD.

Brown, James. "*Star Wars* Debut." *Los Angeles Times*. March 8, 1981.

Brown, James. "*Star Wars* Series to Take to the Airwaves." *The Los Angeles Times*. April 28, 1979, 37.

Browne, Kale. Personal interview. October 29, 2021.

Burton, Bonnie. "Corey Burton: Voicing Villains." StarWars.com. March 20, 2009. https://www.starwars.com/theclonewars/news20090320.html.

Carter, Jimmy. "George Lucas Talks with Jimmy Carter About Radio, Film Editing and Movie Going." YouTube. https://www.youtube.com/watch?v=HycL6kNX2hI.

"Check Out Over 40 Years of *Star Wars: A New Hope* Novelization Covers." StarWars.com. March 9, 2018. https://

www.starwars.com/news/check-out-over-40-years-of-star-wars-a-new-hope-novelization-covers.

Collins, Glenn. "Metropolitan Diary." *The New York Times.* June 16, 1982, C2.

Collins, William B. "New 'Dracula:' Without Fangs Is Delightful, Nutty." *The Philadelphia Inquirer.* October 22, 1977, 6.

Covert, Colin. "Stars in Your Ears." *Star Tribune.* October 15, 1996, 39.

Daley, Brian. "Beyond Light Speed." *KUAT Radio Program Guide.* February 1983.

Daley, Brian. "Episode One: Cry Solo." *Star Wars Part VI: Return of the Jedi.*

Daley, Brian. *Han Solo and the Lost Legacy.* New York: Del Rey Books, 1980.

Daley, Brian. *Han Solo at Stars' End.* New York: Del Rey Books, 1979.

Daley, Brian. Lecture at Jersey City State College. 1990.

Daley, Brian. Letter to Anthony Daniels. September 5, 1995. Correspondences. Brian C. Daley Papers Collection. University of Maryland, Baltimore County Albin O. Kuhn Library & Gallery. Special Collections. Baltimore, MD.

Daley, Brian. Letter to Anthony Daniels. December 6, 1995. Correspondences. Brian C. Daley Papers Collection. University of Maryland, Baltimore County Albin O. Kuhn Library & Gallery. Special Collections. Baltimore, MD.

Daley, Brian. Letter to Lucy Autrey Wilson. December 6, 1993. Correspondences. Brian C. Daley Papers Collection. University of Maryland, Baltimore County Albin O. Kuhn Library & Gallery. Special Collections. Baltimore, MD.

Daley, Brian. Letter to Masakazu Kawamoto. October 11, 1995. Correspondences. Brian C. Daley Papers Collection. University of Maryland, Baltimore County Albin O. Kuhn Library & Gallery. Special Collections. Baltimore, MD.

Daley, Brian. Letter to Owen Lock. April 12, 1994. Correspondences. Brian C. Daley Papers Collection. University of Maryland, Baltimore County Albin O. Kuhn Library & Gallery. Special Collections. Baltimore, MD.

Daley, Brian. Personal letter. 26 July 1995. Courtesy of Lucia St. Clair Robson.

Daley, Brian. "Predators." *Star Wars Galaxy Magazine* 6 (Winter 1996): 32–37.

Daley, Brian. *Requiem for a Ruler of Worlds.* New York: Ballantine, 1985.

Daley, Brian. "Script Treatment." Star Wars: The Empire Strikes Back. Brian C. Daley Papers Collection. University of Maryland, Baltimore County Albin O. Kuhn Library & Gallery. Special Collections. Baltimore, MD

Daley, Brian. Star Wars: Return of the Jedi: *The National Public Radio Dramatization.* New York: Del Rey Books, 1996.

Daley, Brian. Star Wars: The Empire Strikes Back*: The National Public Radio Dramatization* Star Wars: The Empire Strikes Back. New York: Del Rey Books, 1995.

Daley, Brian. Star Wars*: The National Public Radio Dramatization.* New York: Del Rey Books, 1994.

Daley, Brian. *Starfollowers of Coramonde.* New York: Del Rey Books, 1979.

Daley, Brian. "Tatooine Haunts." Star Wars: Return of the Jedi. Brian C. Daley Papers Collection. University of Maryland, Baltimore County Albin O. Kuhn Library & Gallery. Special Collections. Baltimore, MD

Daley, Brian. "Worldrush!" *Droids: The Adventures of C-3PO and R2-D2.* 1984. Brian C. Daley Papers Collection. University of Maryland, Baltimore County Albin O. Kuhn Library & Gallery. Special Collections. Baltimore, MD

Daley, Myra. Personal letter to Brian Daley. July 1, 1967. Correspondences. Brian C. Daley Papers Collection. University of Maryland, Baltimore County Albin O. Kuhn Library & Gallery. Special Collections. Baltimore, MD.

Daniels, Anthony. *I Am C-3PO: The Inside Story.* London: Dorling Kindersley Limited, 2020.

Daniels, Anthony. Introduction. Daley, Brian. Star Wars: Return of the Jedi*: The National Public Radio Dramatization.* New York: Del Rey Books, 1996.

Daniels, Anthony. Personal interview. December 20, 2021.

del Rey, Judy-Lynn. Letter to Al Zuckerman. February 27, 1975. Correspondences. Brian C. Daley Papers Collection. University of Maryland, Baltimore County Albin O. Kuhn Library & Gallery. Special Collections. Baltimore, MD.

del Rey, Judy-Lynn. Letter to Brian Daley. July 7, 1976. Correspondences. Brian C. Daley Papers Collection. University of Maryland, Baltimore County Albin O.

Kuhn Library & Gallery. Special Collections. Baltimore, MD.

del Rey, Lester. Letter to Brian Daley. April 30, 1977. Correspondences. Brian C. Daley Papers Collection. University of Maryland, Baltimore County Albin O. Kuhn Library & Gallery. Special Collections. Baltimore, MD.

The Derek McGinty Show. WAMU. July 12, 1993.

DiBlasio, Myra Daley. Personal interview. March 16, 2022.

Edwards, Bob. "*Morning Edition* Interview with Mark Hamill." *National Public Radio.* June 23–24, 1982. Quoted from Cowan, Lisa, and Lee Vibber, editors. *On the Mark: The Newsletter for Mark Hamill Fans* 1, no. 4 (Fall 1982): 5.

Empire of Dreams: The Story of the Star Wars Trilogy. Dir. Kevin Burns. Prometheus Entertainment in association with Lucasfilm, Ltd. October 2014.

Entertainment Tonight. 1982.

Fardon, Joshua. Personal interview. October 8, 2021.

Ford, Shelley. "*The Empire Strikes Back* Is Back." *Airwaves.* February 1983, 44–45.

"40 Years of *Star Wars.*" Star Wars Celebration Orlando 2017. StarWars.com. April 13, 2017. https://www.youtube.com/watch?v=YI5QodTtlME.

Fry, Jason. "The First *Star Wars* Book I Loved." StarWars.com. October 4, 2012. https://www.starwars.com/news/the-first-star-wars-book-i-loved.

The Graham Norton Show. BBC One. November 24, 2017. https://www.youtube.com/watch?v=xtIiMgMDROg.

Hanauer, Joan. "People There." UPI. *News Tribune.* January 24, 1983.

Harrington, Richard. "Radio Epics." *The Washington Post.* February 22, 1983.

Harrington, Richard. "Radio Notes." *The Washington Post.* April 25, 1981.

"Heading for the Stars: The Empire Is Back." *Dimensions in Sound: The Monthly Program Guide for Supporters of WHRO-FM Program Fund.*

Hill, Steve. "'Empire' Conquers the Airwaves." *The Tampa Tribune.* February 17, 1983.

"The Hot Line." *Des Moines Tribune.* May 2, 1980, 32.

"Interview with David C. Fein." SW Action News. March 2009. http://swactionnews.com/.

Johnston, LaReine. Personal interview. April 22, 2022.

Jordan, Gerald B. "'Star Wars' to Blast Off as a Radio Series." *Kansas City Star.* March 2, 1981.

Kachmann-Geltz, Kim. "Testing the Limits: Ron and Linda Devillier." *Monthly Voice of the Lowcountry.* March 30, 2016. https://www.hiltonheadmonthly.com/people/profiles/3244-testing-the-limits-ron-and-linda-devillier.

Kahn, James. *Star Wars: Return of the Jedi.* New York: Del Rey Books, 1983.

Kerr, Jennifer C. "Aide Announced Kennedy's Death." *The Atlanta Constitution.* October 25, 2014.

King, Perry. Personal interview. September 21, 2021.

Kleiner, Dick. "May the AM and FM Be with You." *St. Joseph News-Press Gazette.* June 30, 1979.

Klinger, Judson. *Playboy.* March 1981.

Kogge, Michael. "30 Years of *Star Wars* Radio Drama Part II: How the Empire Almost Won and the Jedi Returned Late!" *Star Wars Insider* 127 (August 2011).

Lacey, Kellie. "*Star Wars* Writer Explains the Appeal of Non-Jedi Stories Like Mandalorian, Boba Fett." CBR.com. February 6, 2022. https://www.cbr.com/star-wars-mandalorian-book-of-boba-fett-non-jedi-appeal/.

Lewis, Dennis John. "*Star Wars* to Try New Galaxy Via Radio Series." *The Washington Star.* January 3, 1981.

Lindsey, Robert. "Will *Star Wars* Lure Younger Listeners to Radio?" *The New York Times.* March 8, 1981.

L'Officier, Rany, and Jean-Marc. "The Man Inside: An Interview with Anthony Daniels." *Fantasy Empire.* March 1984, 54–58.

Lucas, George, and Carol Titelman. Interview. July 23, 1977. Brian C. Daley Papers Collection. University of Maryland, Baltimore County Albin O. Kuhn Library & Gallery. Special Collections 26. Baltimore, MD.

Lucas, George, and Carol Titelman. Interview. August 5, 1977. Brian C. Daley Papers Collection. University of Maryland, Baltimore County Albin O. Kuhn Library & Gallery. Special Collections 26. Baltimore, MD.

Lucas, George, and Carol Titelman.

Interview. August 11, 1977. Brian C. Daley Papers Collection. University of Maryland, Baltimore County Albin O. Kuhn Library & Gallery. Special Collections 26. Baltimore, MD.

Lucas, George. Letter to Brian Daley. April 31, 1981. Correspondences. Brian C. Daley Papers Collection. University of Maryland, Baltimore County Albin O. Kuhn Library & Gallery. Special Collections. Baltimore, MD.

Luceno, James. Personal interview. November 5, 2021.

"Luke Skywalker Returns." *Missourian*. January 30, 1983.

Lycan, Gary. "*The Empire Strikes Back*." *Register*. February 11, 1983.

Madden, John. Personal interview. November 19, 2021.

Madsen, Dan. Personal interview. October 15, 2021.

Malaspina, Rick. "Prepare for a Vivid View of *Star Wars*—in Mind's Eye." *Tribune*. March 2, 1981.

McKerrow, Steve. "Even on Radio, '*Star Wars*' has the Force." *The Baltimore Sun*. July 9, 1993.

The Making of Star Wars *for Radio: A Fable for the Mind's Eye*. Minnesota Public Radio. 1981.

Miller, Craig. *Star Wars Memories*. Fulgens Press, 2019. Facebook. February 1, 2021.

Miller, Craig. 1-800-521-1980. Lucasfilm, Ltd. 1980.

"National Public Radio." InfluenceWatch.org. https://www.influencewatch.org/non-profit/national-public-radio-npr/.

Newborn, Alex. "A Fan Interviews Brian Daley." *The Star Wars Collector* 13–14 (October 1995). Additional questions by John Hansen, Peter Iorillo, Mike Jasman, Marlene Karkoska, Hans Kummer, and Dan Wallace.

Newman, Kyle. "SWCVI: Smuggler's Gambit—A Live Audio Adventure." StarWars.com. August 22, 2012. https://www.starwars.com/news/swcvi-smugglers-gambit-a-live-audio-adventure

"NPR Strikes with *Empire* in 83." *Starlog* 61 (August 1982): 14.

Palmer, Chris. "NPR Chief Making Gentle (Air) Waves." *Bangor Daily News*. February 3, 1980, ME3.

Prosser, Willets, Jr. "National Public Radio—Let Us Shorthand that to NPR—Is a Sort of Poor Stepsister of Public Television." *Cincinnati Enquirer*, [October?], 1977, 8.

Ralph McQuarrie—Tribute to a Master. *Star Wars UK*. March 5, 2014. https://www.youtube.com/watch?v=tf6oSA28S_U.

Richmond, Ray. "National Public Radio Strikes Back with *Star Wars* Series." *Daily News*. February 1, 1981.

Robson, Lucia St. Clair. "The Etiquette of Ashes." *LuciaStClairRobson.com*. https://www.luciastclairrobson.com/the-etiquette-of-ashes/.

Robson, Lucia St. Clair. Personal interview. January 28, 2022.

Robson, Lucia St. Clair. Telegram to Brian Daley. October 1983. Correspondences. Brian C. Daley Papers Collection. University of Maryland, Baltimore County Albin O. Kuhn Library & Gallery. Special Collections. Baltimore, MD.

Rogers, Julie. "A Timeline of NPR's First 50 Years." NPR. April 28, 2021. https://www.npr.org/2021/04/28/987733236/a-timeline-of-nprs-first-50-years.

Rosales, Lori. "Interview: David Alan Grier." *Sidewalks*. 2018. https://vimeo.com/228580091.

Rosenzweig, Marc. Personal interview. February 1, 2022.

Sachs, Ann. Personal interview. November 12, 2021.

Sachs, Ann, and Samuel Sachs Morgan. Personal interview. November 12, 2021.

Sachs, Samuel Morgan. Personal interview. November 12, 2021.

Sahr, Mel. Letter to Brian Daley. May 14, 1980. Correspondences. Brian C. Daley Papers Collection. University of Maryland, Baltimore County Albin O. Kuhn Library & Gallery. Special Collections. Baltimore, MD.

The Salt Lake Tribune. February 11, 1983.

Sansweet, Stephen J., and Peter Vilmur. *The Star Wars Vault: Thirty Years of Treasures from the Lucasfilm Archives*. New York: HarperCollins, 2007.

Schwartz, Tony. "Financial Troubles Threaten National Public Radio." *Minneapolis Tribune*. April 26, 1981.

Scoleri, John. "The Ballantine/Del Rey Paperback Covers of Ralph McQuarrie: A Checklist (1976–1987)." *BareBones E-zine*. November 22, 2010. https://

barebonesez.blogspot.com/2010/11/ballantinedel-rey-paperback-covers-of.html.

Shah, Allie. "Why Read When You Can Listen?" *St. Cloud Times.* July 23, 1993, 5A–11A.

Silver, Robert. "The Force Returns, but Now It Emanates from a Radio." *Gazette.* March 11, 1981.

Smith, David Hugh. "NPR Brings the Wrath—and Grandeur—of 'Empire' to Radio." *The Christian Science Monitor.* February 17, 1983.

Star Wars: The Empire Strikes Back. Dir. Irvin Kershner. Writer Lawrence Kasdan and Leigh Brackett, from a story by George Lucas. Lucasfilm Ltd., 1980.

"*Star Wars* Radio Broadcast Slated." The *Villager* (Austin, TX). February 13, 1981.

Staten, Vince. "*Star Wars* Is Ready for Invasion of Radio." *Evening Dispatch.* March 5, 1981.

Strickler, Jeff. "Audio Wizard Strikes Back, Readies *Empire* for Airwaves." *The Star and Tribune.* November 5, 1982.

T-bone. "Interview with Ann C. Crispin." T-bone's Star Wars Universe. September 20, 1998. https://starwarz.com/tbone/interview-with-ann-c-crispin-original-posting-september-20-1998/.

Tepper, Ron. "'Cal Tech' Analog Meets Digital Meets Video Meets…" *Billboard.* June 30, 1979.

Toller, Susan. "Radio Drama is Coming of Age." *The Capital Times.* May 13, 1976, 25.

Toscan, Richard. Personal interview. January 25, 2022.

Tozian, Greg. "WUSF Chooses Not to Air *Star Wars* Series." *The Tampa Tribune.* March 2, 1981, 43.

Turgeon, Shane. "Interview with Meco." May 2005. https://www.theforce.net/jedicouncil/interview/meco2005.asp.

Virtue, Tom. Personal interview. September 27, 2021.

Voegeli, Thomas. Personal interview. October 27, 2021.

Warner, Andrea. "The First-ever Oral History of *Christmas in the Stars: Star Wars* Christmas Album." CBC. December 16, 2016. https://www.cbc.ca/music/read/the-first-ever-oral-history-of-christmas-in-the-stars-star-wars-christmas-album-1.5051210.

White, Timothy. "Slaves to the Empire: The *Star Wars* Kids Talk Back." *Rolling Stone.* June 12, 1980.

Wolf, Ron. "Anatomy of NPR: Politic-plagued and Shortchanged." *Tallahassee Democrat.* August 28, 1983, 1G–5G.

Woman's Day. April 7, 1981.

Woodall, Bernie. "George Lucas Goes Back to the Film School He Shaped." Reuters. March 30, 2009.

Woods, Bob. "An Interview with Brian Daley." *Star Wars Galaxy Magazine* 2 (Winter 1995): 24–30.

Zimmerman, Betty. "Central Illinois Debut for Yoda's Herb Stew." *The Pantagraph.* March 9, 1983, 21.

Index